PENGUIN BUSINESS

MODERN MANAGEMENT

Ernest Dale has been president of Ernest Dale Associates and of a council on organization, general management and marketing to many corporations in America, Europe and Asia. He holds degrees from Cambridge and Yale universities and has served on the faculties of Yale, Columbia and New York universities. He has been a Visiting Professor at Wharton School, University of Pennsylvania, and a Visiting Lecturer at the University of Virginia. Dr Dale has had extensive experience as a business executive and as a member of boards of directors. He is the author of numerous books and articles on management and has received the Newcomen Prize and several McKinsey Prizes for his writings. He is a Fellow of the Academy of Management and of the International Academy of Management.

L. C. Michelon has been Director of Public Affairs for the Republic Steel Corporation in Cleveland, Ohio. He attended DePaul University, Chicago Teachers' College and the University of Chicago. He taught at Purdue University and then served as Director of Management Services for the University of Chicago's Industrial Relations Centre; he was Visiting Professor of Management at Ashland College, Ohio. L. C. Michelon has organized programmes in management and executive development and in economic and political education, which have been produced for television. He has served many organizations, including the Ohio State Educational Television Network Commission, the National Association of Manufacturers, and the American Association of Industrial Management.

MODERN
MANAGEMENT METHODS

ERNEST DALE AND
L. C. MICHELON

PENGUIN BOOKS

Penguin Books Ltd, Harmondsworth, Middlesex, England
Viking Penguin Inc., 40 West 23rd Street, New York, New York 10010, U.S.A.
Penguin Books Australia Ltd, Ringwood, Victoria, Australia
Penguin Books Canada Limited, 2801 John Street, Markham, Ontario, Canada L3R 1B4
Penguin Books (N.Z.) Ltd, 182–190 Wairau Road, Auckland 10, New Zealand

—

First published in the U.S.A. by The World Publishing Company 1966
Published in Pelican Books 1969
Reprinted 1970, 1971, 1974, 1975, 1977, 1980, 1983
Reprinted in Penguin Books 1986

—

Copyright © Ernest Dale and L. C. Michelon, 1966
All rights reserved

—

Printed and bound in Great Britain by
Cox & Wyman Ltd, Reading
Set in Monotype Times

Except in the United States of America,
this book is sold subject to the condition
that it shall not, by way of trade or otherwise,
be lent, re-sold, hired out, or otherwise circulated
without the publisher's prior consent in any form of
binding or cover other than that in which it is
published and without a similar condition
including this condition being imposed
on the subsequent purchaser

Contents

List of Figures   7
Preface   9

1. The Job of Management   11
2. New Developments in Human Relations and Leadership   24
3. The Challenge of Organization   43
4. Managing and Communicating by Objectives   66
5. New Dimensions in Organizational Communication   81
6. Long-Range Planning, Financing, and Control   92
7. Government-Business Relations   114
8. Managerial Decision-Making   127
9. Reducing Costs by Value Analysis   142
10. Introductory Statistics for Management   157
11. Payoff Tables and Decision Trees   175
12. Critical Path Analysis – PERT   186
13. Management and the Computer   205
14. Management and the Future   221

Index   231

List of Figures

1.1	The matrix of management functions	13
1.2	Planning ahead for growth	15
4.1	Flow chart of work sequence	76
4.2	Responsibility accounting statement	78
6.1	Financial planning – The income statement	107
6.2	Financial planning – Changes in working capital	108
6.3	Financial planning – Current assets and liabilities	109
8.1	The influence of time span on risk	129
8.2	The three organizational networks	139
9.1	The break-even point for £0·80 variable cost	154
9.2	The break-even point for £0·72 variable cost	155
10.1	The effect of sample size on accuracy	162
10.2	The normal distribution curve	164
10.3	Typical distribution curves and tolerance limits	165
10.4	A control chart with limits set	165
10.5	Plotting the averages of small samples	166
10.6	Temperature and chirps per minute of 115 crickets	167
10.7	Breast-high diameter growth and height growth of twenty forest trees	168
10.8	Yield per acre and man-hours per ton required to harvest broomcorn	169
10.9	Annual production of stainless steel	170
11.1	A typical decision tree	179
11.2	A specific decision tree	181
11.3	Applying expected monetary values to decision alternatives	182
12.1	PERT network of events and activities	188
12.2	PERT event layout	190
12.3	PERT activity layout (connecting events)	191
12.4	Completed PERT network	193
12.5	A theoretical frequency distribution of performance times	194
12.6	Mean and variance of performance time distributions	195
12.7	Calculating mean time for each activity (t_e)	196

12.8	Calculating expected times of events (T_E)	196
12.9	Calculating latest allowable time of an event (T_L)	197
12.10	A list of jobs, job durations, and deadlines	199
13.1	Block diagram for getting to work in the morning	211

Preface

TODAY'S manager lives in a world of rapid change, and yet the rate of change is likely to increase in the years ahead. Unless he can keep up with this change, he's likely to find himself obsolete – perhaps unpromotable or even unemployable.

In recent years there have been many improvements in the art and science of management – in guides to effective human relations as well as in the more quantitative and objective aspects of the subject. But it's difficult for the practising manager to keep up with all of them, for they are reported in publications dealing with a wide variety of fields. The busy manager just doesn't have the time or the opportunity to review them all.

This book overcomes this difficulty by bringing together the important trends in management and the useful new management methods which are coming into favour in progressive companies. It is intended for practical use by managers at all levels – from the first-line supervisor on up.

For example, it reports on the kind of manager who's likely to be in demand in the next few years; on new developments in human relations, communication, and organization; on economic forecasting and planning for company success.

In addition the book explains useful techniques which have been developed to improve decision-making in management: *Value Analysis*, which enables managers to produce direct and measurable savings for their companies; *Payoff Tables and Decision Trees*, a method spear-headed by the Harvard Business School; *Critical Path Analysis – PERT*; *Operational Research*; and the use of the computer.

Finally, the book to some extent anticipates further developments in the years ahead to help the reader prepare himself for the many problems that managers are likely to encounter. However, it avoids the science-fiction approach in favour of a practical explanation of where present trends seem to be leading.

PREFACE

The material for this book has been drawn, in part, from a series of television presentations by L. C. Michelon for the Republic Steel Corporation and the South Carolina Educational Television Foundation. Fundamentally, however, it is the product of the authors' experience, working as management consultants with hundreds of companies in different industries over a period of years.

The authors have been greatly assisted in their work by Alice Smith, a member of Ernest Dale Associates and a former editor of the American Management Association. Miss Smith did much of the basic research, editing, and shepherding the book throughout the publication process.

The authors are also grateful to Mr E. D. van Rest for his work in revising the book for the British market, and to Della Jaffee for typing assistance and to Charles Meloy for research aid (both of Ernest Dale Associates) and to Mrs Cora Benes and Miss Helen Chelos for secretarial and typing assistance.

The responsibility for this book is solely the authors':

ERNEST DALE
Wharton School of Finance and Commerce, University of Pennsylvania; Graduate School of Business, University of Virginia; Ernest Dale Associates, Counsel to Management, New York City

L. C. MICHELON
Republic Steel Corporation, Cleveland, Ohio.

CHAPTER 1

The Job of Management

EVERY manager – from the chief executive to the first-line supervisor – can profit from the body of management knowledge so far developed. The top man can increase his company's chances of success. For the middle manager, management know-how will make the job easier, and will very likely increase his chances of promotion.

Greater management know-how will:

1. Lead to better performance by enabling the manager to increase the output and quality of the work group.

2. Help the manager better understand the objectives and functions of the company as a whole and the thinking of his superiors. As a result he will be more able to 'talk the language' of higher managers, and gain a better hearing for his recommendations and suggestions.

3. Promote a better understanding of the way in which the manager's group fits in with other groups, make him a more effective team worker, and one whom other managers will respect and like to work with.

But he should never expect a set of exact rules that will be applicable under any circumstances. In the management field it is never possible to say: 'If I do A and B, then C will inevitably happen.' The best that he can say is: 'If I do A and B, the result is *likely* to be C. And if I neglect to do either A or B, it is *very probable* that the consequences will be unfortunate.'

Management is not an exact science like physics or chemistry. Although many things have been discovered about it, it is essential that the manager use judgement, based on good sense and experience. And this is not a bad thing. For if he could manage by merely following a set of rules, the management job would be far less interesting than it is.

But what, exactly, is management? Are there certain functions that all managers perform regardless of whether they're company presidents, managers of departments, or supervisors of sections of departments?

If we watch managers at work, we might conclude that their jobs differ so widely in content and scope that no generalizations about management are possible.

One reason for this is that many managers, even top managers, do work that is not management at all. A simple example is the sales manager who actually sells and perhaps has a set of customers of his own, in addition to managing the sales force. Again, the supervisor of a research group may actually perform some of the research himself. Then there's the 'working foreman' or leadman who works right along with the group he's supervising. In these cases the managers are actually spending only part of their time on management itself.

A second reason why it may be difficult to identify the functions common to all managers is that the scope of their activities differs so widely. In some cases the way a manager carries out his functions affects an entire company; in other cases only a small part of it.

Yet if we look closely at managers at work, we can see that fundamentally they are all performing – or should be performing – the same functions during the time they are actually managing rather than doing work similar to that done by those under them. These functions are illustrated in Figure 1.1. It is in these areas that the manager must be skilled.

THE MANAGEMENT FUNCTIONS

Planning. The basic management function is planning, which begins with setting objectives and includes specifying the steps needed to reach them. At the top, of course, the objectives are those of the business as a whole, but top management also must set objectives for each segment of the company.

Naturally the fundamental objective of any business is to make a profit and to increase it. But it is necessary to be much more specific. Each company must decide just how, in view of the resources and talents available to it, it can best carve out its own profit-making niche in the economy. For example, some companies

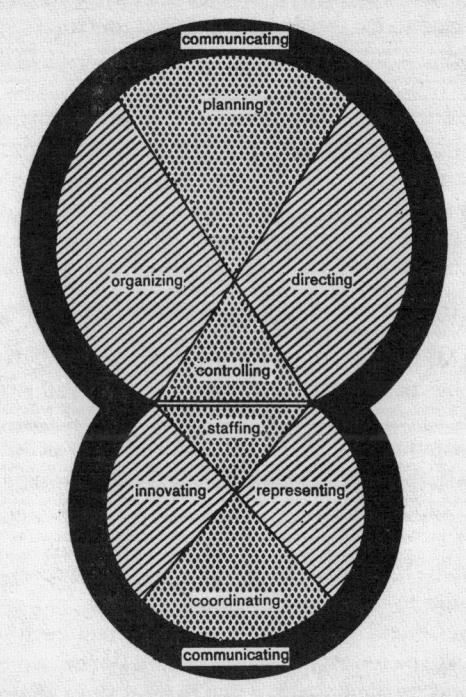

Figure 1.1 The matrix of management functions

SOURCE: L. Urwick and Ernest Dale, *Profitably Using Staff in Organization* (AMA General Management Series No. 165; New York, American Management Association, 1953), and *Staff in Organization*, New York, McGraw-Hill, Inc., 1960.

plan to attract customers by producing particularly high-quality products at premium prices for a selected group of customers. Others aim to serve a clientele that's primarily interested in low prices. Either may be a good objective, depending on the company's circumstances. But objectives of this kind must be re-examined periodically because circumstances change and the market the company is aiming at may be shrinking.

Objectives and plans are both long-range and short-range.

Short-range plans cover the next year or two, while long-range plans may extend for five to ten years into the future. The former are quite definite, and the latter are tentative except in cases where definite commitments must be made long in advance.

Objectives embody definite rates of profit, which are based on what is considered feasible in the light of forecasts of the state of the economy, the position of the industry, and the company's position as compared to those of its competitors.

Increasingly, also, companies are taking an even more fundamental view of objectives by asking themselves: What business are we really in? In other words, what do our customers pay us for?

Thus IBM, one of the best growth companies in the country, defined its business as 'supplying information' rather than as the 'production of office machines'. This led to its successful development of computers, an important factor in its growth.

In contrast, the machine-tool industry has commonly defined its function as 'supplying metalworking and metal-forming machines' rather than as 'providing the means of production'. It has lost ground, relatively speaking, although it has grown somewhat because of the growth of the economy.

Most companies hope to increase their profits each year; hence their plans will include means for doing so. For example, they may strive to increase their share of the market through greater sales effort, the introduction of new products, or improved product performance.

Moreover, revenues and costs must be matched against the plans to ensure a reasonable possibility that things will work out as expected. A sales forecast is important here because most of the revenues must come from sales, which will be forecast in the light of economic conditions, industry sales, and the company's present or expected share of the market.

The planning process will often reveal that if the company continues its past practices, there is likely to be a gap between goals and results. See the illustration in Figure 1.2.

In that event the planners must develop a strategy for filling in the gap through new products, new methods of selling, new markets, or cost reduction. In many cases managers down the line are asked to contribute to the setting of objectives and the formulation of plans for reaching them. For example, regional sales managers may forecast the sales in their territories each year and suggest plans for increasing them. But even where this is not true, every manager must set objectives and plan how to reach them.

The manager far down the line may believe that his objectives come down from above and that he cannot change them. And this is true when objectives are formally stated to him by higher management, in his job description or other directives.

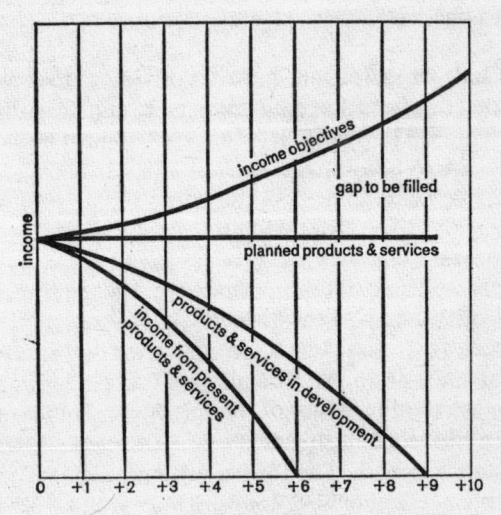

Figure 1.2 Planning ahead for growth

But just as a company must ask itself what its customers really want from it (e.g. 'information' rather than office machines), so the subordinate manager must ask himself what his company really wants from him – what he's actually being paid for. It is remarkable how many subordinate managers never do this.

This brings to mind the young man who had charge of a group of clerical workers who made lists for direct mail purposes. The formal objective given him was to supply the lists when they were needed and to keep them current. This he did. The lists were made up of company officials, and he was careful to ensure that as positions changed hands, the names on his lists were changed. So far, so good.

But in certain cases the lists contained names of top officials at headquarters, and time after time they notified him that all purchasing of the products in question was handled by the divisions. Yet he still kept the names on his lists. It never occurred to him that he should be concerned with the over-all objective of the operation – which was, of course, to make sales – and that it was a sheer waste of time and money to keep sending letters to those who were in no position to purchase.

Organization. Organization includes dividing the work into missions that can be handled by one person, and providing means of coordination. The principal functions that must be carried out if the plans are to become reality must be described and arrangements must be made to prevent the duties of two positions from overlapping and to ensure that various units are not working at cross-purposes.

The broad outlines of the organization are generally established at the top, but each manager down the line must organize his own group in such a way that there is no duplication or wasted effort. In addition he must ensure coordination within his own group and endeavour to coordinate his efforts with those of other managers.

This last is becoming particularly important as companies become more complex. The formal arrangements set up by top management – committees, coordinating groups, and special coordinators – are often inadequate for the policing of every small transaction that may affect another department or group. Hence it is up to the manager of each group to make some effort to coordinate the work of his section or department with that of others.

The manager also should take pains to understand what is known as the 'informal organization' within his own department or group, and in groups whose work is related to his own. The informal organization – which really consists of a network of friendships, alliances, communication channels, and spheres of influence not provided for in the formal organization charts – is sometimes regarded as a bad thing. It's sometimes bad for the company in that it that the manager's job was primarily to ensure that things went along smoothly, without intramural fights or disruptions. Thus some years ago, William F. Whyte, Jr, then an editor of *Fortune*, wrote to 150 personnel men and 150 company presidents asking whether they believed business most needed adaptable administrators, 'concerned primarily with human relations and making the corporation a smooth working team' – or men with new ideas and strong personal convictions 'not shy about making unorthodox decisions that will unsettle tested procedures – and his colleagues'. 50 per cent of the company presidents and 70 per cent of the personnel men voted for the administrator as opposed to the innovator.[1]

But the viewpoint has changed in many companies as competition has become keener, including competition from abroad. In fact, by 1961, a *Wall Street Journal* survey found a decided swing in favour of the innovator.[2]

In the late eighteenth century and almost to the end of the nineteenth century, British managers were the greatest innovators in the world. They got in on the ground floor of the Industrial Revolution, and by their willingness to try and to promote new inventions and new ways of doing things made their country the most prosperous in the world. But many think that they clung too long to the original ways of doing things, to the industries in which they led – production of coal and iron and steel products.

No country and no company can expect to stay on top, or near the top, if it continues doing things in the same old way simply because that way has brought success in the past. And innovation is not a job for the research department alone. Innovations must be developed by every manager who wants to be worthy of the name. A new product or an entirely new production process or piece of equipment is more dramatic than the introduction of a new procedure or a new form of financial control, but the latter may sometimes be of more benefit to a company.

1. William F. Whyte, Jr; *The Organization Man* (New York, Simon & Schuster, Inc., 1956), pp. 133–4.
2. Donald A. Moffitt; 'Maverick Managers: Individualist Displaces Organization Man in Many Corporations', *The Wall Street Journal* (22 November 1961) pp. 1, 23.

We know of one case in which a new assistant was able to produce reports that showed the company president exactly what was happening, and he was instrumental in saving the company from disaster. The president, a man with a good deal of drive and great ambition for his company, was continually branching out into new fields, and the money he lost in that way was draining away the profits of his organization. Many of the other top executives had talked to him but to no effect. It was the new assistant's imaginative and informative way of presenting the figures that finally convinced him.

Innovation may consist of replacing one way of doing things with another, or it may simply mean discarding old procedures that are no longer needed. But whatever form it takes, the drive towards innovation must be continuous. For a company cannot stay in the same place; it must move forward or go back. This is also true of a department.

Representation. In addition to all these functions, the manager must represent his company to the outside world. This has always been a part of the management job, although many books on management do not list it as one of the major management functions. There are many managers who still regard it as a peripheral activity, or believe that they can delegate it to a public relations or public affairs department.

Actually, the manager cannot escape the job of representation – and today, he must represent his company to more groups than ever before. These groups include the financial community, the general public, the local community, labour unions, industry associations, and innumerable governmental bodies.

Not all managers have contacts with all these groups, but they usually have contacts with some, although on different levels. The top manager may represent his company in conference with government officials or Ministers or give evidence before Parliamentary Committees or Commissions set up by the Government. For a plant manager, government contacts may be confined to meeting with local zoning boards or making speeches before community groups. The director of industrial relations may negotiate contracts with the union, but the first-line foreman must represent his company in discussions with the union steward or committeeman. And nearly every manager writes letters to outside groups or individuals.

Communication. In Figure 1.1, communication is shown encircling all the management functions, since none of them can be performed without it. Plans or innovations cannot be carried out until they are communicated to those who will have a part in implementing them. The organization structure is designed to set up 'channels of communication', through which information is passed downward and upward. Organization is sometimes described as 'a system of communication'. In staffing, the manager must explain the job, the skills needed, and the benefits provided to candidates; and the training phase of staffing is almost entirely a matter of communication. Direction and representation, too, are exercised largely through communications, and control systems are actually systems of communication.

WHAT THE MANAGER CAN LEARN

There were good managers, of course, long before anyone ever studied management. But not everyone can be a genius, and the demand for good managers far exceeds the supply of geniuses. Moreover, many of the genius managers of the past – in business, government, the military, and other fields – were deficient in one or more of the management skills and were probably less successful than they might have been if they had not proceeded by trial and error.

A classical example is Henry Ford, who didn't believe much in organization, or in communication for that matter. 'It is not necessary,' he said, 'for any one department to know what any other department is doing ... It is the business of those who plan the entire work to see that all of the departments are working ... towards the same end.'[3] But the Ford Motor Company grew beyond the point where it was possible to operate in this way, and was

3. Henry Ford, in collaboration with Samuel Crowther: *My Life and Work* (Garden City, N.Y., Garden City Publishing Co., 1922), p. 92.

saved from disaster only by a reorganization under Henry Ford II and Ernest R. Breech, whom the younger Ford hired away from General Motors to introduce a more formal structure.

When Henry Ford started, not a great deal was known about the management field, although some work had been done. But in the past few decades a great deal of research, experimentation, and thought has been devoted to the subject. In addition, the computer has given rise to entirely new possibilities. In short, there are a large number of findings that will help any manager – whatever his native ability – to become more competent.

One of the fruits of the study of management has been the breakdown of the management job into the several functions listed above. In itself, of course, this does not tell the manager much about how he can handle his job, but it has the great advantage of making it easier for him to grasp the essentials of his job and to study the subject in a systematic way.

Fortunately, there's much more that the manager can learn in addition to the techniques of his own job and his own industry. The field of management has drawn on sociology, psychology, economics, and other disciplines, and it is in these areas that the manager can learn from study as well as from experience and trial and error. He still needs plenty of intelligence, common sense, and business judgement – and even the inspired hunch may still have a place. But a knowledge of what others have learned about the various aspects of management will help him use his native abilities more effectively. It may even help him determine whether his hunches are inspirations or exercises in wishful thinking.

SUGGESTED QUESTIONS FOR YOUR CONSIDERATION

1. What percentage of your time is devoted to each of these basic management functions: Planning, Organization, Staffing, Direction, Control, Representation and Innovation?

2. Which do you think is most important in your particular job? Why?

3. Why is innovation so important today? What are its effects on the company's over-all operations? On its staff? Policies?

Procedures? Capital Equipment? Capital Requirements? Research and Development?

4. What is 'control'? Why is it necessary? Who should carry it out? What different control methods are used company-wide?

5. Under what circumstances do you represent the company to outside groups? Do you feel your representation is adequate for your position?

CHAPTER 2

New Developments in Human Relations and Leadership

THE human aspect of the manager's job begins with staffing – selecting people for the various jobs to be done. Of course, he will try to get the person best fitted for each job, but often the fit cannot be exact. And for this reason, proper training and direction can do much to improve its exactness.

SELECTION

What techniques are available to improve the hiring process? Well, there is the interview, the examination of the past work record, the reference check, and psychological tests – a great variety of them, with more being produced every day. Occasionally, in some jobs, it is possible to give the candidate an actual tryout.

In many cases these methods are used in combination and they can contribute to better selection if used wisely.

It is important that managers understand, and perhaps better than many of them do at present, just what psychological tests can do to help them to better selection and just what they can't do. Too many managers take the easy way out by relying too heavily on tests. In fact, one large company abolished psychological testing entirely because subordinate managers often hired people solely on the basis of the test results. That was, of course, simply a way of ducking a decision that every manager should be willing to make.

How does one judge the value of a test? There are two measures: (*a*) validity and (*b*) reliability. If a test is *valid*, it measures what it is supposed to measure; and if it is *reliable*, the same person will make the same score each time he takes it, even after an interval of several years. No test is perfectly valid and reliable, but some do improve the batting average in selection considerably.

Now tests are of various kinds. There are intelligence tests, which measure with fair accuracy the extent to which a person is capable of understanding and learning, although they don't tell may result in a tacit agreement among a group of production workers to hold down output. But it also may be good in that it may provide a type of horizontal coordination not supplied by the formal organization. The manager should be able to recognize the manifestations of the informal organization and learn how to encourage the good results it produces and discourage the bad ones.

Staffing. Once the functions to be performed have been decided upon, it is necessary to fill the positions with the most qualified people available. This is a continuing task since some people will be quitting, retiring, getting promoted, or transferring. The purpose, of course, is to have round pegs in round holes because this would solve many of the manager's headaches. But this is difficult to do, particularly when there are shortages of certain skills or when other companies in the area are paying higher rates. Then the manager may have to take people who seem to him the best of a rather poor group of candidates.

If so, he must supplement the abilities of his people by training, and this means that he must never become too preoccupied to observe their performance and to judge where they are deficient. Too often training courses are prescribed for whole groups when only some need them, while others would profit from entirely different types of training.

Direction. Direction is one of the most important parts of the manager's job – that is, telling people what to do and seeing that they do it to the best of their ability. Since the manager must work through other people, he may stand or fall by his ability to get them to produce the needed results.

Because of its importance, some people define management itself as 'the direction of people'. But this is only a half-truth. It is essential for the manager to lead his people well, but it is equally important to lead them toward the right goals by the right route. If the manager hasn't planned well, he may have a happy, hardworking group that is efficiently proceeding towards the wrong objective. And if he hasn't organized well, they may be working efficiently on their own tasks, but a good part of their effort may be counteracted by the efforts of others. If he hasn't staffed or trained well, they may be incapable of producing the results that he and his company are seeking.

Control. Control often suggests the idea of command or direction – and, in fact, this is one of its dictionary meanings. As applied to management, however, it means checking on progress to determine whether plans are being fulfilled. If performance is falling short of what is necessary to fulfil the goals, the manager must take steps to correct the difficulties.

Many of the controls available to management are financial in nature. A simple example is the budget, which is also a tool of the planner, for a budget is a plan to spend certain monies to accomplish certain ends. If actual expenditures overrun the budget, it's an indication that performance is deviating from plans – perhaps justifiably, perhaps not. Similarly, an underrun may indicate that a manager or several managers have been able to turn in especially fine performances and produce results for less money – or it may mean that some of the things that should have been done have not been done – again, justifiably or unjustifiably. If the budget is broken down finely enough, it is relatively easy for a superior, or the manager who is responsible for meeting the budget, to determine what has been happening and whether or not some special action is called for.

Not all controls are financial, however. To mention just a few, controls are needed for quality, for production, for ensuring that deadlines will be met, for sales (like a budget, a sales quota is both a plan and a control). It is even possible to develop controls for such things as training – for example, one might compare the performance of a group that had been given a certain type of training with that of an untrained group doing the same type of work. In that way, one could judge whether the training course is worthwhile, or whether it needs modification, or should be discarded altogether.

Innovation. A great many books on management confine discussion of the management job to the phases listed above. During the immediate postwar period, for example, there were many who felt us to what extent he will apply his intelligence to the job. In some cases people who make high scores even seem singularly lacking in common sense and judgement. There are aptitude tests – such as tests for mechanical aptitude or finger dexterity – which give an indication of the skills a person may find easy to acquire – and there are trade tests that indicate the extent to which a candidate is experienced in a skilled trade. In the case of management candidates, there are tests like the 'in-basket' test, in which participants are given a series of letters and memos, such as a manager might find in his in-basket, and are asked to indicate what action they would take in each case. This is, in effect, a test of judgement.

Finally, there are personality tests, which are more controversial since they are much harder to devise than the other types.[1] This is not surprising, because the personality an individual exhibits on the job is likely to be determined in part by the situation in which he finds himself. Although a person can't fake the answers to the other tests, it is quite possible to guess the 'right' answers to many of the personality tests and to adjust his responses accordingly.

Moreover, the way a person uses his intelligence and aptitudes depends in part on his personality as it develops in the job situation. Thus tests can't be depended upon to do the manager's selection job for him.

The interview is really the crucial part of the selection process, and it is here that the manager can make the greatest contribution to better staffing. Some companies provide interview blanks, which list the questions the interviewer should ask candidates. If this is not the case, it might be well for the manager to jot down in advance the facts he considers important. Some managers find that they have never asked the things they wanted to because they have allowed the candidate to interview them rather than vice versa, or perhaps they have talked too much themselves and never let the poor applicant get in a word.

Probably the best way for the manager to improve his score in staffing – whatever methods he uses – is to determine what the job requires in a realistic way. It would be nice if all jobs could be filled with perfect people, but the real question is not how a candi-

---

1. For some harsh criticism of personality tests, see Martin L. Gross, *The Brain Watchers* (New York, Random House, Inc., 1962).

date stacks up as a human being or whether one would want him for a bosom friend, but 'Does he have what it takes?' And, of course, what it takes differs for different jobs. For some jobs the proverbial strong back and weak mind are sufficient. For other positions there are other *sine qua nons*, and often the man who possesses them is quite deficient in many of the qualities one admires. Many of the most successful salesmen, for example, are money-hungry to an extraordinary extent, and their ability to sell is really the result of a neurotic drive.

TRAINING

One of the simplest types of training, and a very valid method for training in certain types of tasks, is the old JIT (Job Instructor Training) developed during World War II when industry was forced to train thousands of inexperienced people, many of whom had never seen the inside of a plant or office.

In this method the instructor first tells the trainee what he is to do, then shows him (actually performing the task himself), then has the employee repeat the instructions in his own words and watches him and corrects him as he follows these instructions, then repeats the steps until the employee is job-perfect.

Role-playing is another technique, useful where the employee is being trained not in performing a specific task but in handling face-to-face contacts. For example, the sales manager may take the part of a prospect and have the salesman rehearse an interview with a customer with him. Similarly, two supervisors or a supervisor and an instructor may act out a scene, often based on an actual case in which a supervisor must correct an employee. In both instances the role-playing is generally carried out before a group, whose members later offer suggestions for improving the performance. This method of training has the advantage of permitting the salesman or the supervisor to practise face-to-face dealing in a situation in which mistakes carry no penalties in the form of lost sales or disgruntled employees.

Other types of training include group discussions, lectures, and special courses at nearby schools or universities – all of which may be used for either managers or employees.

In the case of managers, the company may use job rotation – that is, the manager may spend a few months working in each of several departments to gain a better overall view of the company. Special assignments are another possibility in management development. So, too, is a term as assistant to a member of top management.

Two comparatively new training techniques are now available: programmed learning and sensitivity training. The first is designed primarily to teach skills and the second to improve human relations.

In programmed learning, which may be used either with or without a teaching machine, the learner is presented with a series of 'frames', each of which presents a very small bit of information, and he does not go on to the second frame until he has mastered the first as is shown by answering all the questions correctly.

There are two types of programmes: 'linear' and 'branching'. In the linear technique, Frame A presents a piece of information, Frame B reinforces Frame A, and adds something new; Frame C reinforces B, and adds a new piece of information, and so on. In the branching technique, multiple-choice questions are often used, and the student's possible misconceptions are anticipated. Then, if he picked wrong answer a, he is instructed to turn to pages that explain exactly why this is wrong. If he chose wrong answer b, he is directed to other pages that clear up another kind of misunderstanding.

The great advantages of the programmed learning technique are, first, that it presents the information so gradually that the student finds it easy to absorb and is encouraged by the progress he makes; and second, that he can learn without an instructor, and proceed at his own pace.

Managers find this technique useful in teaching skills to employees, and may also find it valuable in learning new things themselves. For example, Norman A. Crowder, inventor of one type of branching technique, has published a textbook on *The Arithmetic of Computers*,[2] which will help the manager understand binary mathematics and coding. It may also help him to keep up with his

2. Norman A. Crowder: *The Arithmetic of Computers* (London, The English Universities Press, Ltd., 1958).

children, since many schools are now teaching this form of mathematics.

Sensitivity training or 'laboratory education', as it is sometimes called, is a new form of human relations training conducted for groups of managers. In effect, although there's a leader, the meetings are unplanned and members are encouraged to speak their minds freely to each other, often in a way that results in hurt feelings. The aim of this type of training is to make managers more sensitive to others and to their own effect on others, and many managers claim that it produces excellent results.

Before prescribing such a seminar for his subordinates or taking part in one himself, the manager should understand that it is a controversial technique, and some people believe it does more harm than good. To this end the manager might want to read Chapter 10, 'A Sensitivity Training Group in Action', in *Leadership and Organization: A Behavioral Science Approach* by Robert Tannenbaum, Irving R. Weschler, and Fred Massarik,[3] and also the arguments pro (by Chris Argyris of Yale) and con (by George S. Odiorne of the University of Michigan).[4]

DIRECTION

Assuming the operation has been adequately staffed and the employees have been trained to the point where they are quite capable of doing a good job, the manager's work as a director of people is really just beginning. The fact that his subordinates *can* do the work well doesn't mean that they necessarily will. Both the quality and the quantity of their work may fall short of what they potentially could produce. Only if they are motivated to do their best will they turn in the best performance possible for them.

People may, of course, be motivated by fear – fear of losing their jobs or of not getting a merit increase, or simply fear of a bawling out or a nasty look from their boss. But fear is not a very good

[3]. Robert Tannenbaum, Irving R. Weschler and Fred Massarik: *Leadership and Organization: A Behavioral Science Approach* (New York, McGraw-Hill, Inc., 1961).

[4]. *Training Directors Journal* (October 1963). Reprinted in part in Ernest Dale, *Readings in Management: Landmarks and New Frontiers* (New York, McGraw-Hill, Inc., 1965), pp. 282–90.

motivator since it is impossible for the boss to police every action, and the person who is motivated by fear alone will often find many ways of skimping on his work that will not be apparent to the boss. This is true even in depression times, when fear of job loss is acute, and much truer in times of prosperity when other jobs are available.

Thus a manager can achieve better results if he can be a leader rather than a driver of his people. He may have to use the fear motive in some cases, but he's likely to be a better manager to the extent that he can avoid doing so.

To determine how the manager can and should lead, let's first look at the various factors that have been identified as motivators of people in general and then examine the nature of leadership itself.

THE MONEY MOTIVE

Back in the early 1900s, Frederick W. Taylor, originator of scientific management, thought he had the answer: divorce planning and doing to ensure that each job is performed in the best way possible; use motion and time study to determine what the standards should be; and then pay people more for meeting and/or beating the standard.[5] In other words, use money as the motivator. Piecework plans, which also used money as an incentive, had been in existence long before Taylor's time, but Taylor added a new twist. If a man met or surpassed the standard, he was paid the higher rate for *all* the pieces he produced, not just for those he turned out over and above the standard number.

Taylor's view of motivation was simple: 'Now the workman wants just what we want,' he once told students at the Harvard Business School, 'high wages and the chance for advancement.... Welfare work and all such secondary aids to workmen ... should all come along in their proper time, but I wish to emphasize that they should not be allowed to interfere with doing those things which are necessary in order to give workmen what they want most, namely *high wages*.'[6]

---

5. He advocated that jobs be planned to the last detail by a group of special planners.

6. Lecture now in the archives of the Baker Library at Harvard. Published

Taylor's associate, Henry Laurence Gantt, improved his plan by introducing the daily wage, plus the incentive payments for meeting or surpassing the standard. This did away with one of the bad features of the Taylor incentive system under which rates for those who did not meet the standard were greatly reduced in order to make up for the higher rates paid to the faster workmen.

Taylor confidently expected that his system would produce a 'mental revolution' on the part of both management and labour. Management would make so much more because of the higher production that it would not want to cut the rates. Labour would have a chance to earn so much more that it would find no reason to strike for higher wages. In fact, he felt, there could be no possibility of argument over the wage rates at all since they would be 'scientifically' determined.

In experimental situations some remarkable increases in productivity did take place, but the mental revolution in industry was conspicuous by its absence. Labour unions opposed the plan and succeeded in getting the use of the stopwatch for time study banned from government operations. In one case a superintendent who was a prominent supporter of the scientific management movement introduced the plan and the result was a strike that nearly wrecked his company.

Some thirty years later, Taylor himself admitted that his plan had in no case produced the mental revolution that he had hoped for. Quite naturally, he attributed this to management's failure to use the plan as he had designed it – many managements cut rates as soon as production rose.

But many managements today have made strict rules against the cutting of rates, yet they have not sparked a mental revolution to any great degree. Many incentive plans are successful in raising productivity, but even their most ardent supporters don't claim that they tap the full potential of the great mass of workers or that they have produced any particular mental revolution on labour's

---

in Ernest Dale: *Readings in Management: Landmarks and New Frontiers* (New York, McGraw-Hill, Inc., 1965), pp. 119–20. See also Harold J. Leavitt: *Managerial Psychology*, 2nd ed. (Chicago, University of Chicago Press, 1964).

part. Not only do they fail to prevent strikes over wage rates; they are, in themselves, a frequent source of grievances.

Money is not the only motivator, the only thing the worker wants from his job. What else does he want, then?

THE SENSE OF BELONGING

The next answer management got was diametrically opposed to Taylor's. This was the answer provided by Elton Mayo and his associates Fritz Roethlisberger and W. J. Dickson in the famous series of experiments at the Hawthorne Works of the Western Electric Company in Chicago.

The company already had a group incentive plan in effect; that is, each employee's earnings were in part dependent on the productivity of a group. In the experiments a smaller group made up of half-a-dozen girls was used – and hence each worker's earnings depended more on her individual efforts than before. But the girls were allowed to get used to this before the experiments proper began.

Rest periods of various lengths – sometimes accompanied by light meals – were introduced for weeks at a time; and in one case the work week was shortened. With each change in the schedule, productivity went up, which seemed to indicate the value of rest periods. But when all rest periods, shorter hours, and food breaks were abolished, productivity went up still further.[7]

Mayo's explanation of this was that the girls in the test room formed a cohesive group. What the worker wants, he believed, is not more money but a feeling of 'belonging' to a stable group whose standards he accepts. People were happier, he felt, before industrialization when family and work relationships were less likely to be disrupted. But since it would be impossible and undesirable to return to the practices of the past, management should endeavour to recreate the 'feeling of belonging' that existed until technological developments made it necessary for people to adapt themselves to constant changes. He forgot, perhaps, or did

---

7. *See* Fritz Roethlisberger and W. J. Dickson: *Management and the Worker* (Cambridge, Mass., Harvard University Press, 1939) for a complete account of the Hawthorne experiments.

not know, that even in the old days people did not always produce to the top of their potential. The 'idle apprentice' was a well-known character before the Industrial Revolution.

Roethlisberger and Dickson, however, took a broader view. 'What the employees want' has been described by Roethlisberger, who pointed out specifically how the feeling of belonging may be fostered:

1. People like to feel important and to feel that they're doing important work.

2. They're often more interested in the size of their pay packets relative to those of others than in the absolute amounts of pay.

3. They want to be treated well by their supervisors, to be praised rather than blamed, and not to have to admit their mistakes – at least not publicly.

4. They like to know whether they're meeting expectations – how well they're doing.

5. They like to be listened to, consulted about changes that will affect them, or at least warned of changes before they take place.[8]

Well, this sounds quite reasonable. Aren't these things we all want – managers as well as employees, just as we want the high pay and the chance for advancement that Frederick Taylor spoke of?

Here we have a set of fairly definite guides for the manager that have been made the basis of many of the courses in human relations. But is this the whole story? Perhaps it is, if one examines the implications of the Hawthorne findings searchingly. But often, they have been interpreted too narrowly as meaning only that the supervisor should be 'nice' to employees and treat them politely, listen to their complaints, and advise them on their personal problems.

THE ACHIEVEMENT MOTIVE

Frederick Herzberg,[9,10] an outstanding sociologist, has provided

8. Paraphrased from a speech given before the Personnel Group of the National Dry Goods Association in 1950. Reprinted in W. Lloyd Warner and Norman H. Martin: *Industrial Man: Businessmen and Business Organizations* (New York, Harper & Brothers, 1959), pp. 325–6.

9. An excellent review of Frederick K. Herzberg's and other approaches is

an analysis that may be more helpful. Herzberg characterizes money, pleasant surroundings in the work place, and pleasantness on the part of the supervisor as 'hygiene' factors. That is, just as good medical hygiene removes factors that may be detrimental to health, what he calls the hygiene factors in the job situation remove possible causes of dissatisfaction and poor productivity but do not provide positive incentives to produce. The real motivators, he believes, are such things as the sense of achievement, interesting work, and the feeling that the accumulation of achievement will lead to personal growth and recognition.

The supervisor, Herzberg says, will need to be discriminating in recognizing good work and in rewarding it appropriately. He will need to be pleasant, of course. But in addition, he will have to organize and distribute the work so that each of his subordinates will be given a chance for successful achievement.

This is very much in line with the Y theory developed by Dr Douglas McGregor of MIT, which is that people are really anxious to do a good job and will do so if only management will let them take on all the responsibility they are capable of assuming. This theory he contrasts with what he calls the X theory, that people are naturally passive and lazy and have to be cajoled and/or compelled to work at all.

It is also in line with studies conducted by Dr Rensis Likert and his colleagues at the University of Michigan. They found that 'high productivity' supervisors were employee-centred supervisors whose groups were supervised less closely than the 'low productivity' groups and were themselves less closely supervised by their own superiors. They placed more responsibility on the employees, and thus might be said to be providing the chance for achievement and growth that Herzberg believes is all important.

This is also in line with some very cogent observations of Peter Drucker: 'Satisfaction is, above all, inadequate as motivation. ... Responsibility, not satisfaction, is the only thing that will serve.

---

contained in Saul W. Gellerman, *Motivation and Productivity* (American Management Association, Inc., 1963).

10. For a full explanation of Herzberg's theory, see his book written in collaboration with Bernard Mausner and Barbara Block Snyderman: *The Motivation to Work*, 2nd ed. (New York, John Wiley & Sons, Inc., 1959).

To perform, one has to take responsibility for one's own actions and their impact... one has, in fact, to be dissatisfied to want to do better.'[11]

These later findings don't really contradict the Hawthorne findings; they supplement them. In fact they help to explain them. The girls in the Hawthorne test room, who were under the direction of the researchers rather than that of the regular supervisors, said they could produce more because there was no 'slave driving'. Mayo discounted this remark because the regular plant supervisors were pleasant enough in their approach and by no stretch of imagination could they be considered 'slave drivers'. But in the test room, the girls set their own pace. They could slacken off at times and then make up for it later, and many supervisors make a fetish of a 'steady pace'. It may have been this that gave the girls their sense of freedom.

In addition, many of Roethlisberger's statements of 'what the employee wants' do carry some implication that responsibility and achievement are motivators – for example, his emphasis on participation and on praise for good work. Too much of the failure of the 'human relations approach' in many companies may rest on the failure to utilize it fully.

To cite one example, many researchers have called attention to the fact that 'participation' as practised is too often nominal. Either subordinates are asked to voice their opinions only so that they may be persuaded to accept a decision already made, or the participation is restricted to very peripheral activities, such as serving on bond drive committees or making minor suggestions about the company cafeteria.

It is remarkable, in fact, how some executives can bring themselves to believe that they are practising consultative supervision and allowing subordinates to participate in their decisions when actually they are doing nothing of the kind, and would probably achieve better results if they dropped the pretence. There was one company president, for example, who planned to move his headquarters from the South to California. He called a meeting of his

11. Peter Drucker: *The Practice of Management* (New York, Harper & Brothers, 1954), p. 303. Part Four of this book, comprising several chapters, develops this idea and contains many valuable insights for the manager.

immediate subordinates and asked them to suggest possible locations. About half the group voted for New York, and the rest chose Chicago.

'Well,' said the president, 'since we can't agree on either New York or Chicago, we'd better try a third possibility. We'll move to California.'

And he went through this scene although he knew that he had already purchased land in California and, furthermore, that *some of the men present knew that he had.*

Few company presidents would try such tactics with higher executives, but many subordinate managers act out similar scenes with rank-and-file employees because they believe the latter are not bright enough to know what's happened. But in this managers deceive themselves. You don't have to be extraordinarily intelligent to recognize deception of this sort, and there are always one or two in the group who can.

Unless the manager is prepared to allow genuine participation, he had better stick to old-fashioned authoritarianism coupled with some attention to the hygiene factors.

This doesn't mean that the manager must obey the employees or take a vote on every decision. But it does mean that he shouldn't ask for suggestions unless he really believes the employees can contribute something and is prepared to consider their suggestions seriously. If he has already made a decision, he should merely explain it without pretending that he can be convinced to make another.

Now what about money, which Taylor considered the sure and all-important motivator? Well, he was perfectly right in many respects – particularly, since as many behavioural scientists have pointed out, pay is a status symbol in our society and a very tangible recognition of achievement. But as regards incentive systems, and their failure to produce what Taylor thought they would, some interesting insights developed from studies conducted in a factory in Great Britain.

The researcher found that the workers made a distinction between 'good money' and 'big money'. 'Good money' enables a man to live on a standard that he considers adequate. 'Big money' provides many extras, but to many people it's not really worth the extra effort.[12] Other people continually seek the 'big money'.

Thus it is not always possible to say that *all* people will respond to the same motivators. And this is true of the motivators uncovered by the behavioural scientists as it is of the money motivator.

For example, take participation, or, as it is sometimes called, 'consultative supervision'. In general, its contrast – authoritarian supervision – is very much frowned upon in advanced management circles today. But sometimes it works better.

The Harwood Manufacturing Company is famous for the introduction of participation, and claims excellent results from it. But when that same company tried to introduce it into its plants in Puerto Rico, it found that the girls – who were used to authoritative direction from their fathers at home – were confused and made insecure by it. 'He's asking *us* what we should do,' they said. 'But if he's the boss and *he* doesn't know, how should we?'

It would be nice if a set of rules could be found that would tell the manager how to direct employees and subordinate managers in all cases, but the fact remains that groups and individuals differ and the manager must gauge what is needed and act accordingly. There are certain things everyone wants, but people want them to different degrees and in different doses.

But it is often possible to provide the achievement motive even on very routine jobs, provided the supervisor organizes the work so that each person can see the results of his efforts and get a feeling of satisfaction in his work.

For example, in one supermarket each of the employees who refill shelves as purchases are made is given responsibility for one or more aisles, not only for keeping it filled but for its appearance. A consultant who visited the store on a mission from central headquarters was surprised at the speed and effort the employees were putting into their work. He complimented one boy on the appearance of his aisle, and another immediately said: 'If you want to see a really good aisle, come see mine.' Each took a real pride in his work. Further, the employees said that the workday went like lightning – they were barely conscious of the passage of time

12. T. T. Paterson: *Glasgow Limited: A Case-Study in Industrial War and Peace* (Cambridge University Press, 1960), Chap. 18.

before it was lunch time or quitting time. They had to work hard and fast, and they were happier for doing so.

LEADERSHIP

From the foregoing we may derive some clues to the way in which the manager or supervisor may become an effective leader. Many of the findings of studies of leadership itself are also helpful.

Most people tend to believe in what is known as 'charismatic leadership' – that leadership consists of some intangible quality impossible to describe that is immediately recognized by everyone else. It follows from this, of course, that a leader will lead in all situations, regardless of who the followers are or where he is trying to lead them.

If this theory were valid, the manager who has not been a leader of every group in which he found himself would have to give up in despair. Fortunately both everyday experience and research on the subject by psychologists and sociologists contradict this idea. It is almost comparable to the theory – held by some in Victorian times – that because of his greater intelligence, a man could quell a lion or tiger merely by a direct and fearless glance. If anyone ever put the latter theory to the test, he was probably not on hand to report on the findings of his research.

The classical example of an apparently charismatic leader who was certainly not a leader in every situation is Hitler. According to his own account, he was 'a young ringleader' in his childhood, but since he was not exactly truthful, we may take this with a grain of salt. After he grew up, he failed to achieve a rank higher than corporal in the Army and for a long time afterwards his meetings attracted no more than half-a-dozen people.

Often the childhood leader is one who is good at games, or perhaps taller or stronger than the rest of the gang. Sometimes it is merely the fact he is a year or two older that makes him the 'natural leader' of the group.

Other attempts have been made to define leadership in terms of traits. Thus it has been said that a leader is fair, intelligent, kindly, and so on – that is, he possesses all the traits generally considered desirable. But everyone has met leaders – in business and elsewhere

– who were something less than perfect human beings. Yet this theory is nearer to some of the findings of the psychologists than the charismatic theory, for studies have shown that when a person is esteemed by the group it is more likely to accept him as a leader.

There really are two traits which most leaders do seem to have – intelligence and confidence. Many studies have shown that the leader is likely to be more intelligent than his followers, although too great an advantage in this respect may militate against his leadership. The reason confidence is important is easy to see – if he isn't sure of where he's going or can't act as though he were sure, he can scarcely expect other people to accept his direction without question.

The best-accepted theory of leadership today is that it depends on the situation – some people will lead in one situation, others in another – for leadership depends as much on the nature of the followers and on the situation in which they find themselves as it does on the nature of the leader himself. The leader, analysis tends to show, is the one who can best help the group achieve its objective. One round-up of leadership studies, in fact, came to the conclusion that while leaders were generally superior to their followers in one or more of a wide variety of ways, they had only one thing in common with each other: *superior technical ability in the field in which they were engaged.*

In another case an executive seminar took up the question of leadership, and instead of reading up on the subject, members set down the characteristics of good leaders they had worked for in the past. The only common characteristic found was that the leaders were people who were really interested in getting a job done, not those who were trying to win a popularity contest.

This theory is encouraging to the manager who lays no great claim to charisma. He can acquire superior knowledge of the field in which he is engaged, and the more his knowledge increases, the more confidence he will have in his own decisions, and thus he will acquire at least one trait that will reinforce his ability to gain acceptance of his leadership.

If authoritarian leadership is called for, it will be better accepted if the leader knows his job. There is nothing more disturbing to subordinates than the incompetent autocrat. Because of his lack of competence, they cannot respect him, and therefore they feel humiliated by taking his orders. And because he cannot but be at least slightly aware of his own incompetence, he tends to bluster to cover up his own uncertainty and thus acts more unpleasantly towards his employees.

Further, although employees appreciate praise, as Fritz Roethlisberger pointed out, praise from someone who really knows good work from bad is far more satisfying than indiscriminate and perhaps even undeserved praise. Praise from a boss who really doesn't know good work from bad may give the employee some sense of security ('If he likes what I'm doing, he can't be going to fire me'), but it gives him no real sense of achievement.

If job competence is so important, why have companies become so dissatisfied with it as the sole criterion of promotion? Time after time one hears managers complaining that too much stress has been placed on skill in the selection of supervisors and not enough on 'human relations' and 'leadership' qualities.

One reason is that 'skill' and 'knowledge of the job' have been interpreted too narrowly. The mere fact that a person can perform a manual job extremely well does not mean that he can direct others doing it. If he has true knowledge of the job, he knows how to plan it in the most effective way, what is more important about it and what is less important, and where it fits into the whole job the company is doing. He's interested enough not to rest on his current knowledge, but is constantly seeking ways to improve his methods.

The skilled man is sometimes so satisfied with his own methods, learned perhaps through a strict apprenticeship, that he's unwilling to change them when better methods are discovered. He becomes what higher managers refer to as a 'brittle' supervisor, one who resists all change and is generally a problem to his superiors.

Many people who can do a first-level job can't supervise others because they try to do the work themselves instead of training and encouraging others to do it. Thus the low-productivity supervisors in the University of Michigan studies tended to do more of the work themselves than the high-productivity supervisors, who spent more time advising employees, listening to their ideas, and so on.

These were supervisors of clerical workers, but one might take an example from another field. The star salesman who becomes a sales manager may go out into the field with one of his men, ostensibly to teach him how to sell. But what does he do when they visit a customer? He monopolizes the conversation, and makes the sale. As a result, the salesman gains no rapport with the customer and has no opportunity to learn from his own mistakes.

The proper conduct for the sales manager in this case is to stay more or less in the background, and to take part in the conversation only when he can reinforce the salesman's own presentation. Then after he and his man get outside, he can go over the whole interview, mention any mistakes, commend the good work done, and offer advice that will help the man the next time.

It is partly because of this tendency to grab the ball and run with it that the best salesman may not be the best sales supervisor or sales manager, which is a matter of observed fact.

It may also be because he takes little interest in such things as market surveys, analyses of the potential of various customers, the importance of considering credit ratings, and so on – all of which are part of the knowledge of the job needed by the sales manager.

The ability to delegate, which the manager needs as much as he needs knowledge of the job, can also be acquired, which is again encouraging to the man who may not possess any remarkable degree of charisma. It is acquired, of course, by thought and by practice.

In the matter of thought, another rule of one of the quickie courses – JRT or Job Relations Training – is of value. The supervisor should ask himself, 'What do I really want to accomplish?' In other words, is this one sale – or this one task – so important that I had better do it myself to get it done right, or is it more important to create a good employee?

Another characteristic of a good leader, according to Rensis Likert, is that he sets high standards – standards that are attainable but not easily attainable. Such standards, of course, contribute to the sense of achievement, for no one gains any sense of achievement from doing something anyone can do without half trying.

Now the situational theory holds that the person a group accepts as a leader is the one who can help the group achieve its objectives – and in many business and industrial situations, the objective of most members of the group is in line with company objectives to some extent. That is, most people want to do a job they can be proud of, as McGregor's Y theory indicates. They want a sense of achievement, and they want to grow on the job, get promoted, get such merit raises as may be forthcoming, and so on. And the manager who can help them achieve their ambitions – because he knows more than they do and has the time and patience to teach them – has gone a long way towards winning their acceptance of his leadership. A group of executives, for example, willingly accepts the leadership of a top manager who is instrumental in company growth because they know their own positions and incomes are likely to grow with the company.

But occasionally a manager is faced with a subordinate or a group of subordinates who are completely apathetic towards their work or who even seem to get a sense of achievement from being paid for not working. What then?

Of course there are some people that the manager can't do anything about. Their apathy or recalcitrance may not be their fault, since it may be the result of a lifetime of experience, but the manager can't hope to correct it. In that case he may have to separate them from the payroll as soon as possible. Or if they will perform useful work of some sort provided they're driven to it, then he must drive them.

However, he shouldn't be too inclined to reach such a conclusion about any given person. Many people don't realize their own capabilities and are afraid to try to exercise them. A little encouragement, a little chance to do something on their own and subsequent success at doing it will go a long way to change them.

There are secretaries, for example, who are afraid to try composing letters because they believe that they must be 'writers' or at least college graduates to do so. Yet with some training they can learn to write letters that are not only acceptable, but very good. The manager who takes the time to provide the necessary encouragement and training will subsequently save himself considerable time and effort – for he can simply pass on correspondence to his secretary with a notation 'tell him yes', or 'tell him no', and be confident that the replies will be properly expressed.

Apathy on the part of an entire group may be based on an incorrect view of the job that has been fostered by previous managers. Many managers, confident that the provision of 'hygiene' is all that is necessary, will tell an employee who asks questions beyond the immediate task, 'Well, now, let me worry about that. You don't need to bother with it.' This is actually the hygienic way of saying, as some supervisors did before 'good human relations' received so much emphasis, 'You're not paid to think. You're paid to work.' It may arouse less resentment, but it is equally productive of apathy.

If the supervisor has a group whose ambition and pride in work has been beaten down in this way, he cannot expect to change things over-night. He must patiently encourage each sign of interest and be willing to take the time to listen and to explain.

Further, unless he is supervising a machine-paced job, such as part of an automobile assembly line, he will often reorganize the work so that each person has a 'whole job' instead of little bits and pieces, the final result of which is so far away that no sense of achievement is possible.

SUGGESTED QUESTIONS FOR YOUR CONSIDERATION

1. Do you believe there's such a thing as a 'natural born' leader? If so, what do his leadership qualities consist of?

2. What is meant by the situational theory of leadership? Do you think it has validity? For what reasons?

3. Do you think you could provide your subordinates with more of the achievement motive if you were to change your way of doing things? Where would you start? What, specifically, would you do differently?

4. What can you do to become an even better leader? Would you like to work for someone like yourself if you were one of the employees reporting to you? What would you keep the same? What would you change in your personal approach to employees?

5. Have you ever taken a battery of tests that purport to measure problem-solving ability, personality factors, creativity, and so on? If so, have you examined the results carefully? Have you acted upon them?

CHAPTER 3

The Challenge of Organization

As soon as a man becomes a manager, he must become an organizer. For unless he organizes the work of his subordinates, they will be getting in one another's way and even counteracting one another's efforts – to say nothing of the fact that the way he organizes the work has a great deal to do with the effort his employees put into their jobs.

Organization has been called 'a system of communication', and it has been defined as 'coordination'. It is both, but a more fundamental definition is given by James D. Mooney, a former vice president and member of the Board of Directors of General Motors, in his book, *The Principles of Organization*:[1] 'Organization is the form of every human association for the attainment of a common purpose.' This definition is more inclusive than the other two, for we need communication mainly to ensure that everyone understands what the purpose is, what his part in achieving it is, and why it is to his advantage to help achieve it to the best of his ability. Coordination, in turn, is necessary to ensure that each person contributes to the common purpose without lost motion.

There are two schools of thought on organization – what is sometimes known as the 'classical', 'traditional', or management process school and the social science or behaviourist school. The concepts developed by the first group are based on company experience and logical common sense. Those developed by the second are drawn from findings of sociologists and psychologists, often arrived at through experimentation with companies and other groups.

Since both sets of theories are to some extent based on experience, it might seem that there is no reason why there should be any quarrel between them. Yet considerable differences sometimes develop in discussions on the subject of organization. The classicists

1. James D. Mooney: *The Principles of Organization* (New York, Harper & Brothers, 1939), p. 1.

have evolved certain 'principles of organization', which they believe offer general guides for the organizer, while some behaviourists claim that these guides are not only useless, but actually detrimental to good organization.

One reason is that the two schools of thought have been asking different questions – and, of course, the answers you get depend upon the questions you ask. In general the classicists have asked: What work must be done if an enterprise is to achieve its objectives? Which activities should be combined into a single job? Which jobs may be coordinated by a single executive? The behaviourists, on the other hand, have tended to ask: What do people want from the organization? How do they react to one another as they work in groups? How do the various groups interact with one another? How can we organize people so that their jobs will afford them satisfactions other than their pay packets?

Now it is obvious that the answers to the second set of questions have a decided bearing on the answers to the first. An organization of people is not a machine, and just because the parts are fitted together in what seems like a very logical order, it will not necessarily function as it is supposed to. Each individual has his own goals, which may or may not be in line with the purposes of the organization, and these goals – and the ways in which he sets about reaching them – will certainly be influenced by the interactions within the group in which he finds himself and by the interactions of his group and other groups in the organization.

Classicists, however, have never denied the usefulness of psychological and sociological findings. They believe that these can provide valuable insights for the manager, both in determining the style of direction he adopts and in fitting the pieces of his organization together. But they do believe that in developing an organization structure, he must *first* consider the purpose of the enterprise and the work that must be done if that purpose is to be achieved. And most behaviourists do accept the fact that the organization, especially the business organization, must have a purpose – in fact, many of their experiments have been conducted with the consent or at the instance of company managements who wished to know more about the effect of different types of organization practice on the people within the organization.

Thus there is really no reason for the manager to become a devotee of either one school or the other. He can accept the findings of both where they seem good to him – in the light of his own experience and the situation with which he must cope – and use what will be useful to him.

Now what, exactly, are some of the various theories?

THE CLASSICAL THEORIES[2]

The classical theories are easier to enumerate because they include several distinct principles, or suggestions, since the classicists don't consider them immutable principles but rather guides to be used as the occasion requires.

OBJECTIVES

The first of these is that there must be an objective (or objectives) for the organization as a whole, and for the holder of each position in it. This is, perhaps, a real principle, in that it holds true in every situation. There is no reason for a formal organization of any kind to exist unless people can accomplish something by working or acting together that they cannot accomplish separately. Even a group organized entirely for social purposes has an objective other than organization itself: for example, to run social events that none of the members could swing alone, or to provide for regular meetings so that members will find it easier to get together.

SPECIALIZATION

The second principle is that specialization is needed, and here it is the degree of specialization that the manager must concern himself with, for specialization is well established in modern industry, and the complexities today are such that it would be impossible to operate without it.

The theory behind specialization is, of course, that the greater

---

2. For an excellent treatment of these theories, see Luther Gulick and L. Urwick: *Papers on the Science of Administration* (New York, Institute of Public Administration, 1937). Also see Ernest Dale: *Management: Theory and Practice* (New York, McGraw-Hill, Inc., 1965).

the specialization, the easier it is for a person to become skilled at a job. Also, it is easier to find a person who has the aptitude or skill to perform one specialized task than one who can perform several.

There are, however, limits to the amount of specialization that is technically feasible or economically desirable. If there's room for only one person at the controls of a machine, it is technically impossible to subdivide the operation any further. If splitting up the work would produce a job that can't keep a person busy more than a couple of hours a day, the result would be a waste of time rather than an economic gain.

This is a situation a manager must watch, for sometimes the specialization that was worthwhile in the past is no longer so today. For example, one company employed two men full time to clean cuspidors at a cost of $10,000 a year in wages and fringe benefits. At one time, a great many employees chewed tobacco, so this was no doubt the most economical way to handle the cleaning. But a recent survey showed that there were only 83 men in the entire plant who chewed tobacco and said they needed cuspidors. In addition to keeping about 300 unused cuspidors free of dust, the cleaners were spending a large part of their time just talking. The answer was to unspecialize the job by letting those who used the cuspidors clean them themselves and transfer the specialized cleaners to other work.

Less narrow specialization may also be advisable from the viewpoint of worker morale. A very highly specialized job – for instance, one that is confined to making a few motions over and over – often produces apathy and discontent.

COORDINATION

Like objectives, coordination is essential because there can be no true organization without coordination. A characteristic of the large, complex organization is that it is not possible to rely on a common superior to coordinate all aspects of two or more managers' work. For this reason a number of other coordinating devices must be introduced: committees and/or specialized coordinators of various types.

Any manager can, however, do much on his own initiative to further coordination by maintaining communications with others on his level whom his work may affect. Henri Fayol, the French industrialist, who was the originator of many of the classical principles of organization, pointed out that there's no reason why two managers on the same level who report to two different superiors should not communicate with each other directly, provided they keep their superiors informed of any decisions arrived at. He called this form of horizontal communication throwing 'gangplanks' between positions and illustrated what he meant by a diagram like the following:

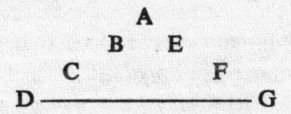

```
            A
         B     E
       C         F
     D ─────────── G
```

In this case, A is the head of a company or a division. If the typical organizational channels were followed, any communication from D to G would have to go all the way up the chain of command and down the other side before it would reach its destination, an obvious waste of many people's time, especially since the chain of command may be much longer than in the diagram. The gangplank was his answer, and he believed that every superior should authorize his subordinate managers to deal with others informally in this way, provided they kept him informed of the decisions made.

Authorizing subordinate managers to throw out gangplanks may be insufficient, however. Many managers never give a thought to anything but their own departments, and are likely to adopt a policy that makes things a little easier for them even though it causes a whole lot of inconvenience or expense to another department. A manager can make himself a great deal more useful to his company by using gangplanks himself and encouraging his subordinates to do so. Further, he may find that others will eventually be ashamed not to reciprocate, and his own job will become easier in consequence of his communication with them.

AUTHORITY

The authority principle implies that each man should have only one boss, and the line of authority should run from the company president straight down through the hierarchy to the rank-and-file employee. This principle is observed when the production worker reports to a single foreman, the foreman to a single production manager, the production manager to one vice president, and the vice president to the president. Henri Fayol called this the principle of 'unity of command' and it is, in many ways, a common-sense proposition. If a man has more than one boss, he may be subjected to conflicting orders and thus become confused.

The fact that a company uses group management at the top, as some companies do, need not prevent observance of the principle so far as most of the members of the organization are concerned. Members of the top group can thrash out differences before they transmit orders or instructions down through the channel, which is often known as the 'chain of command'. By-passing channels by utilizing Fayol's gangplanks is not a violation of this principle, since the gangplanks are designed for horizonal communication rather than communication up and down the chain of command.

Of course each man has more than one boss in that he is subject to the authority not only of his own immediate superior but of his superior's superior and all the bosses on higher levels. But this need not interfere with true unity of command since the higher bosses are supposed to transmit all their instructions down through the chain, and no one is told what to do by anyone except his immediate superior. Thus the production manager, or even the company president, should not bypass the foreman in issuing orders directly to the worker except in an emergency.

RESPONSIBILITY

This principle states that responsibility and authority should be commensurate, or as nearly equal as possible. If a man is held responsible for attaining certain objectives, he should be given the authority to do the things necessary to meet the goals. Conversely, when he has the authority, he should be willing to accept the responsibility that goes with it.

DELEGATION

The principle of delegation is that authority should be delegated as far down the line as possible. The advantages of practising delegation are that those who are closest to the scene of action may be best able to deal with the problems that arise and time is saved by not sending information up the line and directions down again. Perhaps even more important, pushing responsibility down the line is one way of tapping the initiative of everyone in the organization and of keeping people interested in their jobs.

How far down the line is it feasible to push authority to make a given decision? This depends on three things:

1. At what point does the person in the job have access to all the information necessary to make the decision? For example, it isn't expected that the production manager would know whether a change in the design of a product would increase sales sufficiently to offset higher production costs, or that the sales manager would know what the total effect of a design change would be on production. Therefore, a common superior must make a decision on this point.

2. At what point may the job incumbent be expected to have the incentive to decide solely on the basis of what is best for the entire company?

In the case cited above, the sales manager has no incentive to keep production costs down since he is judged on sales volume, while the production manager – who is judged on production costs – has no incentive to make expensive changes simply because they will benefit sales.

3. Is the incumbent personally capable of using good judgement in the case in question?

The first two criteria are easy to apply, but the last one is difficult indeed. The manager may delegate authority and hold responsible the man to whom he delegates, but the manager himself is still responsible to his own boss for the results of delegated decisions.

This is as it should be, because the manager has the authority to delegate or not to delegate.

Many managers, however, are much too cautious about delegation because they're afraid that their subordinates will make too many mistakes, and they have not devised the controls that make it possible for them to correct errors before they become serious. Thus many managers say that they could operate more effectively if their superiors would delegate more authority to them, and that they personally are overworked because their own subordinates are incapable of assuming responsibility.

SPAN OF CONTROL

The principle of span of control calls attention to the fact that a man can directly supervise only a limited number of people whose work is interrelated. As enunciated by L. A. Graicunas, a management consultant, this principle holds that supervision of two men entails six relationships:

First, there are the superior's own relations with each of the two men and his relations with each of them when he contacts them both at the same time – or four relationships altogether.
Second, there are the relations between A and B and between B and A. These may actually be two different relationships since A's attitude towards B may not be the same as B's attitude towards A.

Using this method of calculation, the number of relationships becomes enormous as more subordinates are added. With four subordinates the number of relationships becomes 44; with five subordinates it rises to 100.

This has led some management experts to contend that no executive should supervise more than four to eight subordinates whose work is interrelated. But the real question is whether the superior need be concerned about all these relationships. Shouldn't he really leave something to the men's own initiative? If there's a big fight over a question of policy or procedure, he'll naturally have to umpire it and make a decision. But if his subordinates are reasonably adult, he need give the relationships only occasional attention. He doesn't have to determine exactly how they feel towards each other at each moment. If he does, he's probably a 'snoopervisor' rather than a manager.

At any rate, most successful companies transgress the span of control principle, especially at the top, where a president or an executive vice president seldom has fewer than eight people reporting to him and may have as many as fifteen or twenty. It is true, however, that it is important to consider the span of control in developing an organization structure, since it naturally can't be extended indefinitely without loss of coordination. Some companies, however, still prefer to make the span of control as long as possible because they want to make it difficult for the superior to police things too closely. Thus he's practically forced to delegate more than he otherwise would. In addition, a long span of control makes it easy to observe another principle.

SHORT CHAIN OF COMMAND

Many authorities hold, and with good reason, that a short chain of command is desirable. This means there should be as few levels of supervision as possible between the chief executive and the rank and file. The greater the number of levels the more the chance that objectives and instructions will be garbled before they reach the point where action must be taken, and the more slowly and less accurately information will move up from the bottom to the top.

The short span of control and the short chain of command are likely to be incompatible in a company where there are many different activities and a great many people to be supervised. So it is necessary to strike an optimum balance between them. In fact, *balance* is cited by many classicists as one of the principles of organization – in this respect as well as every other.

LINE AND STAFF

The classical principles we've described would be easier to observe were it not for the fact that industry has become so complex that it has been necessary to carry specialization to the point where we have two different types of executives: *line* and *staff*. Line executives are those who supervise activities that contribute directly to the profits of the company, while staff executives are those who contribute indirectly by providing services or advice to the line organization.

Thus a production manager is a line executive, as is a sales manager. But departments like personnel, accounting, engineering, and production control are staff or auxiliary departments in a manufacturing company. Their job is to assist the line departments. On the other hand, a copy-typing department in a secretarial-services agency, since it actually produces the service which the agency sells to its customers, is a line department.

The existence of staff departments makes it very difficult to keep spans of control short, and it makes it impossible to have a single line of authority running from the chief executive down through the chain of command to the rank and file. This difficulty is partially recognized by the fiction of 'functional authority', which is indicated by dotted lines on the organization chart. But 'functional authority' is usually very real authority – and where its possessors are higher in the organization than the line managers, they in fact dilute the latter's authority even though the plans they devise may be transmitted through a line superior. For example, if a methods department, which is a staff department, reports to the plant manager or the production chief, the first-line foremen will have less freedom to prescribe the methods to be used. Similarly, if the plant is one of many, the plant manager's own authority may be somewhat diluted by policies or instructions devised by staff men at headquarters.

Neither staff executives nor line executives are entirely happy with this situation. Line executives may complain that the staff interferes with their operations and requires them to spend too much time making reports. Staff executives, on the other hand, may find that the line resists their efforts to help, and that they have continuously to 'sell' their ideas to others down the line to get their plans put into effect.

The line-staff difficulty may sometimes be due to higher management's neglecting to define jobs carefully. But even if the extent of responsibility and authority attaching to each position has not been made entirely clear, the line and staff management down the line can do a great deal to ease the situation.

Line managers should remember that staff men can help them with problems that they don't have time to study themselves, and thus make use of staff services to the fullest extent possible. They should keep an open mind about new programmes that the staff suggests, and not condemn them out of hand simply because the staff has suggested them. Nor should they construe staff suggestions as criticisms of the way they have been handling things to date. No one person can be expert in all the specialized skills needed in modern business, and no one is expected to be. In fact, that's why staff men exist.

Staff men, on the other hand, should be content to introduce their projects gradually and shouldn't assume an air of superiority simply because of specialized training. They should be willing to listen to the line's objections and criticisms of their programmes since the objections may be based on very practical experience and thus be well worth taking into account, even to the extent of modifying a programme based on what seems to be very sound theory.[3]

In addition to the specialized staff departments, there are two other types of staff of which the manager should be aware. The first is 'personal staff' – a private secretary for example – and the second is the general staff-man or assistant-to. Both are outside any chain of command, and there's no reason why either should come into conflict with line executives. An assistant-to, it should be noted, is not the same thing as an assistant, who is second-in-command and may have to act for his chief when the latter is absent. The assistant-to has no authority over anyone, unless he has assistants of his own. He merely handles part of the functions that the chief executive cannot delegate. Generally, his role is that of information gatherer and evaluator.

The position of assistant-to the chief executive is often a highly coveted one since it provides an opportunity to learn general management skills that few other positions provide. Also, the incumbent has a high degree of 'visibility' – that is, the man in the

---

3. For a very enlightening picture of line-staff difficulties, see Melville Dalton: 'Conflicts between Staff and Line Managerial Officers', *American Sociological Review* (June 1950), pp. 342–50. Reprinted in part in Ernest Dale: *Readings in Management: Landmarks and New Frontiers* (New York, McGraw-Hill, Inc., 1965), pp. 207–10.

best position to further his career cannot be ignorant of his existence or his abilities. Sometimes the position is used as a training ground for a future chief executive.

The position, however, is one in which the incumbent needs to watch with extreme care his relationships with his chief's immediate subordinates since in the course of his information gathering he may be tempted to assume authority he does not possess and arouse resentment that may result in his ousting.

Another type of general staff-man is the chief of staff, who has authority over all the staff functions in the company. Not many companies have created such a position, however.

USING THE CLASSICAL PRINCIPLES

Now the general classical maxims and the distinction between line and staff provide only general instructions about the actual mechanics of organizing. Have the classicists anything else to offer?

Yes, they have. Specifically, they offer certain guides to the division of work. For example, Luther Gulick has pointed out that work may be divided by:

1 The purpose served
2. The process used
3. The persons or things dealt with
4. The place where the service is rendered.

These criteria may be used at any level in the organization, though not necessarily in the order given, to determine how the work should be divided and then subdivided.

Consider a manufacturing company. The overall objective is to produce tangible products and sell them at a profit. However, this implies two different purposes: *making* and *selling*, which also require two entirely different sets of processes. In addition, the fact that the objective includes making a profit indicates that there must be records kept. So there is still another primary division by both purpose and process: *finance and accounts*. Thus every manufacturing company has at least three main divisions: manufacturing, sales, and accounting or finance. In some companies there are two financial departments both reporting to the president

– the accounting or controller's department and the treasurer's department. This is not illogical, for these two also serve entirely different purposes. The accounting department provides the records for control while the treasurer's department manages investments, stock issues, and borrowings.

If the company has only a single plant, the head of manufacturing may be the plant manager. But if it has several, it will resort at once to a subdivision by place – that is, there will be one executive in charge of manufacturing in all the plants and several plant managers under him.

Now the plant manager has more than one purpose to consider. He must strive for the right quantity of production and also ensure that what is produced is of the right quality, but these two purposes conflict to some extent since it is easier to produce in quantity if he pays no attention to quality. Hence he'll probably want to separate quality control from the management of production.

Production itself may be divided according to processes, each of which may be placed under a supervisor. If the plant is a large one, there may be general foremen over the first-line supervisors. Usually related processes or departments near each other will be placed under one man. Or, if the plant produces more than one product, the division may be by things dealt with.

Now consider another of the primary purposes of the enterprise: *selling*. What processes are used here? Fundamentally there are two: Advertising and face-to-face selling through salesmen who visit the customer. The modern concept is to put the two together under a single marketing manager, and have both the sales manager and the advertising manager report to him.

In sales, also, there is often a division by things dealt with, as when different sales forces are used for different products. This division may even occur further up in the organization scale, so there may be a marketing manager for industrial products and one for consumer products.

The division between industrial and consumer products might also be considered a division by persons dealt with, since industrial products are sold to companies and consumer products to wholesalers or retailers, or sometimes directly to consumers.

Geographical division of the sales force is typical. If the company sells throughout the country, it will generally have regional and district sales managers, and each salesman is assigned an exclusive territory in any case.

Again, an accounting department has the general purpose of providing records that will enable management to maintain control – that is, to determine when deviations from the planned course of action are occurring. But many different processes are used for this purpose – two examples are budgeting and cost accounting, which is the determination of the cost to produce a single unit of the product. Thus further subdivisions of the department may be made if it is a large one.

Division by purpose, it may be seen, enables the manager to set definite objectives for each segment of his enterprise. Division by process, or by people or things dealt with, enables him to bring together the jobs that require the same or related skills. For example, selling industrial products may require a knowledge of engineering, but selling of consumer products may not.

Geographical division of the work is one way of cutting down the manager's direct span of control, and also of reducing the time wasted in travel. And travel time may be within the plant as well as outside it. For example, many plants that are spread over acres of ground have adopted what is known as 'area maintenance' – that is, stationing a maintenance foreman and several craftsmen in each department or at a central point near a group of related departments. This saves travel from the central maintenance shop, which in a large plant may be as much as half a mile or more distant from some of the departments.

DIVISIONALIZATION

A company generally begins by having what is termed a 'functional' organization – with each of the principal functions, either line or staff, reporting to a top executive, probably a vice president, who in turn reports to the company president. But as the company grows, this organization may become increasingly unwieldy as chains of command get longer and longer.

Then a company may resort to what is known as *divisionalization*, which is a new way of dividing the work according to things dealt with. A division manager is appointed to take complete charge of both the production and marketing of a single product or group of products, and is judged not on the amount of production or the volume of sales but on the profit his division produces. His position is comparable, then, to that of the president of a smaller company, except that he's not responsible for raising capital. That's appropriated for him from the general company funds.

Occasionally divisionalization is by place; that is, the division manager is given charge of all operations, including both sales and marketing, in a section of the country. This, however, is less common than divisionalization by products.

Divisionalization has several advantages. It brings major decision-making closer to the scene of action and enables the man in charge to concentrate his efforts on a single family of products. In addition, it relieves the burden on top management.

However, it introduces new problems. One of these may arise because some divisions sell all of their products to other divisions of the same company. How, then, are the prices to be set? If the division manager is compelled to sell at a low price in the interests of the overall profitability of the company, it's hardly fair to judge him on the profit and loss statement. On the other hand, if he's permitted to charge his captive market whatever he wants to, his profits might be artificial so far as the whole company is concerned. One might say, of course, that the price should be the 'market price', but this may be difficult to determine because prices may be set by bidding, and outsiders are not likely to waste time preparing bids if they know they can't get the business anyway.

This problem, however, will affect only certain divisions, and in some companies there may be none that sell only to other divisions of the company. More serious may be the loss of control by top management, which may not know that things are going badly until something very unfortunate happens. Income statements that look good may conceal a variety of shortcomings. Pressure to show increased profits may lead divisions into such practices as letting plants and equipment run down, adding too many bad debts into accounts receivable, or short cuts of various kinds that may bring the whole company into disrepute. These practices are likely to show up in the income statement eventually, but perhaps not until a good deal of harm has been done.

REORGANIZATION

Often an organization has outgrown its current organization structure because many new products and new functions have been added as its size increased. So, thorough reorganization may be needed. But a company may reorganize to align the work more logically and lose more than it gains because of the general disruption entailed when old relationships are suddenly broken up and many people become fearful that the reorganization may leave them in a less favourable position than before.

Therefore it is generally recognized that reorganization should be as gradual as possible. If the present organization is not too unwieldy, the procedure recommended by the classicists is for the manager to chart the 'ideal organization', as he would like to see it if he didn't have to consider people at all and then gradually work towards it rather than introduce the changes all at once. For instance, a company may recognize that since advertising and sales serve the same purpose, they should be coordinated by a single marketing manager. But if the advertising manager and sales manager now report to the company president, both would feel that they had been demoted if another layer of supervision were suddenly inserted between them and the top. For this reason it may be necessary to wait until some of the executives retire before making the change.

BEHAVIOURAL SCIENCE AND ORGANIZATION

Most companies are organized largely along classical lines, although they don't necessarily observe all the principles exactly. And by and large, they have a chain of command with the work divided into specialities according to one or more of the methods suggested by Luther Gulick.

Yet as psychologists, sociologists, and other behavioural scientists have examined situations in industry, they have tended to be critical of the traditional approach, sometimes harshly so. Probably the severest critic of the classical principles is Chris Argyris of Yale, who states definitely that organizations structured along classical lines are not suited to the needs of psychologically healthy people – that the environment created tends to demand that they be 'dependent, passive, and use few and unimportant abilities'.[4]

This is certainly true of some business organizations structured along classical lines, with specialization carried up to the point which is technologically or economically feasible and where those in charge are so fearful of mistakes that they prescribe every action in detail. But this doesn't follow from the classical principle of specialization as we have described it.

Some behavioural scientists have advocated what is known as an 'organic organization' in which jobs are defined only slightly, if at all, and everyone pitches in and does what he can do best. This sometimes works very well in a small group; but in an organization of any size, it is likely to make coordinated work impossible. Moreover, there are many people who, so far from being stimulated by this freedom, are made insecure by it.

Two British researchers, Tom Burns and G. M. Stalker, examined an electronics company whose chief executive contended that jobs should be as little defined as possible so that they might be shaped to the abilities and initiative of those who held them.

All personnel, who numbered around 2,000, were housed in a single one-storey building so that direct access to anyone was possible, and there was a general awareness of the common objective. When necessary, one individual or group obtained help from another, largely by personal discussion and negotiation.

The result was described as follows:

The sheer difficulty of contriving the correct social stance ... for use in different negotiations, the embarrassment of having so to contrive, and the personal affront attached to failure to achieve one's ends by these means induced in managers a nervous preoccupation with the

---

[4]. Chris Argyris: *Personality and Organization: The Conflict between System and the Individual* (New York, Harper & Brothers, 1957), p. 233.

See also the review on Argyris in Saul W. Gellerman: *Motivation and Productivity* (American Management Association, Inc., 1963), pp. 73–82, 94, 102, quoted 179.

hazards of social navigation ... and with the relative validity of their own claims to authority, information, and technical expertise.[5]

Again, an electronics manufacturer in the U.S.A. (Non-Linear Systems of San Diego, California) broke up an assembly-line type of organization in which people were seated at long tables and each person performed a very small part of the total job. Instead, it organized them into groups of about seven people each, placed each group under the direction of an electronics technician, and gave each group kits of parts from which to assemble completed products. People were allowed to divide the work as they saw fit and work at their own pace, and were given responsibility for producing finished, checked, and correctly calibrated instruments.

At the same time the company more or less broke down the fences between the various jobs at the top and defined the executive responsibilities very broadly in such terms as 'productivity' and 'market standing'. No one reported to the seven executives at the top directly, yet everyone reported to each one on some aspect of the work.

What happened? As far as the rank-and-file workers were concerned, the results were excellent. There was an initial period of some confusion which lasted for several months, but eventually productivity reached and then surpassed previous levels. Moreover, the company found that it had created flexible groups capable of building many different kinds of instruments and that the people learned new techniques easily. As a result it could offer customers the exact features they wanted because the employees could build instruments to order without difficulty. And the work force in this case was neither exceptionally brilliant nor exceptionally well educated. It included a good many men and women who had not even graduated from high school.

But the results were less fortunate among the executives in middle and top management. They were not happy with their ill-defined responsibilities, and eventually the company reverted to a more conventional form of organization for its executive group, with more strictly defined duties for each one.

5. Tom Burns and G. M. Stalker: *The Management of Innovation* (London, Tavistock Publications, 1961), p. 93.

At the rank-and-file level the new organization produced sky-high morale and higher productivity, but at the executive level a sense of uneasiness. Why the difference?

The conclusion the company drew from this, according to *Business Week*,[6] was that the more intelligent a man is the more he wants to know where he stands; and since the executives were presumably more intelligent than the production workers, they had a greater need for more exact definitions of their jobs.

One can, however, draw another conclusion. Very few people, however intelligent or unintelligent they may be, can be happy in an *entirely* unstructured job – that is, one in which their objectives and the extent of their authority and responsibility are entirely undefined – at least not where they must work in cooperation with other people, as they naturally must in an organization.

While the people on the assembly line were not told how to go about the jobs, except through the guidance of the technicians, their objectives were clearly defined, and so were their responsibilities and their authority to proceed. Also, as classical theory prescribes, they each had only one boss in the person of the technician who acted as group leader.

The executives at the top presumably had only one boss, the company president, but they apparently didn't know the extent of their authority and responsibility, and where one job left off and another began. For middle management executives there was added confusion in that they reported to several different people. Thus a regional sales manager, who had formerly reported only to the vice president of marketing, had to go 'to one man for market reports, to another for budgets, and to still another for the training of salesmen'.[7]

ORGANIZATION FOR MOTIVATION

Some managers have a saying, 'If you want a good job done, make it somebody's baby' – that is, give him responsibility for success or failure and let him work out his own plan of the best way to go about it. And it should be a job that calls on all his abilities and one

6. *Business Week* (20 March 1965), p. 94.
7. ibid.

in which he can judge his own failure or success as he goes along. That's practically the only way to arouse his interest and get the best from him. Moreover, it can be done without any great violation of classical principles.

The only point in specializing a job to the point where it requires only one motion or only a few motions is that it makes it easier to substitute a machine for human labour.

Peter Drucker, who is neither a classicist nor a behaviourist, but a close observer of industry and an authority on management, has suggested the following guides for the organization of work:

1. Each job should constitute a distinct stage in the work process. The man or men doing the job should always be able to see a result. It does not have to be a complete part, but it should always be a complete step. Final heat treating of a metal part... is such a step. It contributes something visible, important and irreversible.

2. The job should always depend for its speed or rhythm only on the performance of the man or men performing it. It should not be entirely dependent on the speed with which the jobs before it are being done. The workers should be able to do it a little faster at times or a little slower.

3. Each job should embody some challenge, some element of skill or judgement...

4. Whenever a job is too big, too complicated, or too strenuous to be performed by an individual, it should be done by a community of individuals working as an organized team rather than by a series of individuals linked together mechanically.[8]

Only when work is organized so that each portion of it is the 'baby' of some person or group will it be possible to get real motivation, for only in that case can people get the sense of achievement which is the real motivator towards better performance.

And it is only when real judgement must be used that this sense of achievement can be obtained. For example, in one case, girls packing candy were allowed to choose one of three patterns in placing the candies in the box, but they preferred to have one prescribed

8. Peter Drucker: *The Practice of Management* (New York, Harper & Brothers, 1954), pp. 295–6, 298.

pattern instead. The choice they were given was not a real choice — it made no difference which pattern they selected. If the worker's job doesn't allow him to make decisions that affect results, he prefers a job that's completely mechanical and that he can do without thinking at all. It is the lesser of two evils.

To organize work in such a way that it will provide the real motivators described by Herzberg is a challenge to every manager, whether he's the president of a company or the head of a small group. It can be done, and it has been in some companies, but it takes ingenuity, knowledge of processes, and an insight into the capabilities of individual subordinates.

THE INFORMAL ORGANIZATION

The informal organization is sometimes spoken of as though it were one organization pervading an entire company and existing side by side with the formal organization. But the informal organization is not one organization but several. It consists of a number of circles, whose members are in communication with each other and who thus establish traditions, norms, and status systems of their own. Some of these circles intersect each other and others are entirely separate.

Managers have probably paid most attention to the informal organization as it exists in a rank-and-file group under a first-line supervisor in cases where it curtails output. It was in response to a situation like this that Frederick W. Taylor developed his differential piecework plan by which a man could earn more by producing more. The same phenomenon was noted in one of the Hawthorne studies.

Employees explain this restriction on output, where it occurs, by the fear that if they do too much work they will eventually be laid off. Or if they are on piecework or an incentive system, they fear that the rates will be cut or the standards raised if they show that higher productivity is possible.

Although some social scientists have been reluctant to believe that these are the real reasons, they may in many cases be the simple truth. But there may be other reasons, and some developing out of the way the work is organized.

When it is impossible for a man to see real results from his work and he's expected to keep moving at a 'steady pace' throughout the day, performing the same few motions over and over, he may tend to keep that pace as slow as possible so as not to get too tired by the end of the day. On the other hand, if he had some part in planning his work, and could feel responsible for results, he might not work so steadily but might accomplish far more.

At any rate, some cohesive work groups with highly developed informal organizations do attain very high productivity, and this may be due both to the absence of the fears mentioned above and to the way in which the group is organized. Certainly the organization of the work groups at Non-Linear Systems and the responsibility given them had everything to do with the increase in productivity achieved.

The development of 'norms' of productivity – either high or low – is only one manifestation of the informal organization. In many cases it facilitates the attainment of company objectives by making possible more horizontal communication – between people on the same level – than the formal organization channels provide. Another result of the informal organization is that it permits people to 'make their own jobs' to some extent and to use the abilities they possess to the highest degree. T. N. Whitehead, who was one of those who took part in the Hawthorne experiments, pointed this out in his book, *Leadership in a Free Society:*[9]

... anyone with a first-hand experience of factory life will recognize the many unofficial ways in which a foreman creates a small group of collaborators officially denied to him. John, an elderly mechanic, shows some aptitude for training novices and he, unrecognized by the formal organization, is the *de facto* trainer for the shop. Tom is quick at figures, and looks after the foreman's paperwork. ... Without such a shadow staff, the position of the foreman would be quite hopeless ...

Again, the informal organization often enables people to do what's necessary to meet specific day-to-day problems that arise by changing procedures or channels of communication to meet the situation. Often these problems are special and temporary, and it would not be worthwhile to change the formal organization to take

9. T. N. Whitehead: *Leadership in a Free Society* (Cambridge, Mass., Harvard University Press, 1936), p. 114.

account of them, but an informal organization enables them to be solved satisfactorily without any disruption of the formal organization.

SUGGESTED QUESTIONS FOR YOUR CONSIDERATION

1. To what extent are the classical principles of organization observed in your company? To what extent do you follow them in your own organizing work?

2. What is an 'organic organization'? Do you think your group would function more or less effectively if your immediate organization were a little more organic?

3. Do you think you should have more specialization among the members of your group, or that you might get better results if you broadened the jobs and made them less specialized?

4. What is the 'informal organization'? Is it producing good or bad results in your immediate group?

CHAPTER 4

Managing and Communicating by Objectives

IN his novel, *Little Dorrit*, Charles Dickens wrote of a certain government department that he called the 'Circumlocution Department' and whose members he named 'Barnacles':

> When that admirable Department got into trouble and was, by some infuriated member of Parliament, whom the smaller Barnacles almost suspected of labouring under diabolic possession, attacked ... as an Institution wholly abominable and Bedlamite; then the noble or right honourable Barnacle who represented it in the House would smite that member and cleave him asunder with a statement of the quantity of business (for the prevention of business) done by the Circumlocution Office. Then would that noble or right honourable Barnacle hold in his hand a paper containing a few figures, to which, with the permission of the House, he would entreat its attention ... Then would the noble or right honourable Barnacle perceive, sir, from this little document, which he thought might carry conviction even to the perversest mind (derisive laughter and cheering from the Barnacle small fry) that within the short compass of the last financial half-year this much maligned Department had written and received fifteen thousand letters (loud cheers) ... had made twenty-four thousand, five hundred and seventeen memoranda (vehement cheering). Nay, an ingenious gentleman connected with the department ... had done him the favour to make a curious calculation of the amount of stationery consumed in it during the same period. It formed a part of this same short document; and he derived from it the remarkable fact that the sheets of foolscap paper it had devoted to the public service would pave the footways on both sides of Oxford Street from end to end, and leave nearly a quarter of a mile to spare for the park.

An exaggeration? Certainly. But in essentials a good picture of the way some government departments, in Dickens's day and ever since, have viewed their tasks. Can the same thing happen in business? It can and does. Many businessmen are inclined to regard government as inefficient, and business as efficient, and to believe that the type of bureaucracy Dickens satirized in the

Circumlocution Department cannot exist in industry. It arises in government, they say, because the government is not subject to competition, whereas business – which must be efficient if it is to survive and compete – would not tolerate such a department for a minute.

Unfortunately, the facts are against them. More than fifty years ago, Harrington Emerson, an early efficiency expert, reported that he had found groups of clerks on some railroads spending their entire time making out reports that no one ever looked at. Apparently at some time in the past, a company president had requested that certain sets of figures be sent to him regularly. Then he had died or retired, and the new president wanted a different set of figures; and perhaps the next president called for a third set. All three reports continued to be made regularly because no one ever told the clerks to stop working on them, even though the fourth president might be getting all the figures he needed from some other source and neither he nor anyone else ever looked at the reports.

That happened more than a half century ago, and maybe things have since changed. Unfortunately not. Whenever a company institutes a programme of forms control in an effort to cut down the different types of forms, it is likely to find that outmoded reports which no one needs are still being faithfully made out. Management literature is full of examples.

This happens in government and in industry not because the people are naturally inefficient – indeed, they may be quite efficient in making out the useless reports – but because in many large-scale organizations, the people who do the actual work are removed from the policy-making levels and don't understand the objectives of the whole organization. They've been told what they're to do, and often how they're to do it, but not why they're doing it or what the ultimate purpose is. Thus, like the Circumlocution Department, they come to think that their objective is to get out as many letters and memoranda as possible, but are totally unconcerned with what the letters or memoranda are supposed to accomplish.

A NEW APPROACH

Management by objectives is a new approach to management and organization designed to encourage initiative and to prevent the working at cross-purposes, or for no purpose at all, that's likely to occur unless positive efforts are made to communicate the company's objectives down through the entire organization.

Management by objectives shifts the emphasis from cut-and-dried procedures to accomplishing results. It makes it easier to follow the methods of direction and leadership that prove most successful in providing the achievement motive, for it leaves people free to develop better ways of doing things if they find that new methods will produce better or quicker results.

It also makes over-all goals the concern of every manager and helps to break down the narrow departmental view that so many managers take because they know they will be judged entirely on the records of their own department.

Further, it is much easier to evaluate and reward people when the objectives of each job are clear. Many managers don't like to talk over executive appraisals or employee merit ratings with their subordinates because the rating systems in use compel them to evaluate people in terms of traits. It is hard to tell a person that he doesn't possess enough 'tact', 'initiative', 'character', or 'acceptability' – all terms that have been used on appraisal forms. To criticize a man on counts like these amounts to a personal attack of a type that's difficult for anyone to take with good grace.

Moreover, it implies that the man had inherent failings that are so much a part of him that there isn't much he can do about them. When he's judged by the results he achieves, by his success in reaching definite objectives, he's encouraged to use the abilities he possesses to the full rather than sulk over shortcomings the boss has accused him of. It might be added that shortcomings, either of intellect or of personality, are immaterial as far as the job is concerned if they don't interfere with results.

Ideally, management by objectives should begin at the top with the emphasis on opportunities rather than on problem-solving. It should start with consideration of possible markets, and the answer to the question: *What do customers really pay us for?* Or if it is a new business, the question should be: What do people want that they cannot now get easily, or in the form they want it, or at the time or the place they want it?

One very successful management news service is said to have started with the idea: 'What information do managers need on such things as taxes, government regulations, and so on that they cannot get easily in succinct form?' Once this was set forth, the founder determined how it could be supplied.

Many people start businesses with no other objective than 'to go into business for myself'. Then they pick a field simply because they know something about it – or even one they know nothing about – and proceed to sink their savings or borrowed capital into the venture. This is one reason why so many new businesses fail during their first fiscal year, and why few remain in business for as long as five years.

It might be stated as an axiom that no business can succeed or continue to exist unless it fills a vacuum of some sort – unless it supplies something people want that would otherwise not be supplied at all, would not be supplied in sufficient quantity, or would not be supplied at the right time and the right place.

OBJECTIVES V. TASKS

If management by objectives has been adopted on a company-wide basis, the subordinate manager may be asked to suggest possible objectives for his department, and to commit himself to producing certain results that will contribute to the overall objective. But even if this is not the case, he can make use of this new technique in managing his own job and the people under him.

He might first try this little test. He can pick out any of his employees and ask him what justifies his being on the payroll. It is more than probable that the employee will reply by stating what he does rather than what he accomplishes – 'I get out these reports' or 'I operate this machine'. In other words he will be 'task-oriented' rather than 'accomplishment or contribution minded'.[1]

1. See Robert H. Schaffer: 'Managing by Total Objectives', *Management Bulletin* 52 (New York, American Management Association, 1964).

Many job descriptions encourage task orientation rather than orientation toward objectives, even on the part of managers. For example:

The general accountant is responsible for establishing and maintaining the general books of the company and for the preparation of financial and budget statements in accordance with the approved policies and procedures of the company.

The maintenance of general books of account is not an objective. It is a task. The books are not ends in themselves but means to ends. There are many ways in which they can make a positive contribution to profit. To do so they must show not only the historical information necessary for the annual reports to stockholders and for the satisfaction of the tax authorities, but also the data that permit management to know where it stands at any given moment and to determine whether or not its plans are being carried out as expected. And they should provide this information soon enough so that management can take steps to counteract unfavourable trends as soon as they appear.

Perhaps the general accountant is well-trained in his profession and high enough in the organization to understand what management needs in this respect and to realize that he is responsible not only for maintaining the books but for suggesting changes in reporting practices when it becomes evident that management could use more information or information different from what it is now getting.

But even men high up in the organization structure don't always consider objectives. There are organization specialists who are more concerned with the appearance of their charts than they are with the actual functioning of the organization. Thus they may recommend breaking up a job or the insertion of another layer of supervision, not because the organization is not functioning properly, but because a span of control seems to them unduly long. There are personnel managers who recommend the adoption of new programmes merely because other companies have them, not because there is any real assurance that they will contribute to company objectives.

One young man whose job was writing standard practice

instructions produced a set of directions that could mean either of two diametrically opposite things. When this was called to his attention by someone on his own level, he said: 'Well, since no one else has noticed it, I think I'll leave it the way it is.' It never occurred to him that the only reason why the company wanted the instructions in writing was to ensure that everyone understood them in the same way.

But perhaps the epitome of task orientation was demonstrated by a graduate student in a school of business administration who had had some experience in hospital administration and was planning to make a career in that field. In a term paper, he wrote: 'The concept of the patient-centred hospital is all very well, but it should not be allowed to interfere with good administration'. Apparently no one, either on the job or in graduate school, had ever said to him: 'Why do we have hospitals at all? What are they *for*? To provide jobs for administrators?'

Some job descriptions do provide objectives for each job, and this is all to the good. But it is not enough. Each superior should talk over the objective of his group with each subordinate and make plain the contribution expected. In doing so he should relate the objective of each job to broad company objectives and show how it contributes to their attainment.

It may be, of course, that his own superior has never taken the trouble to do the same thing with him, but this need not stop him from doing so. He can analyse the matter for himself, decide what his objectives should be, and then take the initiative in discussing the matter with his superior.

To begin with he should realize that the real objective of the company is not simply to produce X or Y product at a present profit. More realistically he can say: 'We're in business to create and to retain customers by satisfying their wants competitively and profitably.'

This implies a fundamental orientation towards the market rather than a turning inward toward the convenient role of getting out production or simply following procedures. Then he should ask himself the following questions:

1. What wants do we really satisfy? For example, in purchasing the services of an advertising agency, a company is not buying

simply copy, art, placement of it in media. It is hoping to buy increased sales. Agency account executives who realize this often use the knowledge to help customers with their complete plans; and if they succeed in producing sizeable increases in sales, they may turn a small customer into a big one.

2. What advantages do we have over our competitors? Quality? Price? Service? Or if we seem to have no special advantages, what advantages could we provide? When the National Steel Company was organized, Ernest T. Weir (National's founder), knew he could not hope to compete with the U.S. Steel on its own terms. Instead he provided personal attention for smaller customers whom the larger company didn't find it worthwhile to cultivate intensively.

3. What advantages do our competitors have that we don't possess, and is it possible that we could minimize these advantages in some way?

4. What groups of companies and/or individuals make up our present and potential customers? Are their numbers growing or declining? And if the numbers are declining, are there other groups we might serve if we did things a little differently or if we could reduce our costs enough to put our products in their price range? Or could we perhaps fill their orders a little faster?

The next step is to determine where our departmental contribution most logically fits in. A production man can make a distinct contribution to profitability by improving quality, by obtaining more production from the same machines and the same people, or by reducing the lead time on delivery. If the sales department suggests a change in the product to make it more saleable, he can try to think how it could be accomplished without too great added expense or disruption in his department rather than spend his energy thinking up reasons why it can't be done.

The production head of a small but successful chemical company talks on the telephone to the sales manager every working day to be sure he's making what can be sold rather than asking the sales manager to sell what he can make. When the sales manager told him that he had a chance at a big contract if production of a certain product could be tripled within a short time, he immediately called a meeting of his foremen to decide how it could be done.

Together they worked out the way and did the trick without any expensive capital investment, by putting on a second shift and pressing some unused equipment into service.

Sales managers of industrial products frequently score by developing new applications for their products, and those who are marketing consumer products have an opportunity to open up new types of outlets for their company's goods. They can also help by passing on customers' comments about the merchandise. Most sales managers probably think they do this, but frequently their tendency is to pass on complaints when they need an alibi for not selling and to take credit for the sales achieved because of the product's good points.

In everything they do, sales managers should keep in mind the twofold objective of *creating* and *retaining* customers. Some sales managers have instituted contests that focus attention on only one aspect of this objective – offering attractive prizes for new accounts but providing no penalties for losing old ones. As a result their salesmen have neglected good customers while they were chasing after prospects.

Managers of some departments or sections may feel that they're too far removed from the primary functions, production and selling, to make any real contribution to profits. They think of themselves and their groups as necessary evils rather than as positive contributors, and as a result, others in the organization consider them in the same light.

Staff departments are particularly prone to mourn their inability to show direct and measurable contributions, and often develop more and more programmes of the type that irritates the line simply because they feel they must show they're doing something. If they would remember that they make their contribution by helping the line achieve company objectives, they would no longer find it necessary to be active just for the sake of being active. When a staff department is ready and able to provide help where the help is needed, it need not worry about the fact that its contributions are not measurable. Everyone will be conscious that it is something more than a necessary evil.

Once the department head or section manager has analysed his contribution to company objectives, he should check with his superior to ensure that his understanding is correct, and that he has placed his objectives in proper order of importance. Where top management itself does not practise management by objectives, misunderstandings are possible.

'Why don't they let us make good rugs?' a foreman in a floor-covering plant once asked a consultant. 'We know how to do it, but they don't want us to.'

This was during depression times – and to provide products at a price the customers could afford to pay, the company was forced to put out a cheaper grade of merchandise. It was not averse to improvements in quality if they could be achieved without substantial extra costs that would have made it necessary to charge higher prices. If the situation had been explained to the foreman, or if he had taken the initiative and asked his boss about it, he might have been able to think of ways in which quality could be improved without raising costs very much.

After the manager has determined the contribution his group can make to the achievement of overall company objectives, he should next make an inventory of his strengths and weaknesses. Strengths are resources that will help in achieving objectives – such things as money, manpower, materials, machines, and skills – while a weakness is anything that could defeat efforts to achieve objectives unless it is corrected. Strengths and weaknesses together determine departmental capabilities.

ANALYSIS OF OPPORTUNITIES[2]

Once the manager knows his objectives and his capabilities, he can spell out what he can accomplish under certain conditions. This in turn compels him to consider the opportunities that lie ahead. How can he make a greater contribution to the attainment of over-all objectives?

As he analyses the possible opportunities, he can use three simple yardsticks in making decisions about each one:

1. He decides whether the opportunity is suitable. That is, will it help him accomplish his purpose?

2. Rear Admiral Charles H. Smith: 'Objectives as a Communication Device in Management,' *Superior-Subordinate Communication in Management*, Item 6 (American Management Association, Inc. publication).

2. Then he determines whether it is 'feasible' to do it. Can he realistically expect to do it in view of the resources available?

3. He decides whether the idea is 'acceptable'. Are the returns worth the risk, time, effort?

For example, let's say the manager is in marketing. He has examined his resources and found them adequate. In the process, however, he determines that his company isn't giving enough attention to its probable future markets. It may be selling, for example, to an industry that's in what the economists call a secular decline. In other words it is declining gradually but irreversibly over the long term. In any company, too, there's usually the normal attrition of customers, as the old faithfuls die off, as tastes change, and as some part of the market is weaned away by new products offered by some other manufacturer. Thus one company discovered that it lost about 20 per cent of its customers each year. This meant that it had to gain that many new ones just to stay in the same place.

The manager's next step is to write up *how* he intends to overcome this marketing weakness. Are new products needed? New outlets? New methods of selling? Advertising in new media to reach new groups? When he has done so and has his boss's approval, he has formulated an objective for his department.

Let's say the manager is in production. Wages rates and material prices are going up, and there's not much he can do about either. Must unit costs inevitably rise proportionately? Not necessarily. Consider, for example, the following possibilities:

1. Can production be planned more carefully so that less inventory of raw materials is needed?

2. Would any rearrangement of the department make it possible to avoid backtracking in handling materials? One way of determining this is to make a flow chart. (See Figure 4.1.)

3. Would some adjustment of machines reduce the amount of scrap and rejects and save both labour and materials?

4. Is there unnecessary paperwork going on in the department? Does it need all the forms it is using? Could some be combined, simplified, or discarded altogether?

5. Can he save money on utilities? The power bill may depend, in part, on peak usage. Can he reschedule the turning on of

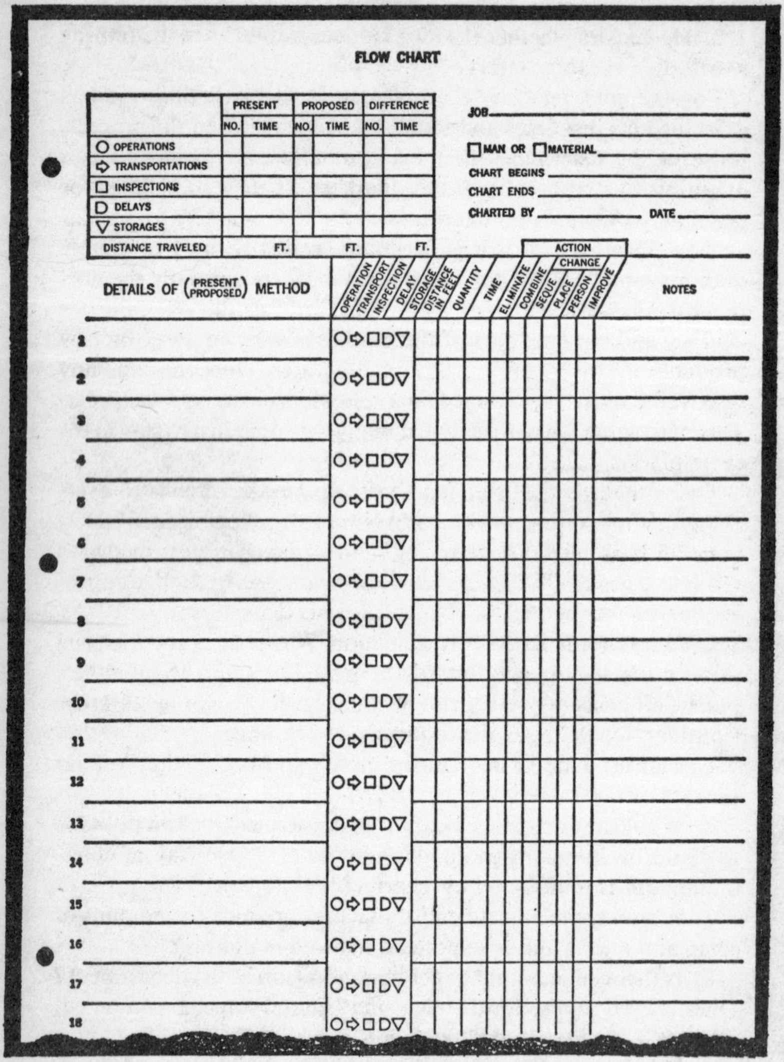

FLOW CHART

	PRESENT		PROPOSED		DIFFERENCE	
	NO.	TIME	NO.	TIME	NO.	TIME
○ OPERATIONS						
⇨ TRANSPORTATIONS						
□ INSPECTIONS						
D DELAYS						
▽ STORAGES						
DISTANCE TRAVELED	FT.		FT.		FT.	

JOB

□ MAN OR □ MATERIAL

CHART BEGINS

CHART ENDS

CHARTED BY DATE

DETAILS OF (PRESENT / PROPOSED) METHOD	OPERATION / TRANSPORT / INSPECTION / DELAY / STORAGE	DISTANCE IN FEET	QUANTITY	TIME	ACTION: ELIMINATE	COMBINE	CHANGE: SEQUE	PLACE	PERSON	IMPROVE	NOTES
1	○⇨□D▽										
2	○⇨□D▽										
3	○⇨□D▽										
4	○⇨□D▽										
5	○⇨□D▽										
6	○⇨□D▽										
7	○⇨□D▽										
8	○⇨□D▽										
9	○⇨□D▽										
10	○⇨□D▽										
11	○⇨□D▽										
12	○⇨□D▽										
13	○⇨□D▽										
14	○⇨□D▽										
15	○⇨□D▽										
16	○⇨□D▽										
17	○⇨□D▽										
18	○⇨□D▽										

Figure 4.1 Flow chart of work sequence

machines that draw heavy current on start-up so that the peak usage is kept down? Can he use process heat for some other purpose? There are consultants who make a business of showing companies how to save on utilities, but many of the possibilities they uncover could be identified by the people within the plant if they only gave thought to the matter.

When the manager has a set of approved projects, he and his boss can decide whether he has allocated his resources properly, and agree on timing and priorities.

Where management by objectives is practised on a company-wide basis, the overall resources needed for each manager's set of projects become the basis for his departmental budget. And when all the department's budgets are put together, they represent the company's plans for the next operating period. In this way management by objectives makes possible what is called 'responsibility accounting', or 'responsibility reporting'. Where this type of reporting or control system is used, the supervisor is made responsible only for objectives he has agreed to and only for resources over which he has control.

At the Bata Shoe Company, every department has its own weekly profit and loss account, and is considered to be using its own 'capital' in the form of machines, power, floor space and so on. Its profit-and-loss account then becomes the basis of its allotment under a profit-sharing plan.

Each successive level of the company gets its appropriate information, and the chief executive is given a neatly summarized performance record in terms of objectives met or not met. Thus he can take immediate action in exceptional areas. Each manager can measure his own progress against his objectives, and is encouraged to use his initiative to develop improvements.

In working with his own subordinates, the manager will find it a great deal easier to practise management by objectives if he has organized the work so that each person has a 'whole job', one that demands a certain amount of planning and some opportunity to vary the sequence in which the work is done. Then each one should be able to answer the following questions in the affirmative:

1. Do I know what I'm supposed to accomplish and why?
2. Has my boss agreed to my objectives?

Name
Position or Dept
Location

— Indicates Unfavourable

Month of February, 1965

Acct No.	Items of Expense	Standard	Current Month Actual	Current Month Variance	Year to Date Actual	Year to Date Variance
	CONTROLLABLE COST					
	Foremen, Clerks-Variable	160	0	160	0	296
	Sweepers and Cleaners	91	0	91	8	160
	Handling & Delivering Matl.	1,941	720	1,221	1,628	1,959
	Idle Time	251	109	142	243	221
	All Other	206	441	235–	956	576–
	Tools and Supplies	365	230	135	971	296–
	Shipping Supplies	891	1,263	372–	1,651	5–
	Total Expenses	3,905	2,763	1,142	5,457	1,759
	PRODUCTIVE LABOUR					
	Direct Labour	22,834	18,880	3,954	39,314	2,890
	Total Productive Labour	22,834	18,880	3,954	39,314	2,890

Figure 4.2 Responsibility accounting statement

3. Has he provided me with the necessary resources?

4. Can I shift the scope and tempo of my effort as conditions require?

5. Can I determine how well I'm doing without asking my boss, but am I free to go to him for help whenever I find I cannot solve problems myself or when I'm not sure I'm on the right track?

Edward C. Schleh, author of the book *Management by Results*,[3] has suggested some guide lines that will help make management by objectives work for any manager.[4] Among these are:

1. Goals should be realistic. They should be attainable in the light of all the circumstances, and the subordinate should be expected to attain them if his performance is to be considered adequate. Then the manager may set higher goals as marks to shoot for, with the proviso that their attainment will be considered outstanding performance.

2. When objectives for all positions have been tentatively set, the manager should write them down and cross-check to see that they all blend with one another. Attainment of the objective set for each man on the lowest level should contribute to the attainment of the first-line supervisor's objectives; the objectives for each first-line supervisor should contribute to the objective to be reached by his superior, so that all objectives contribute to the general objectives of the company. Similarly, short-range objectives should contribute to long-range objectives.

3. The objectives must seem fair to the man to whom they are given. If possible, he should be asked to participate in setting them, to suggest objectives for his own position. Often people set higher objectives for themselves than their superiors would set for them.

4. There will in most cases be more than one objective for each job, but the subordinate should be expected to reach each of them. Outstanding results in one or two areas should not offset less than adequate performance on other areas.

5. There should be no more than two to five objectives for each job. If there are too many, the man may try to accomplish a great

---

3. Edward C. Schleh: *Management by Results* (New York, McGraw-Hill, Inc., 1961).

4. *The Management Review*, published by the American Management Association, Inc. (November 1959).

many of the easier ones, which may be of minor importance, and hope that this will offset his failure to reach major objectives.

SUGGESTED QUESTIONS FOR YOUR CONSIDERATION

1. What is management by objectives?

2. Do you think you could reorganize the work of your immediate subordinates in such a way that it would be more possible to utilize management by objectives?

3. To what extent do you understand the way in which the objectives of your group fit in with the objectives of the company as a whole?

CHAPTER 5

New Dimensions in Organizational Communication

SINCE World War II, management has been deluged with books and articles on communication. It has also spent a great deal of money on communication tools: employee publications, newsletters, and meetings of various kinds. Yet communication in industry is as serious a problem as it ever was, and there are good reasons to believe that the situation may get worse.

One reason for the increasing difficulty of communication is the growing size of companies. As ideas and instructions from the top are transmitted through the various levels of management, misunderstandings are likely to be cumulative as each person makes his own interpretation. The same is true of information moving up from the lower ranks to the top.

Moreover, the further a person is from the source of information, the less likely he is to recognize what Mary Parker Follett, a famous writer on management subjects of the 1920s, called 'the law of situation'.

This law may be illustrated by the case of a fire in a scrapbasket. No one would have to be told to put it out, since obviously it is to everyone's advantage to do so before it spreads. What the insurance people call a 'hostile' fire, in contrast to a 'friendly' fire – like a fire in a furnace – is everyone's enemy and everyone knows it. Everyone, therefore, obeys the law of the situation and tries to put it out.

But it is far less easy to discern the law of the situation in relation to such things as careless work or wasting time. In the end these things affect company profitability, and hence the company's ability to provide jobs and high wages. But, the connexion between what is done in one small job and the final balance sheet of the company is tenuous to most people, especially where jobs are highly specialized and workers are task-oriented rather than results-oriented.

The current emphasis on communication has arisen in part

because the law of competitive situation, which is so apparent to managers, is often invisible to the rank and file because of their distance from the top and the specialized nature of their jobs. In part, too, it stems from the philosophy of the 'soft manage', which has sometimes been carried so far as to foster the idea that the chief job of a supervisor is to make his subordinates happy by maintaining as close relationships with them as possible in order to give them a 'feeling of belonging'.

The latter view has led almost to the belief that communication is an end in itself. It is amazing how many communication activities are undertaken because communication is considered the thing to do, because someone else is doing it, because the brochure or pamphlet looks nice, or because it can be sold to the boss.

But the only way a company's communication effort can be made effective is to make it precise in terms of needs and objectives.

Actually the main purpose of communication is to change *someone*, *some group*, or *some thing*, or to head off unfavourable trends. We can say, then, that the purpose of communication is to induce action or to secure inaction.[1]

THE MENTAL SET

Now a person's 'attitudinal bias' or mental set predisposes him to action or inaction in any given situation. His attitudinal bias, in turn, is the result of stored information, social and economic background, beliefs and prejudices, corporate background and experience, and other factors.

Some of the factors that go to make up a person's total attitudinal bias are stable and tenacious, and it is almost impossible to change them entirely. But even these viewpoints may be modified in intensity by new experience, new information, new personal contacts. In other cases the attitudinal bias is less deeply rooted and can be completely changed over a course of time.

Since what a person does in a given situation depends on his attitudinal bias, this bias may precipitate him to action when the circumstances in which he finds himself and/or the information he

1. See L. C. Michelon: *New Dimensions in Organizational Communication* (Cleveland, Republic Steel Corporation).

receives impel him towards his predisposition. The extent to which he acts will depend on the seriousness of the situation, and the *amount*, *type* and *persistency* of the information.

Fortunately, it is not necessary to change a person's attitude completely if its intensity can be reduced below the 'critical action level'. And it is much easier to reduce intensity than it is to get a person to change his attitude completely.

For example, in some plants minor infractions of union work rules are ignored when it is obvious that the 'law of the situation' demands that one man lend a hand to another in a different craft if the work is not to be unreasonably delayed. Yet perhaps both men may believe in the necessity of the rules as a means of job security and would resist any attempt to modify them. But because they have a reasonable sense of job security anyway, the intensity of their feelings is less. They are not, therefore, aroused to the critical action level, at which they would absolutely refuse to transgress the rules, and perhaps walk out if they were ordered to break them.

Attitudinal biases determine almost every action of any consequence that a person takes, and every position he supports in an argument. About the only time any of us has a truly open mind is when we're presented with a case that's entirely new to us, and on which we have no preconceived opinions at all.

We must, therefore, know a person's attitudinal position on many issues or we cannot predict the action he may take in any situation or adequately prepare the circumstances, the content, and the form of the message. One way of determining a person's psychological 'set' is to learn to listen, something few people really know how to do because their own attitudinal bias gets in the way, and they hear what they want or expect to hear, and disregard the implications that contravene their previous opinions.

When the girls at Hawthorne told interviewers that they were able to produce more because they 'felt freer', Elton Mayo concluded that the cohesive work group gave them a 'sense of belonging', which was really in line with his own ideas. But if he had been able to escape from his own psychological set, he might have thought of other possible explanations: their freedom to vary their pace and the effort that went into interesting them in the experiment, which may have made them to some extent 'results-oriented'.

Again, sometimes what people actually say is not the full story, and it may be necessary to let them talk at considerable length before learning the true meaning behind their words. The ostensible cause of a complaint, for example, may be quite different from the real cause. But this facet has been so strongly emphasized in recent years that perhaps this type of interpretation has been overdone. In some cases, people mean exactly what they say, and they will be satisfied only with a straightforward, logical answer.

THE COMMUNICATION PROCESS[2]

What does the manager himself want to communicate to his subordinates? Through communication he wants to ensure that they are able to do a good job, which means that his instructions must be clear, and he wants to stimulate their will to work and raise their standards so that they will try to do outstanding work rather than merely get by.

Fundamentally, the communication process implies:
(a) A sender
(b) A receiver
(c) A message
(d) A motivating climate.

Each of these plays an important role and can make or break the entire process.

First the receiver must have some confidence in the sender. If the sender has not been truthful in the past, no message will get across – in fact, the communication may produce an effect exactly opposite to that intended. Sometimes a sincere manager will be distrusted because his predecessor has dealt insincerely with the subordinates. In that case, it may take time to build up confidence, but it can be done. When people see that their manager gives honest answers to their questions and does not promise more than he can deliver, they will eventually begin to trust him.

2. See the many materials available through the Industrial Relations Centre of The University of Chicago. See also Compton, H. and Bennett, W.: *Communication in Supervisory Management* (London, 1967).

The mere fact that receivers consider the sender honest, however, does not always mean that they will be greatly influenced by his communications. The message he delivers – its content and its form – is equally important, and so are the circumstances, which may or may not provide motivation to act as he wishes them to.

To get an idea across, you must first of all talk about something the other person is interested in or relate it to his own personal benefit. Otherwise, he will not really listen at all – or if he does, he will soon forget.

But how can a manager do this when he must often talk about the economic problems facing the company, which may seem remote to employees in the lower ranks? About the only way to do so is to relate the communications to the individual's inner drives and goals.

Basically, we have *economic* and *non-economic* wants.[3] Economic wants include:

1. A useful job
2. A rising standard of living
3. Economic security.

Non-economic wants include:

1. Personal development
2. Social recognition
3. Personal freedom.

If we relate communication to these basic drives, we will create a favourable listening climate and our communications will be effective.

COMMUNICATION BY ACTION

Now some people feel that what a company or a manager does is a more important form of communication than any written or spoken communication. And it is true that everyone communicates by action as well as by words. It is of little use to urge employees to put more effort into their work if the manager himself wastes his time or wastes theirs because he hasn't planned properly.

3. See L. C. Michelon: *Basic Economics* (Cleveland, The World Publishing Company, 1960), pp. 14–15.

One manager was very disturbed about early quitting, and was continually giving his employees talks about this. But a union steward managed to get a picture of him leaving with his golf bags with a clock in the background and its hands pointing to 2 o'clock. He was too embarrassed after that ever to mention the subject again.

Of course there are cases when a manager may seem to be wasting time but is not really doing so – and in that case, he should unobtrusively make clear what he is doing. An advertising man told this story:

> When I worked for someone else, it always seemed as though there were drones around who never did any work. I made up my mind that when I had my own agency there would be nothing like that. Then, when I started my agency, I began working 14 to 16 hours a day. In the morning, I went to see clients and prospective clients. After lunch, I went to the office and thought up ideas. My writing I did in the evening. But one day I heard someone say, 'Of all the drones! That guy doesn't come in till 1.30. Then he just sits there doing nothing, and quits promptly at 5.'

WRITTEN COMMUNICATION

Written communications are good for shop orders, detailed instructions, or routine production matters which people can't take in all at once but must refer to continually. They are also good and often required for reports to higher managers.

Many managers dislike to write because they feel that writing is somehow different from talking, and that a special form of literary language must be used. This is a big mistake. The only difference between writing and talking in business is that special efforts must be made to make the meaning of written communication clear. It isn't as easy to correct misunderstandings of a written communication as it is to clarify a spoken statement or to know when clarification is necessary. If a manager is talking to a small group or to an individual, he can generally tell whether his audience is with him – and if he invites questions, he can see whether there are misunderstandings. But if he sends out a memo or a report, he may never know whether the receiver misunderstood it. Thus, if his written instructions are unclear, he may find out only when people begin to make mistakes.

Managers are often advised to keep their sentences short and this, in general, is a good rule for those who are unsure of their writing ability. Naturally it is much easier to get tangled up in a long sentence than in a short one.

But long sentences don't necessarily make difficult reading. Take the quotation from *Little Dorrit* that appears at the beginning of the last chapter. Dickens used very long sentences, but it is comparatively easy to follow his meaning.

Writing becomes hard to understand when the reader has to get to the end of a long sentence before he takes in the meaning at all. This is often true when the subject of the sentence is far removed from the verb. That's why some legal writing is so difficult to read. For example:

That no part of any appropriation made under this Act for the following purposes, namely conduct of customs cases; defending suits and claims against the United States detection of prosecution of crime, defenses in Indian depredation claims; enforcement of antitrust laws; suits to set aside conveyances of allotted lands, Five Civilized Tribes; enforcement of acts to regulate commerce; for payment of assistants to the Attorney General to the United States district attorneys, employed by the Attorney General to aid in special cases ... shall be used for payment of any salary, fee, compensation, or allowance in any form whatever to any person who holds any other office, place, position or appointment under the United States Government or any department thereof. ...

The trouble with this sentence is not merely that it is appallingly long. It is also difficult to understand because the reader must keep remembering the words 'no part of any appropriation made under this Act' through several lines until he finally gets down to the verb, 'shall be used', and the information on what it can't be used for. The passage would be much easier to read if it were recast in this form:

No part of the appropriation made under this Act shall be used for the payment of any salary, fee, compensation or allowance in any form whatever to any person who holds any other office, place, position or appointment under the United States Government or under any United

States Government Department if the appropriation is made for any one of the following purposes:
1. Conduct of customs cases
2. Defending suits against the United States ...

The reader would at least know what the sentence was all about in the beginning. Then he could examine the cases to which the restriction on payment applied to see whether the case in which he was interested might fall under the ban.

Much of the written material distributed by companies today is written to satisfy lawyers or top management committees. The main objective is to get the material cleared rather than to make the meaning clear to the reader. As a result, the employee is given printed material that's quite uninteresting and impossible to understand.

All written material should be prepared with the reader's vocabulary and educational level in mind. If you make a mistake here, no vital communication can take place.

One company compelled its dealers to sign contracts agreeing to take a certain amount of products over a period of time. An old couple who ran a small store wrote in asking to be relieved of the contract because they were unable to sell the merchandise they already held. Since the salesman reported that the store was a poor outlet anyway, the company was willing to scrap the contract. Then someone in the company answered the letter saying, 'We're taking your name off our dealer list.'

The old people were puzzled by this, so they wrote back: 'What do you mean you're taking our name off your dealer list?' They simply wanted to know what the phrase meant, but the man who got the letter thought they were protesting, 'Whad'ya mean you're taking our name off?' He answered: 'We're very glad you have reconsidered, and want to continue the contract.' And he had the company continue to ship the product. A considerable amount of extra correspondence was necessary to straighten the matter out.

Conversely, one should never insult anyone's intelligence by obviously writing down to him. It is quite possible to write simply without sounding condescending.

A good way to judge a written communication before you issue it is to read it over, trying to put yourself in the place of the recipient.

This is helpful whether you're writing a report for top management, a letter to a customer, or a communication to the rank and file. Ask yourself as you read it: Would I be interested in this if I were in the place of the reader? Have I said clearly what I meant to say, and not included points that are of no possible interest or value to the reader? Have I raised questions in his mind and not provided the answers? What kind of an impression of the writer does it leave with the reader?

The total impression left by the communication is very important, and it is something the writer can judge only by putting himself in the place of the reader.

SPOKEN COMMUNICATION

Oral communications are probably the most effective way of changing attitudes, beliefs, and feelings, and it is as necessary to devote as much thought to them as to written communication. Many people begin to talk without 'pre-thinking' what they're going to say. They ramble, back-track, ramble again, take a detour and generally leave people in a state of mental exhaustion and confusion. Their conversation is sprinkled with phrases like the following:

'Last Thursday – no, it must have been Wednesday – '

'Before that I forgot to say – '

'Do it this way. No – perhaps that way would be better in this case.'

By planning talks in advance, this sort of thing can be avoided. You can also plan to use sketches or diagrams and other visual aids that make the discussion more interesting, and may help to clarify some of the things that are hard to express in words.

Again, some people fail to put their points across because they don't listen enough to learn how the receiver is reacting to their remarks. As a result, they have no real clues to how their words are going over, what's important, or who's involved. Walther Rathenau, an outstanding German manager and President of the German General Electric Company, once offered the following pointers on face-to-face communication, pointers that are valuable to any manager in dealing with subordinates, superiors or equals:

Always put yourself in the place of your opposite. Propose only what you would accept in his position.

A great ability consists in recognizing in advance which points are likely to cause the greatest difficulties and clarifying these points in the beginning.

He also cautioned that no one ever convinced anyone else simply by out-talking him or arguing him down. Or, as sales managers often phrase it, 'Win the argument, and lose the customer'.

POINTS TO REMEMBER[4]

To summarize briefly some of the ways in which a manager can improve his communication skill:

First, don't oversell an idea.

Second, don't give up too soon in your communication efforts ... Persistence pays off.

Third, watch your timing. Choose an auspicious moment to put your story across.

Fourth, plan your communication carefully before you write or speak.

Fifth, keep your language simple and to the point.

Sixth, use sketches or diagrams that help make a report or talk more interesting and its meaning clearer.

Seventh, anticipate objections, and have well-prepared answers ready.

Eighth, invite participation by the other person.

Ninth, learn to listen intently as you converse.

Finally, leave enough time for discussion.

4. Robert J. Tiernan: 'Ten Ways to Sell Your Ideas', *Nation's Business* (June 1965), pp. 84–90.

SUGGESTED QUESTIONS FOR YOUR CONSIDERATION

1. An employee comes to you as mad as can be at something another employee did to him. He demands that you take immediate action. If you don't, he says he'll quit. What do you tell him?

2. An employee expects to get his boss's job as soon as the boss retires. But the promotion goes to a younger man with less experience but far better education and potential. How do you explain this to the older employee when he asks you about it?

3. Your company is having a rough time competitively and feels it ought to get its story across to the workforce through its supervision. A meeting is held at which all supervisors are asked to suggest a course of action. What do you suggest?

4. You need new equipment for your department. What points would you stress in submitting a request for it?

5. A good customer wants something that's not the company's policy to provide – let's say extra service beyond what the company has agreed to. Write him a letter telling him why you can't do as he asks. Then, read the letter over, putting yourself in the customer's place. What impression would it make on you? Remember, as a customer, you're not interested in whether the company follows its policies.

6. What do you know about the mental set of each of your immediate subordinates? First, can you recognize each person's particular set? Have you seen its effects in the work situation?

CHAPTER 6

Long-Range Planning, Financing, and Control

A NUMBER of developments are forcing management into planning five, ten, or even twenty years ahead. These include the:

1. Increasing rate of technological change
2. Growing complexity of business
3. Intense world-wide competition.

Technological change is shortening the life cycles of products to the point where a company must continually plan for new products or services to hold on to its markets.

Now there was a time when a company producing a fairly stable product or service could count on a market for it for decades. Today, however, a product may begin to lose sales within two to five years because it is being replaced by new products developed by competitors in the same industry, or by products developed by other industries, or even by entirely new industries.

This shortening of the life-cycle of products requires quicker management decision-making and much more careful planning. It is less and less possible to watch what others do and then imitate them. And it may not be long before only the first company to introduce a product will be able to make money on it. By the time the imitators get into the field, the product may be approaching the end of its life cycle.

Business is becoming more complex because of technological changes, and also because it is growing larger. Both trends have increased the need for new specialities, and managers need to comprehend the possible contribution that each might make. Also, large size has increased the interest that government and other outside groups take in business discussions, and this demands the consideration of more viewpoints than in the past.

For example, if Frederick Taylor were to read the 'Help Wanted' advertisements today, he wouldn't know what a great many of them were talking about. He would be gratified, no doubt, to find companies advertising for time study men and methods men, but he wouldn't be able to make much of such titles as 'cryogenic engineer', 'EDP systems engineer', or 'programmers of real time systems' – all new jobs growing out of technological advances. He would be hard put to understand such titles as 'organization planner' or 'group managing director' – jobs growing out of complexities of size.

Finally, it is apparent that intensified competition on a worldwide scale has come about because of a resurgence of industry in Western Europe, where percentage increases in productivity have been greater than those in the United States in recent years. And since a number of the underdeveloped countries are working towards industrialization, competition will increase even further in the future.

DEFINING OBJECTIVES

In developing a long-range plan, the first essential is a clear statement of company purpose. This, in time, involves an answer to the question: *What business are we really in?*

For example, when IBM consciously decided that it was in the information-gathering and processing business rather than in the punch-card business, this deceivingly simple change in objectives revolutionized the entire future course of the company. Or to take another example, the O. M. Scott Company finally decided that it was in the business of providing its customers with good lawns rather than simply selling grass seed. As a result it expanded its product lines to include fertilizers, weed killers, spreaders, and mowers.

Again, if an electric company defines its business as 'supplying light and power' rather than 'supplying electricity', it will be alert to the possibilities of new sources of power, such as atomic energy, or even gas if that appears feasible. Some electrical utilities, in fact, have already built atomic power plants.

The main purpose of long-range planning is to ensure that the company replaces itself instead of waiting for someone else to replace it. But a long-range plan is also necessary to ensure that there will be time to take the steps needed to provide new products or services or to meet increased demand for old ones.

Sometimes the changes needed are very drastic, like the change from the carriage to the automobile. More often, however, the need is to add new products or to improve products or adapt them to new uses.

The lead time needed for these new products and services varies among industries and among companies, and with the rate at which the demand is expected to grow. For example, Robert P. O'Brien, of the Southern California Edison Electric Company, has pointed out:

Installation of a service drop and meter can be taken care of with little or no delay. Short extensions of the distribution system may take several days to several weeks. Major extensions of the transmission system and distribution substations may require several months to a year or longer. Additions to generation may require from two to three years for steam plants and even longer for hydro plants. Development of new and different types of energy resources involves even longer periods.[1]

In a company which furnishes a service, it may be possible to add services almost overnight if the knowledge needed to provide them is already available within the company. For example, the personnel employed by accounting firms learn a great deal about the management of different companies and different industries in the course of their audits. Thus it may be possible for such a firm to add management consulting services to its 'accounting line' without much difficulty, and the expense involved may be comparatively small. The firm need merely do some direct mail advertising to let clients and prospective clients know that it has the service available, and perhaps hire a new man or two to relieve some of the more experienced men of their accounting work.

DECIDING WHAT WILL BE NEEDED

How does one determine the nature of the markets five, ten or twenty years from now and their location? Of course, there's

1. George Steiner, ed.: 'Planning at the Southern California Edison Company', *Managerial Long-Range Planning* (New York, McGraw-Hill, Inc., 1963), p. 293. Copyright© by McGraw-Hill Book Company, Inc. Used by permission of McGraw-Hill, Inc.

no way of being certain about the future, and the further ahead you plan the greater the uncertainty. Thus even five-year plans must be tentative, and plans for a longer term are more tentative still.

However, an examination of trends will provide some clues and at least reduce the possibility of surprises. Even the crash of 1929, which seemed to most people to occur without the slightest warning, had been foretold by some economists well in advance of its occurrence.

In cases where it is necessary to make irrevocable commitments – for example, when you must spend money to build a new plant to meet demand anticipated two years from now – there's always considerable risk attached to the decision. But the risk of ignoring the trends may be greater. A company that lacks the capacity to meet a larger demand may lose more than the profit it might otherwise have made. If customers are unable to get its products when they want them, they may turn to its competitors or to alternate products – and in the end, the company may not even be able to sell what it can supply. Suppose, for example, that a company producing automobiles were unable to produce as many cars as it could sell, while competing makes were in ample supply. Unable to get the car of their choice, customers would turn to other makes. Then, since there's usually a larger trade-in allowance on an old car if the customer rebuys the same make, they might be tempted to stick with their second choice, to say nothing of the possibility that they might like the car better than the one they wanted originally.

Or consider the field of packaging, where a great number of products from different industries compete for the customer's order. In this case the customer can choose among glass, paper, steel and a number of plastic materials. For exterior packing which is designed for protection rather than appearance, the choice is often between corrugated containers, wood and steel. To shift from one material to the other may require changes in equipment or methods; but if one of the materials is in short supply, the shift may be forced. Then unless the material used earlier has distinct advantages, the customer may not feel it worthwhile to shift back.

LONG-TERM TRENDS

Now what long-term trends are in evidence today that will affect every industry?

First of all, there are the trends in population: *growth*, *age distribution* and *geographical location*. Also important is the way population is divided between city, suburban and rural areas.

Today's population explosion may not continue at the same rate, since the birth rate may fall drastically in the years ahead. However, an increase in population is practically guaranteed because there will be more people in the 18-35 age groups than ever before. So even if the average couple has fewer children, there will be an increase in population, especially since the birth rate is much higher than the death rate.

The present composition of our population suggests two facts about its future age composition – the average age will be lower than it is today and the percentage of people over 65 will be larger.

Another long-term trend is the movement of population away from the farms to the cities and suburbs. Today about 70 per cent of our people live in or near urban centres as compared to 5 per cent in 1790, when the first census was taken.

These facts are very important because different age groups have different needs and the wants of an urban population differ from those of a farm population.

For a utility company, for example, estimates of population in its area are of the utmost importance. So are estimates of the extent to which land will be used for residential, commercial or industrial purposes.

Finally, the market for any given product depends on how many people want it and on how much money they have. Nearly everyone wants things he can't afford to buy – and if incomes drop, more products enter this class for each of us. So an attempt must be made to forecast rises and falls in income.

If a company is selling industrial products, it must determine which of the industries among its customers are declining over the long term and then try to replace them by adapting its products to uses in other industries or by producing entirely new products.

One approach is to try to predict what economists call the 'Gross

LONG-RANGE PLANNING, FINANCING, AND CONTROL

National Product' in future years. This is the sum of all goods and services produced in the country, expressed in terms of money. Future GNP for the next five years may be estimated by considering the trends to date and modifying them according to any likely changes. Over a period of years the percentage of GNP accounted for by certain industries remains relatively constant or rises or falls only gradually. Then if a company knows its own share of the market, which may also be fairly constant, it can predict fairly well what its sales will be and how much production it will need to meet the future demand for its products.

Another approach is to consider *national* and *personal income*. The first is the sum of wages, salaries, income from rents and interest, and corporate profits. The second figure excludes corporate profits, but includes social security payments and military benefits. But perhaps the best figure to use in considering what ultimate consumers will actually have to spend is 'disposable personal income', which is personal income after taxes.

Another matter to consider is possible sources of supply. If a company believes its present sources of raw materials are likely to dry up as, for example, when mines are being depleted, it may want to become more self-sufficient or engage in 'backward vertical integration' by acquiring its own sources of raw materials.

The probable location of markets and of future sources of supply are two important considerations in the location of new plants. While transportation is easy, it costs money, and the nearer a company is to both markets and sources of supply, the lower its costs. Where a choice must be made between the two, the decision generally hinges on whether it is more expensive to transport the raw materials or to ship the finished product.

Still another consideration in long-range planning is the extent to which it would be wise for the company to engage in 'forward integration' – that is, in performing operations that will bring it nearer to the final consumer. Thus a company producing leather might decide that it would make it up into leather products, or even go all the way to the final consumer by opening up retail outlets.

In considering backward and forward integration, the company must keep an eye on Board of Trade policy on mergers since these and similar arrangements are subject to its veto. Also, integration is generally undertaken more for considerations of safety and stability than because of possible future profits to be made by undertaking more stages of production. That is, the company wants to guard against shortages of supplies or a lack of outlets for its present products.

Integration has its dangers, however, because it reduces flexibility. Unused capacity costs money because it ties up capital that might be earning a return in some other way and because unused facilities require a certain amount of maintenance if they're not to deteriorate. Thus if the market contracts, the company's losses may be greater than if it were less integrated.

A third consideration in long-range planning is the extent to which a company should diversify, and thus avoid putting all its eggs in one basket. One way of diversifying is to build new facilities for producing entirely new types of products for new uses, and then hiring new managers to manage them. But the same result may be obtained by purchasing the facilities of another company and retaining its management.

In either case a company is well advised to consider its own management resources and know-how before it proceeds, since entirely new fields are full of traps for those unfamiliar with them. The best acquisition may be one to which the parent company's management can contribute something in the way of technical or market know-how. Thus it might purchase a company that made a product utilizing somewhat the same technology or one sold to the same markets but for different purposes.

MAKING THE PLAN

When the long-range plan is tentatively developed, it is necessary to work back from the five-year or ten-year goal, decide what must be accomplished each year if it is to be met on schedule, and then determine what resources in money, manpower, and facilities are available and whether they will be adequate. It may be necessary to modify the long-range plan at this point.

The sales forecast is perhaps the most important part of the one-year plan, because it is sales that will determine the amount of revenue that will be available and also the amount of production needed.

There are various ways of building up a sales forecast. One way is to ask each salesman how much he thinks he can sell in his territory. This is a little risky, however, for salesmen may keep their estimates low to be sure that they will be able to meet their quotas or overestimate because they're naturally optimistic.

For this reason most companies prefer to use other methods instead of, or in addition to, the salesmen's forecasts. For example, in the automobile industry, the forecasters look first at the factors indicative of general business conditions: trends in GNP, industrial production, personal income, wholesale prices, consumer prices, and the ratio of sales to manufacturing inventory. Then they examine trends that are particularly important to their own business: the prices of cars as compared with industrial prices; the prices of used cars as compared with new car registrations; the percentage of disposable income that's being spent for cars; new car registrations as a percentage of cars on the road; the size of the car-buying population (people between ages 18 and 69, and especially those in the 18-to-24-year-old bracket who are likely to be buying their first cars); the ratio of instalment debt to disposable income; and the percentage of all spending units with instalment debt.[2]

Again, a manufacturer of lamps and lighting equipment watches closely the figures on construction awards, building permits, and new housing starts since new homes will require lighting fixtures and often new lamps. The trend in the number of marriages also may be important to companies making products for the household. When young people are living with their parents they can use the family's television set, vacuum cleaner, and refrigerator. But when they marry and start a home of their own, they're likely to buy new appliances of their own.

2. *Business Week* (14 September 1963), p. 24. A spending unit is a family, any two or more persons who live together and pool their incomes, or an individual living alone.

FORECASTING THE BUSINESS CYCLE

A great deal of the long-range planning done by companies is necessarily done by what is called 'extrapolation' – that is, projecting the trends of the past into the future. So if GNP has grown by 3½ per cent a year during the past five years, it is assumed that it will grow at much the same figure for the next five.

How do forecasters know that this will be the case? How can they be sure that there won't be a serious recession, or even a big depression like that of the 1930s?

The answer is that they can't be, but some methods of forecasting business cycle turns have been developed. An important one is known as the 'lead and lag method', which is based on the theory that certain factors in the economy, as measured by published statistics, rise or fall several months in advance of an upturn or downturn, while other factors change only as the turn becomes evident, and still others lag behind the turn. The important figures are, of course, those that most commonly show a change several months before a general change in the economy. These are:

1. Business failures, bankruptcies and their liabilities. 2. Indices of share prices (e.g. *The Times* and the *Financial Times*). 3. New orders for durable goods. 4. Building contracts, residential, commercial and industrial. 5. Average hours worked. 6. New firms registered. 7. Wholesale price indices.

SOURCES OF STATISTICS

Where does one find the figures, those used in the lead and lag method and the other statistics mentioned earlier? Most of them are to be found in the *Monthly Digest of Statistics* and *Financial Statistics* published by the Central Statistical Office (HMSO). Centralized publication of business statistics has recently been undertaken by the Business Statistics Office of the Board of Trade. A new quarterly, *Statistical News*, will inform users of changes and will also contain articles of special interest; a new edition of *Sources and Methods for Official Statistics*, has been published; the

Monthly Digest of Statistics and the *Annual Abstract of Statistics* are to be overhauled.

The *Ministry of Labour Gazette* gives more detailed (by towns) figures on stoppages, incomes, prices, employment, productivity, not published elsewhere. This publication is also useful in giving rates of wages and weekly hours of work arrived at under voluntary collective agreements in various trades, besides the Statutory Orders under the Wages Council Acts as they are made.

The weekly *Board of Trade Journal*, besides giving selected indicators of the economy, gives a general assessment and much information for exporters. Periodically, as available, it publishes the statistics of business failures. It also reports new Acts as they are prepared in advance of possible legislation. An Export Services Department lists export opportunities from inquiries received and offers specialized foreign mailing lists.

There are a number of non-government publications which, besides giving various index figures of their own devising, also provide in their columns general assessments and interpretations. Such assessments, being made by those who are continually engaged in studying the statistics they report, may be more valuable to many businessmen than the underlying statistics themselves whose interpretation is fraught with difficulties and reservations. In this connexion the value of averaging should not be overlooked. Just as numerical estimates from chance, variable processes benefit in precision (see Chapter 10) from averaging, so will these more general, non-quantitative forecasts. In other words, a general consensus adds to the confidence to be placed in a forecast. These observations do not rule out the value of an individual watch on a particular sector of the economy; a firm may be able to draw conclusions applicable to itself from its own studies which are not apparent in the more general, national studies.

The *Financial Times* (daily), *The Times Business News* (supplement, daily except Saturday), *The Economist* (weekly), *Management Today* (B.I.M.), and the Reviews published periodically by the leading banks (ask your bank manager) provide, besides statistics, much light on trends generally and from time to time in special sectors. Similar review articles appear in the *Economic Review* and other publications of the National Institute of

Economic and Social Research. The Economist Intelligence Unit produces surveys of special sectors.

Note also the existence of two useful books: A. J. Wilford: *Guide to Reference Material*, Library Association, and W. A. Bagley: *Facts and How to Find Them*, Pitman. ASLIB, the Association of Special Libraries and Information Bureaux has access to a vast store of information and has staff to make it available to inquirers.

BUDGETING

Once a sales forecast has been developed, the company can go ahead with a definite plan for the year ahead. This will make plain:

1. What the company will do that year. 2. How it will go about it. 3. When each phase of the plan should be completed. 4. Who will do what. 5. What costs will be, overall and for each department, as expressed in the form of budgets. 6. What return is to be expected and when.

Budgets will be of two types: expense and capital budgets. Expense budgets cover labour and material needed for the amount of production forecast, plus overhead to cover such things as salaries and interest on debt. Revenues must at least equal the sum total of all expense budgets if the company is not to run in the red.

Capital budgets, on the other hand, cover such things as new plant and new equipment that need not be paid for out of the current year's income. If a company spends part of its reserve funds for a new plant, it has not decreased the total amount of its assets. It has a plant instead of cash in the bank or investments in stocks and bonds. The money is used up only as the plant begins to depreciate and decline in value; hence, only part of it is really being spent each year. This is taken care of by depreciation, which means setting aside each year a sum equivalent to the amount of value the plant is expected to lose each year. This depreciation must be included in the expense budget as part of the overhead.

An important difference between expenses and capital expenditures is the tax treatment of them. Expenses are wholly deductible for tax purposes; capital expenditures only to the amount that they are depreciated each year. Thus a manager who charges what is really an expense to his capital budget is costing his company money unnecessarily.

Another form of budget is the cash budget, to which companies are giving increasing attention. Income is not constant over the year, so it is important for the company to know how much cash it will have during each period. If cash will be short at certain times, it may have to borrow to meet its current bills, or draw on its reserves, and it must plan ahead for this. Also, in certain periods more cash will be on hand than is needed to meet current bills, and leaving it in a current account would be to lose the opportunity of earning interest by short-term investment.

Once a company has established its revenues and costs, it can determine what its rate of return will be and how much it will probably have to pay in taxes on the income. From this figure it can calculate how much it can put into its reserves after paying the stockholders an adequate return for the use of their money.

This, together with the current amount of the reserves and projections for the next few years, will determine whether it can finance its plans for expansion, diversification, and so on, out of its own funds and still leave enough money on hand as a cushion against the unexpected. If the sum will not be sufficient, it need not necessarily abandon its plans. It can raise money either by borrowing or by equity financing.

Borrowing may take the form of borrowing from banks or an issue of bonds. Equity financing is obtained by issuing new ordinary shares or stock. Either may be the more advantageous depending on the circumstances.

The advantage of financing by borrowing is that the interest on the debt is tax deductible as an expense, whereas dividends to ordinary share and stockholders are not. While a company, if it does not earn a good return in any year on the money invested is free to cut or omit dividends on the equity capital, it must continue to pay interest on bonds or debentures. And if prices decline, interest payments will probably represent a greater proportion of the company's income than they did originally. On the other hand, if prices rise, the interest will remain constant and will constitute less of a burden than it did at first.

PLANNING FORMAT[3]

Different companies may use different formats for their plans, but one approach is to include three sections:

1. A strategic plan
2. A corporate development plan
3. An operations plan.

The strategic plan contains the answer to the question: *What business are we really in?* It also sets objectives or targets, quantitative and qualitative, for the period the plan covers. Finally it covers the strategy to be used in taking advantage of opportunities and in averting threats, and provides for marketing research and intelligence reports from the field to help it identify both opportunities and potential threats. In addition, it spells out internal areas where the company should be strengthened.

The corporate development plan covers research and development, plans for diversification, plans for divesting the company of unprofitable products or sections, the new business needed to meet the profit objectives and where it will come from, special assignments that must be carried out to meet the plans, and the controls to be instituted.

Finally, there's the operations plan which covers the things each section of the company is to do: the five-year goals and the goals for the year ahead, with the necessary budgets. This might cover such things as:

1. The annual sales and earnings goals
2. The annual marketing plans for each major product
3. The strategic plan assignments
4. Capital expenditures
5. The five-year budget.

HOW ONE COMPANY PLANS

The development of a long-range plan may perhaps best be illustrated by reference to one company's planning procedure. This is a

3. See *Formal Planning – The Executive's Role* (Menlo Park, California, Stanford Research Institute, 1964).

steel company that is a 'big company' by most standards, but only of medium size as compared to U.S. Steel.

The original basis of the plan is top management's belief that the company should at least maintain its share of the market. This figure is arrived at from past history, present position, and management's desire to maintain profitable status in future markets.

The company tries to forecast the future markets for steel five – and sometimes ten – years ahead, including the market for different types of steel. Then it predicts the total tonnage, the type of tons, and probable location of the demand for these tons for the next five years.

The next step is to compare the company's capacity to produce the tonnages projected. Here an analysis is made to determine whether the tonnages needed at the various locations are reasonable.

In some areas it may be unrealistic to expect to sell its share of the market because of heavy competition or for other reasons. In other areas, it may be possible to increase its share somewhat.

From these studies the company works up revised figures that indicate the growth rate it may actually expect.

Then the task is to analyse each plant's capacity to produce what will be required of it. This study will cover the equipment available and its condition, and will indicate whether the plant will need new equipment, more equipment, or additions to the plant, and whether any new plants will be needed and where.

Once plant and equipment requirements are determined, the money part of the programme is brought into focus. If more money is needed than the company will have, in the light of realistic forecasts of earnings and the borrowing it can undertake, the overall programme may be cut back.

Also, if a particular plant will need too much new equipment to handle the extra tonnage required, some other plant may be asked to handle part of the demand. Or the product mix may be changed to bring the total tons back up to the company's original market objective.

At this point the company can calculate what extra equipment will be needed to bring each steel-making district to the point where it can produce the amount and type of tonnage required.

Meetings are then held to discuss each phase of the programme in detail – to make sure that everyone is in accord and understands the requirements. After that the plans are referred to the financial department, which starts a new set of studies to determine how the money can be made available.

The financial department develops a long-range financial forecast to show how the proposed plans will affect the company's balance sheet three, five, or ten years in the future. Will enough money be generated internally to support the working capital requirements? Will the company run out of cash – and if so, when and why? If it will, how much money must be borrowed and how long will it take to pay it back?

The answers to these questions determine top management decisions on the various projects that make up the plan. It may decide to defer or abandon some of them if too much borrowing would be required.

The financial department also prepares a short-term forecast showing the expenditures and expected receipts by months for the year ahead. This helps to prevent sudden needs for cash that will mean unplanned short-term borrowing and enables the financial department to plan ahead for investment of surplus cash so that it can be used in the most profitable way.

The financial people must depend largely on other people's estimates. The big problem, therefore, is to obtain accurate forecasts of trends on which the financial position of the company will depend. For this reason a great amount of time and effort is devoted to getting an agreement on future sales, prices, labour costs, costs of plant and equipment, and so on.

The long-range financial forecast is then prepared in three sections:

1. A projected net income statement
2. A projected statement of working capital
3. A projected partial balance sheet, showing current assets and current liabilities.

The first is determined by multiplying the projected shipments by the estimated selling price per ton, adding other income, and deducting the estimated expense items. Of course this is more

PROJECTED INCOME STATEMENT

	Actual 1964	Projected 1965–70
Ingot production (tons)	1,021,000	
Shipment (tons)	671,100	
Selling price per ton	£18.965	
Sales (less discounts allowed)	£127,274,200	
Cost of products sold	105,294,200	ESTIMATED FIGURES ARE ENTERED IN THIS COLUMN
Gross profit	£21,980,000	
Other income	1,139,400	
Total Income	£23,119,400	
Expenses, depreciation, interest, and other deductions	12,271,700	
Income before income tax	£10,847,700	
Provision for income tax	3,620,000	
Net Income	£7,227,700	

Figure 6.1 Financial planning – The income statement

complicated than it sounds because there are many different types of steel costing different amounts to produce and selling at different prices. But essentially the statement shows that if so many tons are produced and so many shipped, income after taxes will probably be so and so.

From this statement working capital can be projected. This will show whether the company's financial position will be adequate to carry out the plans. Depreciation, depletion, and amortization – which are shown as deductions from income – produce increases in working capital because they are part of what the financial analysts call 'cash flow'. They are funds available as working capital although they don't contribute to net income because they don't represent gains, merely changes in the form of an asset. If a machine costs £1,000 and has a ten-year life at the time of purchase, the company has a machine worth £1,000 instead of its equivalent in cash. But at the end of the first year, it has instead a machine worth £900 and should have at least £100 in its depreciation account to make up for the depreciation on the machine.

PROJECTED CHANGES IN WORKING CAPITAL

	Actual 1964	Projected 1965–70
Working Capital – Beginning of Period	£26,005,400	
Increases		
Net income	£7,227,700	
Depreciation, depletion & amortization, etc.	6,013,400	
Insurance loan	7,500,000	
Other items	71,500	
Total Increases	£20,812,600	ESTIMATED FIGURES ARE ENTERED IN THIS COLUMN
Decreases		
Property expenditures	£10,500,800	
Repayment of debts	5,331,100	
Total	£15,831,900	
Dividends declared	3,151,200	
Total Decreases	£18,983,100	
Net increase in working capital	£1,829,500	
Working Capital – End of Period	£27,834,900	

Figure 6.2 Financial planning – Changes in working capital

It will be noted also that working capital was increased by the amount that the projected loan (£7½ million) exceeds the loans repaid (£5,331,100). This additional money is available to the company for use in the business, but of course it will have to be repaid. In increasing its working capital through borrowings, a company has generally decided that it can make more by investing the money in needed inventory or in plant and/or equipment than it will have to pay out in interest. If this is true, borrowing will produce a net gain: *the difference between the interest rate and rate of return expected when the money is invested in the business.*

The third financial statement shows current assets and current liabilities. The assets are not the total assets of the company but those in the form of cash or assets quickly convertible to cash. Similarly, current liabilities don't represent total liabilities – only the amounts that will have to be paid within a short period – such as taxes, money owed for materials, and the amounts needed to pay interest on long-term debts plus the amounts by which they must be amortized (paid off) each year.

PROJECTED CURRENT ASSETS AND LIABILITIES

	Actual 1964	Projected 1965–70
Current Assets		
Cash	£5,150,000	
Short-term securities	3,010,000	
Total Cash Items	£8,160,000	
Tax funding	1,240,000	
Total Cash and Funding Items	£ 9,400,000	ESTIMATED FIGURES ARE ENTERED IN THIS COLUMN
Receivables	11,080,000	
Inventories	27,450,000	
Total Current Assets	£47,930,000	
Current Liabilities		
Accounts payable	£13,090,000	
Income tax	2,430,000	
Other taxes, interest, and long-term debt	4,720,000	
Total Current Liabilities	£20,240,000	
Net Working Capital	£27,834,900	

Figure 6.3 Financial planning – Current assets and liabilities

Naturally any forecast of the future involves many uncertainties, especially the figure for sales. Therefore this company revises its forecasts every three to six months. In fact, the more frequently a long-range forecast is revised, the better the management is able to focus on the immediate future.

MAKING THINGS HAPPEN

Managerial planning is a means of determining what is likely to happen, but it should also make things happen. Let's say that other companies seem likely to enlarge their share of the market at your company's expense, or that the market itself is not growing as fast as necessary if your company is to grow at satisfactory rates. What can you do about it?

For example, how do you determine the point where a product is reaching the peak sales of its life cycle and can at best hold its own in the years ahead? One thing to watch here is the extent to which the market is a replacement market. What proportion of the customers are buying the product for the first time, and what proportion are merely buying, say, a replacement for products of the same type that are worn out?

Another point is the extent to which new products are coming up that serve the same purpose and appear to be finding favour with the customers.

Because all products have life cycles – some long, some short – a company must try to have new ones coming up to take the place of old ones whose sales are likely to begin falling off. That's why so many companies have research departments. And since research takes a long time, it must be started well before the old products have begun to decline.

A manufacturer of typewriters, for example, decided that the market for typewriters was becoming largely a replacement market, even though as population and businesses grow there is bound to be some growth in the field. Since computers were already coming into use, it considered the possibility of providing computers for the offices to which it was supplying typewriters.

However, there were major obstacles. IBM had a head start, and it was a much larger company and could afford to spend more on research. The smaller company simply didn't have and couldn't raise the capital to compete with it on equal terms. Therefore, it decided that the best bet was to supply some of the peripheral equipment associated with computers and to concentrate research in those fields. In this way it was able to introduce new products in line with current trends despite its smaller size.

Sometimes an innovation in marketing practices is needed rather than, or as well as, a change in products. For example, if a company is seeking to reach a mass market, it must get its products distributed through such outlets as supermarkets, shopping centres, discount houses, and department stores. On the other hand, if its product goes to a limited but highly profitable market, it may want to concentrate on speciality stores.

There are three variables that affect profits:

1. Sales
2. Labour and material costs
3. Overheads.

Thus a company may increase its profit by increasing the first and decreasing the second and third.

To accomplish this, it must study its processes as well as its markets, for a change in process may make it possible to produce more saleable products and decrease labour costs. The introduction of new equipment for this purpose will, however, increase overheads by increasing depreciation, so it is necessary to balance the gains and losses.

CONTROL

Planning and control are closely related because management must develop systems of determining when deviations from plans are occurring in time to take steps to bring actual results into line with the plans or to revise the plans in the light of changed circumstances.

One control tool is sales analysis – an analysis of sales by type of product and by type of customer, and it is important that records be kept in such a way that these can be easily determined. For example, if sales of certain types of products or sales to certain types of stores are so small that they don't pay their way, it may be wise to stop selling to these outlets or to drop some of the products, unless it is believed that potential future sales justify continuance of the practice.

Performance against budget is another important control tool, since it shows whether the company is spending more than it is expected to.

The value of this measurement depends on two factors: how the cost is broken down and how often comparisons of actual and budgeted amounts are available. It would be of little value for management to learn at the end of the year that it had spent £10 million more than it had expected to if there were no way of tracing down the reasons. Thus reports of performance against budget must be issued often enough so there's still time to do something about them and must be detailed enough to make it possible to determine why variances have occurred.

For example, wage costs may go up because rates have risen or because more labour was needed to produce more products to take care of greater sales. If rates have risen unexpectedly, plans may have to be revised. But more often the rise will have been considered in the planning, because management knew the union contract was to be reopened that year or had made provision to take care of a rise expected because of a general trend. If the rise is no more than is warranted by the increase in production necessary because of higher sales, the variance is in the sales figure – and since that is a favourable variance, it is not a cause for concern. But if labour costs rise without a corresponding increase in either wage rates or production, then the change should be looked into because it may be due to poor utilization of labour – too much avoidable overtime, for example.

Because the level of sales and hence of production is likely to vary from plans, companies often use variable budgets that allow for variable expenses, which are those that vary with level of activity, in contrast to the fixed expenses, which continue to some extent no matter how much or how little the company produces and sells.

On the sales side, there are such control figures as sales quotas to be compared with actual sales, and sales expense allowances to be compared with actual selling expenses. To the extent that it is possible to calculate the share of market that the company is getting in each area, this percentage will also provide a useful control figure.

Planning and control are complementary techniques, and both are essential to good management.

SUGGESTED QUESTIONS FOR YOUR CONSIDERATION

1. Do you think the markets for your company's present products are likely to grow or shrink in the next five to ten years? Why do you feel that way?

2. What business is your company really in? If its present markets are shrinking or not growing as fast as desirable, what other products or services could it furnish to maintain a healthy growth rate?

3. What would these new products or services require – in capital facilities, manpower, technology, funds, and so on?

4. Have you made an effort to forecast what your department should be doing for your company next year? Or five years from now?

5. How might your company improve its products or services to get an edge on its competitors? Can you play a vital role in this competitive struggle?

CHAPTER 7

Government–Business Relations

MOST managers grumble from time to time about government regulation of business, and many of them seem to believe that about the only way to improve the situation is to find some way of getting the laws they object to repealed outright. But this is unrealistic. Few, if any, of the laws that business finds irksome are likely to be stricken completely from the books within the foreseeable future.

It is quite possible, however, that either the laws themselves or the way they're interpreted by enforcement agencies may be changed at any time. Thus it is important that managers become familiar with the content of these laws and determine whether the trouble lies with the statutes or with the interpretation of them by the regulatory agencies.

It is always difficult to write a law in such a way that it will ban undesirable practices and still not interfere with other practices that are justified and in the public interest. It is virtually impossible to draw up a statute for all possible cases, and provide the necessary exceptions. This becomes the function of administrative agencies and the courts.

That's why managers – both as managers and as citizens – should concern themselves with proposed laws or amendments while they are being formulated. They should present their views to legislators, and persuade others to do so.

Very few people do this, however. They read about a new law when it is first suggested, or after it is passed, and decide that they're for or against it, but they don't follow its progress sufficiently through the law-making bodies as provisions are added or subtracted, or as it goes back to a committee for revision. When it finally emerges, it may be quite different from what it was originally, and only those who have taken the trouble to consider it in detail and have written or otherwise contacted the legislators have an influence on the shape it finally assumes.

IMPORTANCE OF ADMINISTRATIVE LAW

Statute laws are not the only regulations that affect business. There is also what's known as 'administrative law', which is the body of rules and regulations drawn up by the government agencies charged with administering or policing the laws. Because the actual implementation and interpretation of a Statute is by means of Statutory Orders and Regulations which the appropriate Minister is empowered by the Statute to make from time to time, this 'administrative law' is often more pertinent to one affected by the law than the Statute itself.

Consider the anti-trust laws; these are designed to prevent monopoly and safeguard competition. The relevant Acts are The Monopolies and Mergers Acts of 1948 and 1965 and The Restrictive Trade Practices Act of 1956. The first of these set up a Monopolies Commission which was to decide whether a merger (or, since 1965, a proposed merger) was 'against the public interest or might be expected to operate against the public interest'. The second outlaws price agreements between suppliers who would otherwise be competitors. Any such agreements that can be shown to be in the public interest can be registered if approved by the Restrictive Practices Court.

But it will readily be understood that the meaning to be attached to such wording as 'might be expected to operate against the public interest' is very much a matter of opinion. There are no figures laid down as to what constitutes a monopoly. Courtaulds, since its purchase of British Celanese, has enjoyed 98 per cent of the U.K. rayon market but the only attention it has received from the Monopolies Commission has been in respect of price differentials between its customers.

While on the one hand politicians set out to encourage mergers (through the activities for example of the Industrial Reorganization Corporation) for the opportunities they offer of economies of scale in research, production and sales, on the other hand they discourage through the Restrictive Practices Act similar rationalization through Trade Associations (the agreements needed are held to remove competition). Firms are often reluctant to bring about similar rationalization through their Trade Associations for fear of their efforts being nullified by an order under the Restrictive Practices Act. The Building Trades Association, for example, is reluctant to recommend its members to adopt a standard form of contract although asked to do so by a Government body (the National Economic Development Sub-Committee dealing with the Building Trade) for this very reason. Similarly the members of the British Paper & Board Makers Association were prevented by the Restrictive Practices Court from agreeing among themselves on a guaranteed minimum price for purchasing waste from local authorities which would have encouraged many more to install the necessary sorting facilities. It is true that the Court gave as its reasons that better prices might be obtained by individual agreements but the disincentive to action remains and many local authorities still do not sort out paper from other waste, a state of affairs which still causes concern to the little 'Neddy' concerned.

On the whole it suits both Industry and Government to implement policy by cooperation in the shape of voluntary agreements rather than by Statutory Order. In fact, the Government will sometimes use the threat of an Order to bring about a voluntary agreement among the members of a Trade Association on lines indicated by the Government. For example, in 1954 the Minister of Supply extracted an undertaking from the Cable Makers' Association that common-price agreements should be terminated and that information should be available to the Government sufficient to satisfy them that prices charged, either to the British Electricity Authority or to other customers, were reasonable.

In addition to this 'administrative law' local authorities receive many circulars on subjects under their administration which are policy directives because they indicate the kinds of plan and conditions under which Exchequer grants will be made.

There is in the shape of The Parliamentary Commissioner (the so-called Ombudsman) a resort for appeal against individual decisions made under administrative law.

One needs to be aware of all this machinery not only for its possible effect on the individual firm but in order to understand the extent to which the ultimate decisions will depend on the political climate at the time.

HOW MUCH REGULATION IS NECESSARY?

As companies become larger and as population increases and people live closer together, there are likely to be more possibilities of contention and more of the feeling that 'there ought to be a law' to govern this or that aspect of behaviour on the part of individuals or companies. A man who retires to the backwoods and lives by himself can do practically as he pleases, and no one cares. Similarly, when industry was small with few employees and small markets, no one cared particularly what one company did. But the larger a company grows, the more people it affects and the more interest the public and the lawmakers are likely to take in what it does or what it might do.

The theory of free enterprise is simple and direct. A large number of companies compete for the consumer's money, which the consumer is free to spend as he pleases. He buys what he likes when the price is right for him; and if the price isn't right or the quality or service doesn't come up to expectations, he buys something else and the company that didn't give him what he wanted must eventually change its ways or go out of business. The economy, therefore, is largely self-regulating.

But, the argument goes, self-regulation could break down if one company were to dominate a given market so completely that entry of new competitors would be impossible. They could not find retail outlets or compete successfully in the face of the dominating company's great resources. It might, for example, cut prices until it had driven its smaller competitors out, and then raise them when the public had no other sources of supply. Similar effects would result if all companies in a given industry combined to curtail supply by cutting production and raising prices and to ensure that the public could get no better quality or service from one company than from another.

These things can happen, and they're the reason for the anti-trust laws. But the fact that regulation is needed to protect customers and companies alike doesn't mean that more regulation is better. The problem is to determine how little rather than how much regulation will accomplish the desirable ends sought.

This is somewhat parallel to the decision every manager must make regarding rules and regulations within his company. Some rules are necessary – and, in some cases, it is necessary to develop a procedure for handling certain situations and permit no deviations from it. But as was pointed out earlier, rigid procedures induce apathy in employees and reduce productivity rather than increase it. In the same way, too much regulation can produce apathy in the economy. We have to be especially careful to watch these points both in the economy at large and within companies if we're to avoid a society where there's practically no freedom at all.

Consider, for example, the amount of regulation to which the economy is presently subjected.[1] To recapitulate the laws that affect business in every respect would require endless volumes of small print. It is only possible therefore here to consider possible changes in the laws themselves or in the interpretation of them in a few respects. Here are some matters worth thinking about:

1. The Monopolies and Mergers Acts. Taken literally this might outlaw all economies to be gained from size, integration of functions both horizontally or vertically. In practice some are allowed, some not.

2. In considering which mergers to allow the proportion of the market held by competitors is taken into consideration. But is the market to include that for competing products as well? For example is the market for aluminium cable to be taken as that for cable generally including copper for which aluminium is a competitor, or more narrowly for aluminium only? As many companies have pointed out competition exists between industries (e.g. gas, coal and electricity) as well as within them, between different materials, between road and rail, between different forms of amusement.

3. The relatively new institution of Corporation Tax taxes the income of members of an enterprise (the shareholders) both as the income of the enterprise and a second time when it is distributed to the members (as dividend).

4. The cost to business of a rise in a minumum wage rate may be greater than the rise actually awarded because of the need to maintain existing and desirable differentials with other rates.

5. The Selective Employment Tax in differentiating between

[1]. See 'Business and Government', *Nation's Business*, Special Report, Edition, January 1965.

those employed in production and those engaged in providing service ignores the contribution made by 'services' to 'production' and, further, differentiates between service employees in the same building as production workers and those in separate buildings.

6. The collection of this SET tax and of some other taxes (e.g. purchase tax) involves industry in giving an interest-free loan to the Exchequer for the period between payment and recovery (either from the Revenue in the case of SET, for production workers, or from the customer in the case of Purchase tax).

7. Retail Price Maintenance is allowed on some goods, not on others.

8. Support for the Agricultural Industry by way of price guarantees and production grants increases over the years yet we still have a farm problem.

9. The Government through the defence departments, the nationalized industries, the Post Office and the Health Ministry is a major customer of the manufacturing industries and can therefore affect prices, market stability and investment decisions.

10. What is the Government's proper role in the fields of education, health, welfare, defence, communications, research, transport?

11. Investment grants, tax relief, export rebates are given preferentially to regions and industries.

12. Credit restrictions operate from time to time and are operated under instruction from the Government by the banks whose livelihood is gained by making loans. Hire purchase restrictions are imposed by regulation in order to control the home economy.

13. Price changes are liable to be vetoed by the Prices and Incomes Board.

14. The Government has an influence on rates of interest and money markets in general.

All these activities require Government agencies to administer and interpret the law. Thus we have The Monopolies Commission, The Wages Council, The Bank of England, The Prices and Incomes Board, The Restrictive Practices Court. Unpredictable changes in the Regulations make forward planning far from precise.

All together the local and national governments employ, including those in the armed services, nearly two million people, roughly one in sixteen of those available. If those in industry manufacturing supplies to be purchased by government agencies or compiling statistics for government use or accounting for tax collected on its behalf are added, the proportion is even larger. The effects on tax rates and on basic economic freedom are obvious.

Many of the laws that these agencies administer were designed to accomplish results that everyone would agree are desirable, and if you have a law you must necessarily have an agency to administer it. But once an agency is organized, those in charge of it quite naturally want to extend their domain and to gather more and more subordinates about them. This often happens in business as well, as department heads strive to improve their positions. It is only human nature to want to improve one's status. But the difference is that what a department head in a business does affects only his own company. In government, however, this extension of power affects every one of us – our pocket-books and our freedom.

EFFECT OF ELECTIONS

Of course a change in elected representatives can lead to changes in the laws or their interpretation. Hence it is important that managers take an active interest in elections and understand the issues clearly so that they can explain their viewpoints to others.

It is difficult, obviously, to pin candidates down on any clear-cut issue. Naturally they want to gain as many votes as possible, and are therefore likely to try to be all things to all men. But since they want to gain votes, they're likely to answer letters, or have them answered, when voters write asking their views on current questions.

But to know just what the answers mean, it is sometimes necessary to read between the lines. 'I consider this question very important, and will certainly give it thoughtful consideration', means either that the candidate is opposed to the writer's viewpoint or that he is not particularly interested in the point at issue and is not likely to press for the changes that the writer would like to see made.

Another clue is each candidate's past record, and it is here that close attention to what has happened while laws were in process of formulation will pay off. 'I voted for the such-and-such Act,' may not be much of an indication that the candidate really favoured it. He may have also voted for amendments that emasculated it, or have voted to keep it bottled up in a committee, and approved it only because he knew it was going to pass and felt it well to get on the bandwagon.

Another point to remember is the importance of local elections. A parliamentary election, especially a general one, is exciting and few people are uninterested in its outcome. There is less interest in local government elections but it is important to be alert to the personalities and the issues in both. There may, in fact, be more satisfaction in working for the candidate of one's choice in a local election. Each vote counts more and each person can have a real influence.

Also, local issues and the attitudes of local Councillors can touch the operation of a business very closely. Consider, for example, the effect of building codes, which are often a hodge-podge accumulated over the years, zoning laws, laws regarding disposal of wastes, and real estate taxes. The type of education provided by the local education authority's schools is important to the manager, even if he has no children or sends his children to private schools, because it helps to determine the quality level of employees that will be available to the company.

Also, local councils may as bodies be able to influence the local member of parliament. Thus, helping to elect those who will do a good job may contribute to better representation at the national level.

DEALING WITH ELECTED REPRESENTATIVES

But one cannot always be on the winning side in national or local elections. There may be no chance for some years of displacing either the elected officials whose decisions affect a great many aspects of a company's operations.

Some managers seem to believe that representatives for whom they didn't vote, or who were appointed by the opposing party, are ogres determined to make things as difficult as possible. Thus they either avoid them altogether or approach them with truculence with no real hope of getting them to see reason.

This is a big mistake. Most of them are conscientiously trying to do a good job and welcome the expression of different points of view. They can't know the effect of their various interpretations and rulings in each case unless public opinion makes itself felt. When the facts are explained to them, they may modify their attitudes in some respects.

Nor need the contacts always take the form of protests. There are many instances in which positive suggestions from managers have been adopted to the benefit of both business and the community in general. Many school boards, for example, are definitely anxious to prepare their students for jobs available in local industry, and would welcome advice from managers on the subject. There are many cases of this nature in which the interests of a company and the local community coincide so obviously that cooperation will be easy to obtain.

THE PUBLIC DECIDES

Most important of all in determining the laws that are passed and the way they are interpreted is the viewpoint of the general public. Managers are, of course, part of the general public, but they are in a minority. Hence they can get their viewpoints across only if they can influence others. What can the manager do about this?

First of all, he should read the papers so that he knows what's happening, and then talk to his employees and others with whom he comes in contact. He should be sure of his facts, and think through the implications of moves on the part of the legislative bodies and administrative agencies so that he will be able to explain to others exactly what the consequences of these moves are likely to be. And he should not confine himself to matters that affect only his own particular company or his own job. The affairs of the nation and the local community are everyone's business.

Second, he can work for the candidates of his choice at election time – by talking to others, perhaps by helping to get people to the polls, and by contributions to the party of his choice.

Another way in which managers can help head off stricter

regulation is to avoid doing things that make people believe 'there ought to be a law'. Many managers think this depends only on top management, which makes decisions on mergers, on prices, on product quality, and so on. And naturally, top management does have a major responsibility in this respect.

But the responsibility does not stop there. There is much that middle and lower management can do.

For example, take the matter of air and water pollution, which is arousing increasing interest on the part of the general public and local and national officials. There is legislation already, both local and national, on both air and water pollution, and it may become more strict in the future as the population grows and pollution grows with it.

Whether to install an expensive waste disposal system may be a decision for top management, or at least for plant management. But much still depends on those in direct charge of the operation of the processes.

For example, in one detergent manufacturing plant, an entire batch went wrong, and the supervisor in charge had his men sweep it all down a drain that led into a river. As a result the stream was a mass of bubbles for miles, the fish were killed, and protests arose from residents of the area as well as from other companies that were accustomed to using the river water in their processes.

The amount of air pollution, too, depends not only on the amount of equipment provided by top management but on the way the production processes are operated. A mistake on the part of operators can cause much more pollution than is necessary – in one instance, for example, ashes settled on a parking lot and destroyed the finish on hundreds of cars. The fact that the company had to pay damages for this was perhaps less important than the feeling the incident created in the minds of the car owners that the laws governing air pollution should be stricter.

THE COMPANY IMAGE

Incidents like those just related help create an unfavourable image of the company and the industry in general. An enterprise that is the only large company in a community comes to represent industry in general to the people of that community – and even where there are a number of large companies in the vicinity, each contributes something to the image that the general public holds of industry as a whole.

A good point to remember about 'images' is that, once created, they're very difficult to erase, for people don't like to change their minds once they've made them up. Unfortunately, too, it is easier to create a bad image than a good one – one bad experience will often do the trick so far as an individual and his friends are concerned.

Every manager is a representative of his company, and so every manager has a part in creating the image people hold of his company and of industry in general. Most managers are conscious of this as far as employees and good customers are concerned, but they never think sufficiently of the many other people who are gaining an impression of the company from them.

For example, if a company has a job to fill, it generally considers more than one applicant. This means that some people must be turned down, and naturally they're not going to feel too good about it. But the way they're turned down may make all the difference in the world about how they feel towards the company and even towards industry in general.

If they think that the company has honestly considered their qualifications and treated them courteously and fairly, they will not hold the turndown against it. But if they feel that the manager who interviewed them was prejudiced against them for some reason, or that he didn't give them a chance to state their qualifications, or was abrupt or discourteous in any way, they're likely to be angry at the company as well as the manager.

Ensuring good treatment of applicants is not a matter for the personnel department alone. Every manager is likely to do some interviewing – and to the extent that he does, the company's reputation is in his hands.

Curiously, some very simple things can make the difference. One researcher asked several people who had applied for a number of jobs to show him the letters of turndown that they felt were the most understanding and courteous. It developed that a two-paragraph letter, merely because it was a little longer, created a better impression than a note of only one paragraph. The one paragraph letter, it appeared, seemed abrupt to them.

Again, what about customers? Every manager is probably conscious of the need to treat good customers well, but how does he deal with those who don't seem to be good prospects or even prospects at all? Does he brush them off? That may save his time at the moment – but quite aside from the fact that they might become good prospects later, they're members of the general public to whom the company wants to present a favourable image.

And what about suppliers? In this case the company is the customer, and the manager may believe that as the customer he is always right. But suppliers and their representatives are also members of the general public.

Finally, the manager must consider the various civic organizations in his community. If he can be active in some of them he has a large opportunity to influence public opinion as well as to create an image of a company that's genuinely interested in the welfare of the community, and doesn't simply regard it as an adjunct to the plant or office operations.

There are also cases in which delegations from various groups will call on a manager to complain about inconveniences – air or water pollution or traffic problems occasioned by the plant itself.

If the manager brushes them off, argues heatedly with them, or counter-attacks, he's helping to solidify the feeling that 'there ought to be a law'. If, on the contrary, he explains what's being done about the nuisance they complain about and why the company can't proceed any faster than it is doing, and solicits their suggestions, he's creating the opposite impression.

The company image and the image the public holds of business and industry in general are only partially moulded by top management and the public relations department. Every manager has the power and opportunity to build good images, or to tear down good images that have cost a great deal to build up in the past.

SUGGESTED QUESTIONS FOR YOUR CONSIDERATION

1. Have you ever written to your M.P. regarding proposed legislation which you support or object to?

2. Have you ever written him about matters other than legislation?

3. Have you made it a point to meet with him personally at any time? Do you know him sufficiently to discuss problems frankly and informally?

4. Has he ever visited your plant or place of business? Have you ever extended an invitation for him to do so?

5. Do you make it a point to check the issues and candidates in all parliamentary elections and generally vote in them?

6. Do you vote in local elections? Do you encourage your employees to do so?

7. Under what circumstances do you act as the legislative or governmental representative of your company?

8. How could your company improve its image in the local community? In the minds of the general public? What can you yourself do to further this improvement?

9. Do you now have a legislative or other programme in mind to improve the business climate of your locality?

10. Does industry appear to be moving in or out of your immediate area? Why?

CHAPTER 8

Managerial Decision-Making

A MANAGER is responsible for the men, machines, materials and methods at his disposal. These are resources he uses to reach his objectives. And in determining how he will use them, he must constantly make decisions.

A decision always involves a choice among alternatives. It is not necessary to make a decision when only one course of action is feasible. The same is true when one course is obviously the best one, for in that case the situation dictates the decision. A real decision is required when there's some uncertainty about choosing one course rather than another – when the manager can't really be sure that it is better to decide one way rather than another. Thus true decision-making involves some degree of risk.

Perhaps that's why some people find it hard to make decisions. They're afraid of making the wrong decision, and the result is they let things slide whenever they can.

Actually, they're not eliminating risk. For as Chester I. Barnard points out in *The Functions of the Executive*,[1] they're really making the decision 'not to decide'. And the decision not to decide may be as risky as the decision to act – for if a problem is ignored, it may become more serious than it was at first.

Consider a company whose product is approaching the end of its life cycle. It is confronted with the question: *What new products shall we introduce?* There are, let's say, several possible products, but uncertainty exists as to whether one is better than another. Each requires new capital investment, and it is impossible to know for sure how much of any one could be sold. None the less, if management keeps postponing a decision, and the sales of its old products keep falling, the company may find eventually that it doesn't have the working capital necessary to start producing any new products at all.

1. Chester I. Barnard: *The Functions of the Executive* (Cambridge, Mass., Harvard University Press, 1956), p. 193.

Or let's take an example that might occur further down the line. A subordinate manager is authorized to make decisions in certain cases – but because he feels so keenly that he takes a risk every time he decides, he passes the buck to his superior whenever he can. In making the decision to avoid responsibility, he believes he's eliminating risk. But he isn't. He's running the risk, and a bad one, that his superior will come to think of him as indecisive and lacking in initiative. Thus he may be passed over for promotion.

DEGREES OF RISK

Long-range decisions involve greater risk than short-range decisions because the uncertainty is greater. The consequences of many decisions will not make themselves felt until several years in the future, and it is difficult to tell whether the results will be appropriate to the circumstances at that time.[2]

If management decides not to organize a research department, for example, it will not know the consequences until the results of its competitors' research become known. If its competitors succeed, after several years, in developing revolutionary new products, it may be too late for the company to catch up. But again, it may spend a large amount of money on research without producing any significant breakthroughs, and the result may be merely a reduction in profits for a period of years.

On the other hand, the decision to use one man instead of two on a given job may be a short-range decision. As soon as the man is well started, the manager can check to see how he's getting along – and if it is clear that two men will be needed, he can immediately assign another man.

However, some decisions that seem short-range at the time they are made may have far-reaching consequences. For example, when a supervisor makes a decision on the disposition of a grievance, he may be unconsciously giving away the right to decide otherwise in similar cases – not only his own right, but that of other supervisors as well. It is well known that unions are likely to seize on any concession and use it as precedent; and arbitrators, too, lean

2. See *Formal Planning—The Executive's Role* (Menlo Park, California, Stanford Research Institute, 1964).

heavily on precedent in their decisions. Thus what seems like a short-range decision involving only a single incident may actually have the effect of modifying the union agreement. And the modification may be carried over into future contracts.

Another important factor in the amount of risk attached to a decision is the proportion of the company's resources that must be used to carry out the decision. Committing £1,000 to a project may be fatal for a small company if a decision doesn't turn out to be correct, but such a loss would not be too serious in a large company.

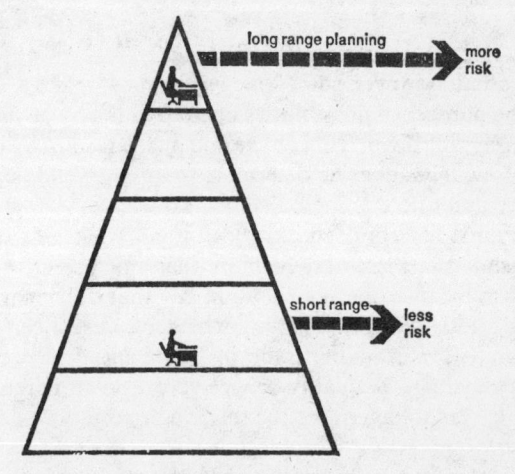

Figure 8.1 The influence of time span on risk

Where decisions commit a large proportion of the company's resources to a project, the commitments should be made by those in a position to see the whole picture. That's why companies frequently set money limits on the amounts that executives at different levels may spend for capital improvements. Large appropriations may well require the approval of the president and the board of directors. And this is as it should be because only the very top executives are in a position to see the entire situation. Also, they're the ones who are ultimately responsible for the company's survival and growth.

Then, in every company, there are streams of decision-making because an individual decision made at one point produces the need for decisions at other points. Thus if top management decides to produce a new product, decisions must be made by different people on the manpower, machines, materials, and methods to be used, on the sales strategy, on the money needed for all this, and where it should come from. Certain decisions will be sequential; that is, they will be in part dictated by other decisions. Thus once it is decided to use certain materials, this narrows down the number of different types of machines that can be used.

THE PROCESS OF DECISION-MAKING

At every point, however, some one person must make a decision, though the number of possibilities open to him may be limited by directives coming down from above and by the resources available to him. How, then, does he determine what he should decide?

The key point here is the objective. To decide what should be done, he must always keep clearly in mind what he's trying to accomplish. Also, there may be more than one objective, and he may have to balance one against another – that is, he makes what are called 'trade-offs'. In deciding whether to use a certain process, he may, for example, trade off some speed in production against an increase in quality or vice versa. So to make a good decision, he has to determine the relative importance of each objective.

The next step is to make an analysis of the situation in the light of objectives. Suppose, for example, that the company's objective in a given case is to raise production to meet increased demand. Before it can decide what to do, it must seek the answers to such questions as: How much more production do we need? Where is the demand coming from? Is the rise in demand likely to continue and at what rate? What's likely to be the effect on competition? Can competitors take away most of the new markets if they really try?

The third step is to consider possible alternatives. In the case of rising demand, these might be:

1. Build a new plant
2. Buy better equipment

3. Add an extra shift
4. Authorize overtime.

The fourth step is to consider these alternatives in the light of the situation and weigh them against the probable consequences. These consequences would include the costs of the various courses of action, both present and future. If analysis shows that the demand is only temporary, it wouldn't be worthwhile to build a new plant or even to purchase new equipment. Thus adding a second shift or authorizing overtime might be the most profitable course. Using overtime would have the advantage of making an immediate increase in production possible, although it would, of course, require extra labour costs and this would have to be taken into account.

It is not always easy to determine what competitors are likely to do, but we can try to find out what they can do and how quickly they can do it in the light of the resources available to them. The neglect of some companies to consider this point thoroughly has resulted in over-capacity in some cases.

For example, one foreign automobile company that had been experiencing an increasing American demand for its small cars decided to build a new plant to produce more cars, neglecting to take into account two important and easily obtainable facts:

1. The car was not American consumers' first choice among foreign cars. Many of them bought it simply because their first choice was not easy to obtain.
2. American automobile manufacturers had the resources to go into the manufacture of small cars as soon as it became clear that there was a sizeable demand for smaller cars.

The outcome was that production at the new plant had to be drastically curtailed shortly after it was completed.

The fifth step in the decision-making process is the decision itself, which must generally be made without being entirely sure of the outcome.

And the sixth and final step is to determine what should be done to put the plan into effect and issue the necessary orders and instructions to see that it is carried out.

Obviously, where the decision may mean the commitment of important resources for quite some time in the future, it is worthwhile to spend considerable time and money on the analysis and the consideration of alternatives. In other cases the decision may be made quickly since the alternatives are well known to the decision maker. This is more difficult than it sounds, however.

Consider the case of a supervisor who discovers that an employee has made a mistake. His first instinct may be to bawl the man out; but if he's to make a rational decision, he must first consider his objective. As the Job Relations Training Programme phrased it, he must ask himself, 'What do I really want to accomplish?' A brief reflection will convince him that his objective is to ensure that the mistake doesn't occur again, not simply to relieve his feelings. With this in mind the next step is to analyse the situation and determine *why* the mistake occurred, or to use the JRT language again, 'Get all the facts.' Was the mistake due to misunderstanding of instructions? To trying to work too fast? To lack of proper training? Or to negligence?

When he has the facts, he will know better what to do. He may still decide on a stern approach because his analysis of the situation and his knowledge of the employee may indicate that this is the best way to ensure that the mistake does not happen again. But his decision will then be rational rather than instinctive. It will be, as A. R. C. Duncan of Queen's University in Canada has pointed out, 'an intelligent decision that can be defended if necessary. The supervisor can say "This is what I did, and these are the reasons why I did it." '

MATHEMATICAL DECISION-MAKING

In dealing with people, the manager is dealing with intangibles; but in many cases the data on which management bases its decisions can be, in part, reduced to numbers, and it is a good idea to use numerical techniques whenever they are applicable. The manager should remember, however, that numbers may not tell the whole story. There's always a tendency to depend too heavily on them because there can be no argument about whether one number is greater than another. That's probably why many managers place too much weight on psychological test scores in hiring, rather than using them as one factor in the selection process.

Mathematical calculations are probably of most value in decisions on capital investment, but even here there are pitfalls because the figures may not present the true picture.

For example, in many companies, the method used to determine the worth of a capital investment is the payout or payoff period. Managers try to determine how long it will take an investment to pay for itself, and the shorter the payoff period the better the investment.

Consider this simple illustration. Let us say the capital investment in a new machine to replace hand labour will save £1,000 a year in labour costs. From this, of course, the manager subtracts the extra costs of the machine to arrive at the net gain to be achieved each year.

Let's say the machine costs £2,000 and the extra costs – depreciation on the machine, maintenance, and the power required – will amount to £200. The net saving is then £800 a year, so it will take the machine two years and a half to pay for itself. If a choice had to be made between this purchase and another investment that would take five years to pay off, one might conclude that the first approach is better. But is it?

Not necessarily. Under the payoff method we leave at least two important factors out of the calculations: *the time value of money* and *the total return on investment*, for returns may continue long after the investment has paid for itself.

The time value of money may be illustrated in this way. Suppose the £2,000, the money the company is proposing to pay for the machine, were put in the bank instead. At the end of the machine's useful life, it would amount to more than £2,000 because it would be earning interest in the meantime. At 4 per cent interest, between £96 and £97 on hand today is worth as much as £100 received a year from now. Therefore, the present value of the £800 the company will have next year is only about £770. Tables are available to find present values at varying rates of interest.

Again, the investment with the longer payoff period may not pay for itself so quickly, but it may produce a better return over a longer period. Also, the returns from one investment may be larger in the first year or two and smaller in subsequent years or vice versa.

One method of deciding between two different investments that will return different amounts in different years in the future is to calculate the present value of the returns over the life of each investment, discounting the amounts to be received in the future by appropriate percentages. Then the total present value of the return is compared to the investment to determine the profitability index for each one. Thus if an investment of £1,000 will yield over its whole life a return whose *present value* is £1,500 the profitability index would be 1·5, and it would be considered a better investment than one with an index of 1·25. If the index were less than 1, the investment would not be made because the present value of the money to be used is greater than the present value of the expected return.

In this case the percentage by which future income is discounted is a predetermined rate, usually equal to what the company may normally expect to earn on its investments judging from past experience, the cost of capital, and similar figures.

By itself, however, this method is incomplete, for it ignores the risk entailed in committing capital for long periods in the future. For example, in ten years, the process the machine is designed to be used for might become obsolete. Therefore the profitability index should preferably be used in conjunction with the payoff and some management judgement regarding future prospects.

MANAGEMENT SCIENCE – OPERATIONAL RESEARCH

There has developed, under the name of *management science*, a body of sophisticated mathematical aids to the making of decisions. These, mostly, are of assistance in providing better predictions of the probable effects of change. A characteristic of the modern outlook is to regard the business or firm, or each part of it under study, as a *system*. This concept ensures that all the interrelated and perhaps interlocking parts are taken into account both for diagnosis of present trouble and for prediction to help future improvement.

An important development in parallel with the concept of the *system* and *systems analysis* is the science of *operational research* which, with the objective of optimizing the functioning of a system makes studies, often mathematical, and certainly involving simplified models of (i.e. theories about) the system. The need for OR lies in the poor results to be obtained by synthesizing piecemeal studies of parts of a system in order to predict the performance of the whole. OR originated, in fact, in the discovery that a particular equipment (radar) when first put to use in 'the field', failed to function as well as had been expected, not because of any technical shortcomings in the apparatus itself but because the operational conditions and links had not been designed to match the main purpose of introducing the equipment. This in fact illustrates the outstanding characteristic of OR that, while adopting the familiar scientific approach to problems, it insists on studying the problem at issue as a whole. In several of the war-time examples of its success this characteristic led to a reformulation of the problem at issue. In the case of radar the problem was changed from that of detecting the approach of enemy aircraft to that of intercepting them; in the case of Coastal Command's maintenance procedure, from that of ensuring maximum readiness to answer a call to maximizing the patrol–for–detection time.[3] In a similar way a firm may realize that the maximization of immediate profit is not the desired objective but instead the maximum utilization of resources or of profit in some future period.[4] This requirement that the objective should first be stated is a useful discipline not always imposed by older methods. OR usually attempts to optimize the performance of a system: in order to make our meaning clear we first explain the words *optimum* and *system*.

The *optimum* is the best answer possible in view of the many different factors in a situation. Thus it will not be *ideal* in every respect. For example, the ideal situation would be one in which advertising expenditures could be cut to the bone and sales raised at the same time. But other things being equal, cutting advertising is likely to cause a decline in sales. Therefore, one cannot do both, but must find the optimum point where enough advertising is done

3. W. E. Duckworth: *A Guide to Operational Research* (Methuen, 1962).
4. B. H. P. Rivett and R. Ackoff: *A Manager's Guide to Operational Research* (Wiley, 1963).

to maintain or increase sales and yet advertising costs are not excessive.

A *system* is any unit in which varying factors interact. For example, a machine is a system, for a change in one part of it will affect the other parts. But it is also part of the production system of the company, and the production system is part of the company, which is another and larger system. The company, in turn, is part of an economic system, which will be affected – to a greater or lesser extent – by what each company does. And changes in the economic system affect the possibilities open to the company.

In theory, OR men or systems analysts employed by a company should work for the optimum so far as the entire company is concerned, but in practice their work is generally concerned with 'sub-optimums', that is, the optimums for particular systems, such as inventory systems or automated systems of production.

Now in any system many of the variables are so interrelated that if we change Variable A, this will mean a change in other variables, and these changes will produce further changes in Variable A, which may or may not further the end we were trying to achieve by the initial change. Since this is so, it will be helpful in decision-making if we can know in advance exactly how a change we are proposing to make in one factor would affect the whole system we are tinkering with.

In OR, an attempt is made to quantify each of the variables, assign a numerical value to each, and then produce a mathematical model that will show the final effect of any proposed change.

A mathematical model is simply a representation in mathematical terms of the various factors involved in a situation. It may be as simple as $P = R - C$, meaning that profits equal revenues minus costs, or it may be very complicated and require higher mathematics and the use of a computer. In operations research or systems analysis, which attempts to take into account the actions and reactions of many different variables, the problem is usually complicated, so a computer is used to make the calculations.

One of the major applications of OR is to the allocation of resources. In World War II Great Britain used scientists skilled in different fields to determine how it could best use its limited air force and anti-aircraft guns to combat the German bombers. The ideal, of course, would have been to have enough guns and fighter planes at every point to shoot down any attacking force that might appear. But since resources were limited it was necessary to determine the *optimum* sites, taking into account the weather, the speed of the aircraft, the distance at which bombers could be shot down, and many other variables.

In management, too, the problem is often the allocation of resources and balancing various advantages and disadvantages of various courses of action in such a way as to achieve the optimum results with the resources available. For example, in developing a production plan the manager must consider such things as stock levels, amount of sub-contracting done, utilization of machines and labour – all of which affect each other.

OR may also be used in marketing to good effect. For example, International Minerals and Chemical Company has devised a mathematical model of the market for fertilizers which takes into account the demand for various products, the timing of the demand, the constituents of the soil, the different cost inputs, and the influence of the weather.

In some types of OR problems, the various quantities are known – for example, the cost of carrying a given amount of stock. But in other instances, the OR men must work with probabilities. One very well known type of problem of this nature is what is known as the queueing problem.

For example, how many tool issue points should there be? When mechanics wait for tools, their time is not being used productively. But having more tool issue points raises costs since it means more attendants. And the number of mechanics needing a tool at any one time is not constant. At certain times there may be quite a few workers waiting in line, at other times none at all. What, then, is the optimum number of tool issue points?

How many toll booths should be at the entrance to a parkway to prevent undue tie-ups of traffic, and not raise costs unnecessarily by adding too many booths and attendants? This is a problem (posed by the New York Port Authority) whose solution involved OR.

In some cases OR clearly points to the most profitable course of action and so makes the management decision clear-cut, in others it can only claim to provide the comparative data that will assist management in arriving at its decision.

Alain Enthoven, Deputy Assistant Secretary of Defense in the U.S.A., reserves the term 'operations research' for cases in which the mathematics are believed to dictate the right answer, and uses 'systems analysis' for those in which human decision-making is required after all the facts are in. An example is a case where systems analysis would show that 89 targets, on the average, would be destroyed by 324 missiles, but 340 missiles would be required to raise the average to 90. The responsible human being would have to decide whether it was worth the price of 16 more missiles to destroy one extra target. He might decide to trade off the probability of destroying one more target so as to use the money for other defence purposes. Even for the government, resources are not inexhaustible.

IMPROVING DECISION-MAKING

Mathematical decision-making techniques contribute to better decisions not only by requiring better knowledge of the situation and marshalling the facts available but by providing a methodical procedure which ensures that all alternatives are considered and their outcomes compared. The fact that often much of the information that would be desirable in a particular case is only available in part or is imperfect in some way can be coped with by the use of statistical methods which are designed for just such situations. Irwin D. Bross's book *Design for Decision* (Macmillan, N.Y.) is well worth reading where one is bothered by the imperfection of the information available.

As A. R. C. Duncan points out, the decision makers who seem to make uncannily good decisions merely by intuition depend only partially on a 'born knack'. They combine with this (*a*) skill acquired through intensive training; (*b*) unusually extensive knowledge of the field built up perhaps over many years; and (*c*) interest in the job. 'Hard work combined with intelligence and interest will do all that is ever claimed for intuition,' Duncan says, and he is very likely right. Few, if any, people make good intuitive decisions in fields of which they are ignorant.

MANAGERIAL DECISION-MAKING

Another factor in good decision-making may be the extent to which organization facilitates communication of the facts upwards and downwards. In this connexion some experiments conducted by a group of professors at Massachusetts Institute of Technology are pertinent.[5]

To study the effects of organization on the speed and flexibility of decisions, they used three different organizational networks: the Star, the Star-Circle, and the Circle-Chain. Then they designed

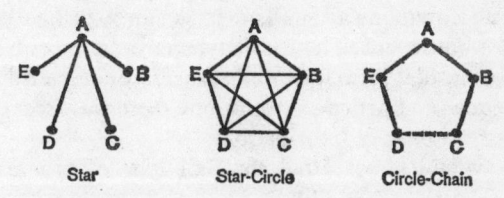

Figure 8.2 The three organizational networks

SOURCE: Harold J. Leavitt, Carnegie Institute of Technology, Pittsburgh

three poker tables with plywood partitions isolating each member of each of the three groups of participants and specified that communication could be only by written messages dropped through slots in the partitions.

The table for the Star group was constructed so that *B*, *C*, *D* and *E* could communicate only with *A*, and he could communicate with each of them. In the Star-Circle and Circle-Chain organizations, messages could go to the left or right, except that *D* and *C* in the Circle-Chain could pass and receive messages from one side only. Each member of each group had six marbles, all of different colours, and the problem was to find out which one of the colours was common to the other members of the group.

Hundreds of different trials showed that in the Star group the answer was determined most quickly and most accurately. The Circle-Chain had the next best score, and the Star-Circle was last.

---

5. Adapted from materials in an unpublished manuscript by Harold J. Leavitt, Carnegie Institute of Technology. Also see Harold J. Leavitt: *Managerial Psychology*, rev. ed. (Chicago, University of Chicago Press, 1964).

The Circle groups were found to be most likely to adopt new ideas, but they were less likely to originate the new ideas.

Then the experimenters decided to impose a change. Instead of marbles of different colours, the groups received marbles that were different shades of pink. When this happened, the number of messages increased tremendously because new communication symbols had to be devised – the participants had to decide how they would describe the varying shades of pink.

This time the Circle groups did much better than the Star group, in which all communications had to go through Leader A. He became the bottleneck. The Circle type of organization was also found to be the best form for training successors because everyone became acquainted with everything, and there was freer exchange and better feed-back of information.

Thus it would appear that the Star type of organization is perhaps the best where conditions are likely to remain the same for a long time, but the other types will be more useful for situations where flexibility and frequent changes are desirable. This is a point the manager must consider in deciding on the form his organization will take, and the channels of communication he will endeavour to keep open.

If one were to prescribe a method of improving decision-making, however, perhaps the best advice would be to consider the objectives and analyse each situation as it arises, spending as much time in getting the facts as the decision warrants but no more.[6]

To focus his thought processes and make better decisions, the manager might ask himself the following questions:

1. Do I really understand the problem involved?
2. What am I trying to get done?
3. Is this the best way to do it?
4. What may go wrong when I put my decision into effect?

It might be a good idea for the manager to make a conscious use of these questions for a month or so. Quite likely he will find that he's digging into decision-making situations much more quickly

6. *Nation's Business* (May 1964), pp. 122–4, 126. Joseph G. Mason: 'Tips on Improving Your Decisions', *Management Review* (American Management Association, July 1964), pp. 52–4.

and easily, and spending less time in unproductive thought and worry.[7]

SUGGESTED QUESTIONS FOR YOUR CONSIDERATION

1. What are the most important decisions you generally make in the course of your work?

2. Can you think of any cases in the past in which you have made the wrong decision? Why? Did you neglect to consider your true objectives? Or to get as many facts as you could without undue expenditure of time and money? Did you consider *all* the possible alternatives? Do you think you could have done better if you had followed the procedure outlined in this chapter?

3. Can you think of any problems your company might use OR to solve?

4. Do you have an organized way of solving problems? Can you list your approach in several simple sentences?

5. Do you believe the managers you know approach their problem-solving and decision-making in a scientific manner? Or do they rely heavily on intuition and hunch?

---

7. John E. Swearingen: 'The Nature of the Executive Decision', *Business Topics* (East Lansing, Michigan, Michigan State University, Graduate School of Business Administration, Spring 1965), pp. 60–65.

CHAPTER 9

Reducing Costs by Value Analysis

SUPPOSE you're putting up a temporary building to store tools and equipment while construction is in progress. You intend to tear it down as soon as the project is finished, which will be in about 15 months. A roofing salesman comes along and tells you: 'We have a roof that's guaranteed to last ten years without any need for repairs. Naturally the price is a little higher, but just think what you're getting.'

Would you buy his roofing for your temporary building? Probably not. The fact that it will last ten years is immaterial because you intend to tear the building down in a short time. His company does provide an extra value for the extra money for other applications, but not for yours.

Now any manager would make the same decision in this case because it is so clear-cut. Yet many companies spend thousands of pounds unnecessarily in similar cases where the lack of value, as far as they're concerned, is just as great.

Value analysis is a technique for uncovering instances in which this is true and doing something about them.

There are a number of methods of cost cutting, but many of them entail penalties that may cut profits rather than increase them. If a company reduces its sales force, advertising, or the quality of its products, it may in the end lose many of its customers. If it postpones buying new machinery too long, it may suffer breakdowns that cause it to miss delivery dates and lose sales – and it may increase its maintenance costs as well. If it tries to cut wages, it may have an expensive strike on its hands. If it cuts salaries, it may lose some of its best people.

With value analysis there are no penalties. The main cost is the time spent in implementing the technique, and this should be more than offset by the gains. Frequently the time required is relatively small because the manager who is conditioned to value analysis may use it to arrive at good ideas during the course of his regular work.

Routine methods of cost cutting, like reduction of scrap and avoidance of overtime, are good, but there are limits to the improvements that can be achieved by these means. Value analysis, however, offers almost unlimited possibilities.

For example, Lawrence D. Miles, a nationwide authority on value analysis, tells of a company that spent $40,000 a year for covers for a temperature control instrument. The purpose of the covers was to keep dust and other extraneous material out of the mechanism. One day, someone got the idea that a cover made of a cheaper material would accomplish the same purpose, and this simple change saved the company $15,000 a year.[1]

It is, of course, possible to cheapen any product by simply reducing its ability to do what it is supposed to do. But this is not the aim of value analysis. It is a scientific technique designed to make possible *the same or better* performance and customer satisfaction at lower cost. Frequently the product is improved by the process.[2]

Suppose the product is furniture. The values the customer seeks are appearance, comfort and durability. It would be possible to produce a cheaper product by shaving one of these qualities, but that would not be the value analyst's approach. Substitute materials would be used only if they would provide as much or more of all three values as the original materials.

In some products durability is not a factor in customer satisfaction. The roof on a temporary building is a case in point, for it need be only durable enough to last until the building is torn down. In other cases appearance may be unimportant – for example, in a component of a machine that no one ever sees except when the machine is torn down.

Value analysis may be applied to the design of a product or a component since design changes will often simplify production and make it possible to eliminate some of the processes used. This is sometimes called 'value engineering', but the terms 'value analysis' and 'value engineering' are more often used interchangeably.

1. Lawrence D. Miles: *Techniques of Value Analysis and Engineering* (New York, McGraw-Hill, Inc., 1961), p. 2.
2. Arthur Garratt: 'How to Get Value for Analysis', *Management Today*, BIM London, May 1967. W. L. Gage: *Value Analysis*, McGraw-Hill.

THE VALUE ANALYSIS TECHNIQUE

Value analysis seeks the answer to the following questions, which may be asked about a complete product, a part of it, or a process:

1. What must this item or process do? What is its function?
2. What else does the item do?
3. What does it cost?
4. What else could perform the same function?
5. What do the possible substitutes cost?

What must it do? Generally, the primary purpose of any device can be described in two words. For example, the function of the cover for the instrument described above was to 'provide protection'. The primary function of an electric light bulb is to 'provide light'.

Then an item may have important secondary functions as well. The function of paint may be to 'provide protection', but in other instances painting may be done to improve appearance as well as to provide protection.

What else does the item do? If the item performs functions that are not needed, this is a symptom that there's waste somewhere.

The answer to the first question – 'What does it do?' – would have eliminated the unnecessary reports Harrington Emerson found the railroad clerks making (see Chapter 4), since the original informative function was no longer being carried out. No one read the reports, so they weren't supplying information to anyone.

The answer to the question 'What else does it do?' might make it possible to simplify and shorten reports which are read, since the original reports may supply more information than is actually needed.

What does it cost? In the case of a purchased item, the answer to this question is easy. But if an item or a component is manufactured within the plant, it may be more difficult to determine its actual cost.

For example, standard costs include overheads, which will

encompass a great many costs that cannot be eliminated merely by eliminating an operation. Any saving in material costs is likely to be a real saving – but if production of a part is used as 'fill-in' work, it may not be possible to save the full amount of the labour costs by eliminating part of the work.

What else will do the job? Here it is important to get as many answers as possible. One technique often employed is brainstorming. Where this method is used, a group of people meet and give the imaginations free play. The rule is that no suggestion offered is pooh-poohed, but is written down as offered. It may not be practical as first stated, but it may suggest something practical to some other member of the group. When the group runs out of ideas, the more promising suggestions are evaluated.

Other methods include looking over the latest books and trade magazines to determine what new materials have come out and what new or improved processes are available. Consulting with specialists or vendors is another possibility. Trade shows are also a source of valuable ideas.

Plastics may have been rejected in an earlier application because none of those available had the necessary properties. But thousands of new plastics come out each year, and one of the newer ones may be as useful for some applications as more expensive materials.

Or a company may be continuing an expensive machining operation because it was unable to get castings with the proper tolerances. But this may no longer be the case since precision casting methods have been improved. Sometimes a standard 'off-the-shelf' part will fill the bill just as well as a custom-made product. It may not have been available when the product was first designed.

What will the alternatives cost? When one or more feasible alternatives have been developed, the costs of each should be determined to see whether they will produce a worthwhile saving.

Of course, one must take into account such factors as new equipment or changes in equipment that will be needed; whether more skilled labour will be required; whether time will be saved and how much; any extra space that must be provided; or conversely any space saving that will be realized; and all other factors that go into costs.

The accounting department may be of help here, and the manager should not hesitate to consult it, or to consult heads of other departments to determine how a change will affect their operations.

For example, the way products are classified may affect the freight rates the company pays. In his book, *Techniques of Value Analysis and Engineering*, Lawrence D. Miles tells of an electric clock factory in which the clock faces were referred to in freight bills as 'crystals', although they were actually made of window glass. This was just a matter of habit. When value analysis was applied to determine what reductions in freight rates would be possible, the investigation showed this: a change in the nomenclature on specifications, orders and bills of lading resulted in a substantial saving in freight rates because glass travels at a much lower rate than crystal. The only function the term 'crystal' actually performed was to raise the rates.[3]

WHOSE JOB?

Value analysis is a tool that may be used on the plant management or corporate level, on the departmental level, or by individual managers. Many successful changes have been made in each way.

Some corporations have value analysis groups made up of people from different fields. One big advantage of this is that it may be possible to increase standardization. In some cases, too, once an item has been selected for challenge, special task forces are organized made up of people with the know-how needed – for example, representatives of purchasing, engineering and manufacturing.

Value analyses may also be conducted by almost any department. Many purchasing departments, for example, have either one or more value analysts, and some train all purchasing agents in the technique. Design engineers may be trained to challenge their designs by answering such questions as: Have unnecessary parts or functions been eliminated? Has the design been simplified as much as possible? Has the item been designed for lowest manu-

3. Miles, op. cit., pp. 40–41.

facturing costs? Have tolerances been relaxed as much as possible?

But many individuals have also made major contributions. In fact, no matter how the company has organized for value analysis, the more knowledge every manager and every employee has of the technique the better the chances of success. Many companies that have value analysis groups or departments make a point of encouraging everyone to submit suggestions to them.

At a value analysis seminar conducted by the U.S. Department of the Army in 1961, representatives of several companies reported on the results they had achieved. The value analysis manager of one of the suppliers to the Department reported the following important savings:

A purchasing agent worked with his company's engineers in the value analysis of an air vane casting for the Pershing missile. As a result of a change from a welded item to a casting, $182,000 was saved and it was estimated that the savings achievable on future purchases would add up to about $5 million.

The supervisor of the tool crib proved that military specifications for the maintenance of gauges could be relaxed somewhat without sacrificing quality or reliability. The saving from this one idea came to $250,000.[4]

Ordinary suggestion systems generally depend on sudden inspiration, which may or may not occur. With the value analysis technique, the search for improvement is a systematic one – and if the technique is constantly employed, some improvements are practically bound to come to mind.

AREAS OF EXAMINATION

In selecting a problem to which value analysis is to be applied, the common procedure is to consider the high-cost items first. If the item is a purchased part, it need not necessarily be one with high unit cost. For example, it would be possible to save more by shaving a few pence off the cost of a tenpenny item that is purchased

---

4. Robert L. Bidwell (Martin Orlando), in *Report on Value Analysis Seminar*, Oct. 1961, at the Pentagon, by the Department of the Army (Washington, DC, Management Analysis Division, Office of the Chief of Research and Development, Department of the Army), p. 39.

by the million every year than by cutting, say, £100 off the cost of a part costing £1,000 that's likely to be purchased only once in two years.

The technique may be applied not only to the design of tangible items, and the materials and methods used in their manufacture, but to almost anything the company does. In one company it was applied to the development of process layouts, which required a good deal of engineering and drafting time. Among other things the task force discovered a 40-page document that had been made up for the sole purpose of setting forth a process for 'assigning blame if something went wrong'. Hours of expensive time had been wasted on its development. Needless to say, it was made plain that no more time should be spent on projects of that nature.

In the same company a study was made of the transportation of people, parts, prints and paper among seven related plants scattered over an area of several square miles. The entire procedure was revised, resulting in a measurable annual saving of $25,000 plus other benefits.[5]

RELATED TECHNIQUES

Actually, value analysis is the application of known concepts plus a few new ones.

One of these is work simplification, which has been in use for a number of years, and is actually a value analysis of the steps required in performing a task. In using this technique, the manager simply watches what is done and writes down each step.

Then having ascertained what's being done, he determines whether it is necessary to do the job at all by asking such questions as: What purpose is served? Is the work duplicated elsewhere? What is the worst that can happen if the work isn't done at all?

If an entire task can be eliminated, so much the better. Sometimes the manager discovers that the cost of procedures designed to prevent certain losses is greater than any possible loss that can

5. R. L. Crouse, 'Value Engineering in Plant Engineering and Maintenance' in *Techniques of Plant Engineering and Maintenance*, Vol. XVI (New York, Clapp & Poliak, Inc., 1965), p. 91.

occur. As Peter Drucker has observed: 'One should never spend more than 99 cents to gain a dollar.'[6]

To illustrate: many maintenance departments have placed nuts and bolts and other inexpensive parts on free issue and allowed the mechanics to take what they need for their work without going to a storeroom and signing requisitions or getting their foremen to sign them. The time spent in travelling, handling the paperwork, waiting for the foreman's o.k., and so on is worth more than any loss of the inexpensive material that's likely to occur.

More commonly it will be found that while the task itself is necessary, certain parts of it are entirely dispensable.

One plant manager[7] tells of a foreman who made a written record of what one of his best diesetters did in setting up a foot press to stake the staff of a volume control. Here's what he wrote down:

SET UP FOOT PRESS TO STAKE VOLUME CONTROL STAFFS
What Was Done
Rises from chair at foot press and to Parts Storage Rack – 10′
Picks up parts in tote pan
Returns to press – 10′
Places parts on press bench
To die cabinet for staking die – 18′
Locates and picks up die
Returns to press – 18′
Places die on bench
To next production line for wrench – 60′
Secures wrench
Returns to press – 60′
Places wrench on bench
Returns to die cabinet for washers – 18′
Picks out washers from box
Returns to press – 18′
Places washers on bench, sets up die to stake staff, stakes trial staff
To blueprint file for print covering job – 36′

6. Peter Drucker, *Managing for Results* (New York, Harper & Row, Publishers, Inc. 1964), p. 85.
7. W. Clem Zinck, Arbogast & Bastian, Inc., Allentown, Pa. 'Developing Supervisors to be Improvement Minded' in *Techniques of Plant Engineering and Maintenance*, Vol. XVI (New York, Clapp & Poliak, Inc., 1965), p. 74.

Locates and picks out print
Returns to press – 36′
Places print on bench. Inspects staff against print. Tightens nuts to secure die press, and picks up die from previous job
Returns to die cabinet – 18′
Places previous die in proper location
Returns to press – 18′
Picks up wrench
To next production line to return wrench – 60′
Returns wrench
Returns to press – 60′
Picks up print
Returns to blueprint file – 36′
Locates position and places print in file.
Returns to press – 36′
Instructs operator on how to properly perform the operation.

After this the supervisor saw to it that all diesetters kept their kits of tools complete and had their trucks supplied with all sizes of nuts, bolts, clamps and so on needed to set up the machines assigned to them. He also gave each man a talk about using his head and saving his feet.

Note that this is entirely different from the type of motion study developed through the use of scientific management methods. The supervisor didn't tell the diesetters what motions to make and prescribe their every step. They still used their own judgement. In fact they were encouraged to use more judgement to make their work less taxing. But by ensuring that they had the tools and parts they needed close at hand, he made it more likely that their judgement would not lead them to do unnecessary walking.

Use of the flow chart shown in an earlier chapter is another technique closely related to value analysis. This shows up unnecessary transportation through backtracking in the flow of work – transportation that actually serves no useful function. A very large proportion of factory costs is accounted for by materials handling. Some people have even put the figure as high as 80 per cent in some instances.

Something very close to value analysis is also practised when companies make what is known as a lubrication survey. Each machine manufacturer generally supplies lubrication instructions along with each piece of equipment; and if the special oils and greases recommended for each unit are purchased, the company will find itself with an enormous and diversified inventory of lubricants, many of which must be purchased in small lots.

When a lubrication survey is made, the actual properties of each lubricant are determined – and since many different products will be essentially the same, it is possible to buy fewer lubricants and larger quantities of each, which generally means a considerable saving. The storage problem is also simplified.

Again, one company has a group whose sole purpose is to study new materials as they come on the market and experiment with their use. It is estimated that it has saved $3 for every $1 it has spent. Very often the savings are dramatic. A change in the material used in fume hoods in the laboratories reduced the cost per hood from $2,000 to $58 without any loss of function, appearance, or durability. Substitution of one type of piping for another produced a clear saving of $200,000. New and stronger adhesives developed in recent years have eliminated expensive fastening procedures.

IMPORTANCE OF VALUE ANALYSIS

The following simple formula applies to any company in any industry:

$$(P-C) \times \text{Volume} = \text{Profit}$$

In other words, the *Price* of a product minus its *Cost* multiplied by the sales volume gives us the profit on that product before taxes. And under highly competitive market conditions we find the following:

Price is determined by customers in the market place; and therefore, it is independent of the costs of production and largely beyond the control of the company. A company is, of course, generally free to change its price if it wants to, but since customers are equally free to pass up the product if they think the price is too high, a price rise may have the effect of reducing rather than raising the profit.

Volume of Sales is also affected by many factors that are not under management's immediate control: the number and aggressiveness of competitors, the company's product mix, the total size of the market, and so on. If the company does influence its volume of sales, it will most likely do so by providing 'more value' at given market prices: better quality, improved performance, or other features that make it more acceptable to potential customers.

Costs may be affected by circumstances beyond the control of management, but of all the factors in the formula they are most susceptible to management action and offer the greatest scope for managerial decision-making.

Moreover, a cost reduction may have a greater effect on profits than the same percentage rise in sales. This may be illustrated by the following elementary example.

Suppose a company makes an item at a total unit cost of £1·00 and sells 10,000 units at £1·10. Then its profit will be £1,000:

Revenue: 10,000 × £1·10	£11,000
Costs: 10,000 × 1·00	10,000
Profit before taxes	£ 1,000

The costs may be divided into two types: *fixed* costs and *variable* costs. The *total* of the fixed costs – rent, depreciation on the equipment, and so on – does not change appreciably with the number of units produced. But the *unit* fixed cost does change with the volume because the amount of the fixed cost charged against each unit is obtained by dividing the volume – in this case, 10,000 units – into the total figure for fixed costs.

Let's say the fixed costs in this case amount to £2,000. At a volume of 10,000 units, this means that £0·20 of the total unit cost, £1·00, is fixed cost and £0·80 is variable cost, chiefly labour and material. The total variable cost naturally rises with volume since each unit produced adds £0·80 to the figure. With a 10 per cent increase in sales to 11,000 units, then the total figure will be:

Fixed Cost:	£2,000
Variable Cost:	8,800
	£10,800

Thus with a 10 per cent rise in sales, the company's profits will be:

Revenue: 11,000 × £1·10	£12,100
Costs:	10,800
	£ 1,300

But suppose sales volume remains at 10,000 units, and the company succeeds in reducing its variable costs by 10 per cent. Then its costs will be:

Fixed Costs:	£2,000
Variable Costs: £72 × 10,000	7,200
	£9,200

In this case its revenue would remain at £11,000, but its profits would be increased more than by the 10 per cent increase in sales:

Revenue: 10,000 × £1·10	£11,000
Costs:	9,200
	£1,800

Of course if fixed costs were a larger proportion of the total cost, the difference might be less. But often the cost reduction is more worthwhile because every increase in sales involves an increase in variable costs, whereas a cost reduction is a net saving.

It will be noted also that the percentage increase in profits was larger than the percentage increase in sales.

Conversely, a very small percentage rise in costs or a very small percentage drop in sales has a much greater percentage effect on profits. That's why a slight recession or a slight percentage rise in costs may cause profit to disappear altogether.

The effect of changes in costs and sales on profits may be illustrated by the break-even chart, which is a device often used in management planning and control.

The break-even point is the sales volume necessary for the company to break even on its operation. If it sells any less than that volume, it loses money; but after that point, profits increase more than proportionately with the sales volume. This is because the fixed cost is spread over a greater number of units.

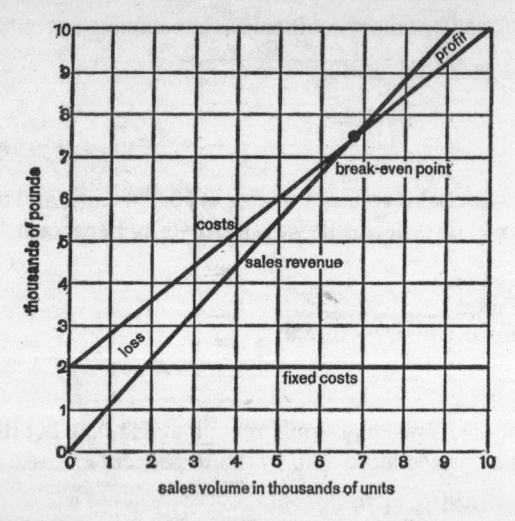

Figure 9.1 The slope of the costs line is the variable cost per unit; here it is £0·80. The break-even point is at production of 6,666 units

Before the company has sold a single unit, it has already incurred the fixed cost of £2,000; and the variable cost multiplied by the number of units must be added to that figure to determine the total cost. For this reason the cost line in the chart *starts* at the £2,000 line and rises with sales, as each unit produced adds £0·80 to the total cost of the operation. The sales revenue line starts at zero, and the total sales revenue increases by £1·10 for each unit sold. The point where the two lines cross is the break-even point at which the company neither makes any profit nor suffers any loss. After that point the profit margin on total sales widens as sales increase.

If the variable costs are £0·80 per unit, the break-even point will come when 6,666 units are sold. If the company sells less than that number, it will suffer a loss. (Refer to Figure 9.1).

But if the variable costs are reduced by 10 per cent to £0·72 a unit, the cost line will rise less steeply and the two lines will cross at a lower sales volume, when about 5,263 units are sold. And the profit margin above that point will be much greater at *any* given volume. (See Figure 9.2.)

REDUCING COSTS BY VALUE ANALYSIS

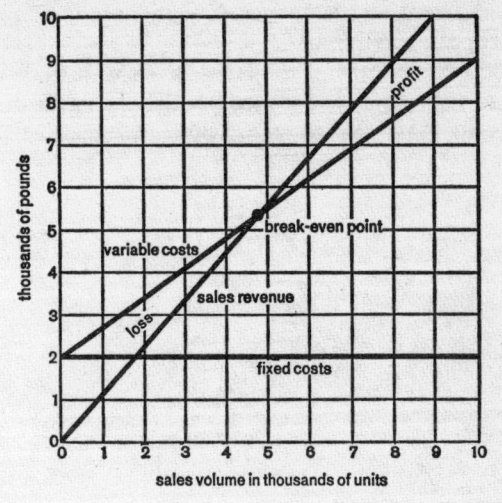

Figure 9.2 Here the variable cost per unit (the slope of the cost line) is £0·72 and the break-even point at 5,263 units

SUGGESTED QUESTIONS FOR YOUR CONSIDERATION

1. If you are in production, consider one of your company's products. What functions does it perform for the customer? What values are important to him – performance, durability, appearance, or any combination of these values?

2. What materials go into the product? What other materials might be substituted for them? What would they cost in comparison with the materials being used at present? If cheaper material could be used for any part of the product, would the values provided for the customer be lessened?

3. Could the parts be made or the product assembled in some simpler way than at present?

4. If you are not in production, consider some procedure your department or section is using. What's this procedure designed to accomplish? What does it cost? Is every step in the procedure necessary, or could one or more of the steps be eliminated and the

same result accomplished? Could the same end be accomplished by some different and simpler procedure? How many possible alternatives can you think of?

5. Read two or three of the latest issues of a trade magazine devoted to your field, and glance through the advertisements as well. Has anything new come out or been suggested that your company might well investigate?

CHAPTER 10

Introductory Statistics for Management

AT a national political convention some years back, a speaker who had been mentioned as a Presidential candidate stated that the cost of living had risen 182 per cent, basing his statement on the fact that the U.S. Department of Labor's Consumers Price Index stood at 182. Only one news commentator caught him up on this, while most of the others saw nothing wrong with his statement.

Well, what was wrong? Briefly, the speaker didn't understand the meaning of index numbers as used in government statistics. It is true that the Consumers Price Index shows the percentage rise in living costs as compared with some earlier period, but the figure for the earlier period is arbitrarily set at 100. Thus the rise was 82 per cent, bad enough certainly, but far less than 182 per cent.

The speaker who made the mistake was an educated man. He or his speech writer merely shared a prevailing ignorance of statistics that makes it possible for some people to deceive themselves or others because they don't understand the significance of statistics or the ways in which they're calculated.

If we look at the Consumers Price Index today, we would find it much lower than 182 because the figure 100 now represents the cost of living in recent years when prices were much higher. If one didn't know this, one might conclude incorrectly that the cost of living had gone down.

AVERAGES, MEDIANS AND MODES

Let's start with the word 'average' – also known as the *mean* or the *arithmetic mean*. As everyone knows, the average of several figures is obtained by adding them up and dividing their total or sum by the number of figures used. So if we want to find the average of 10, 20, 30 and 40, we simply add them up, get 100, divide by 4, and come up with the average of 25.

Everyone knows this procedure, but the word 'average' is so loosely used that we sometimes come to think of it as meaning 'typical'. The average *may* be typical, or it *may not* be typical.

Consider this situation: A salesman is selling a fairly expensive item, and his territory includes a small rural community of 100 families. Someone tells him quite truthfully that the average family income is £12,170 a year. From this he might conclude that the community was filled with good prospects.

But suppose the incomes stack up like this. One family has an income of £1 million a year; forty-nine families each have incomes of £3,000; twenty have incomes of £2,000; and thirty have only £1,000. The average income, in this case, entirely misrepresents the typical income of families in the community.

More nearly representative of the true picture would be the *median* or the *mode*. The median is the central point in a group of figures – where half the figures are smaller than the median and half are larger. The mode is the point around which the largest number of cases cluster. In the previous example the median income would be £2,500, since fifty families have more than that and fifty families have less. The mode would be £3,000 because the largest group of families has incomes of this size. Either the median or the mode would give a truer picture of the sales prospects in the community than the arithmetic average.

Then there is the *weighted average*, which is an arithmetical average in which cognizance is taken of the relative importance of various factors in the true picture. For example, if you were constructing a cost-of-living index, it would be silly to give as much weight to a rise in the cost of needles and thread as to a rise in the cost of food, because people spend a greater percentage of their incomes on food than they do on needles and thread. Therefore, you take this into account, by using a weighted average.

One way of doing this is to multiply the percentage rise in each commodity by the weight given it, and then divide by the number of weights. How the weighted average may differ from the average percentage rise is shown opposite:

If one were to average the percentage rises, the total rise in the cost of living would be 31 per cent (155 ÷ 5 items), whereas the weighted average rise is only 19·75 per cent (1975 ÷ 100). These are not actual figures, since they have been purposely chosen to illustrate how widely the two averages may differ.

Similarly a company that had raised prices of different products by varying percentages would have to weight each one according to the number sold to calculate the average percentage rise in its prices. Whenever one factor is more important than another, it is better to use the weighted average than the simple average.

	Percentage Rise in Prices	Weight	The Two Multiplied
Food	10	40	400
Shelter	15	25	375
Clothing	20	20	400
Medical Care	50	10	500
Entertainment	60	05	300
	155	100	1,975

Still another type of average is the *moving average*, which is useful for showing trends when seasonal fluctuations in sales or costs are normal. You might, for example, take a twelve-month moving average. Then the moving average at the end of January of the current year would be the average of the sales or costs in that month and in the last eleven months of the past year. At the end of February, the figure would be the average for January and February of the current year and the last ten months of the past year. The average keeps moving on, dropping one of the previous year's months as a new month of the current year is added.

If the sales last year were £120,000 – that is, at an average rate of £10,000 a month – and sales in January of this year were only £8,000, it might seem as though the total this year would be less. But if January were ordinarily a poor month, last year's January sales may have been only £6,000, and the moving monthly average would then be over £10,000.

$$120,000 - 6,000 \quad \frac{114,000}{8,000}$$

$$122,000 \div 12 = 10,166$$

Thus if the company does only as well as it did last year in the next eleven months, it will still be ahead. The moving average can be shown as a single trend line on a graph, whereas the comparison with last year would otherwise have to be made by showing two lines.

SAMPLING

One of the most important uses of statistics in industry is in sampling. Instead of questioning all customers and potential customers about the product features they want, a market researcher will endeavour to question merely a group that's representative of the whole.

Again, in statistical quality control, parts are sampled as they come off the production line, and we infer the quality level of the whole batch from that of the sample. This is the same process that political pollsters use. They question a sample of voters and infer that their opinions are representative of those of all the voters.

But the conclusions drawn on the basis of sampling will be valid only if the sample is representative of the universe the sampler is interested in. In the case of a quality-control sample, the universe is all the products in the batch; in the case of market research, all the customers and potential customers; in the case of a political poll, all the voters.

But if the sample is to be representative of the whole it must meet two tests:

First, it must be large enough. If you were to walk down the street and question the first ten voters you met, you might by chance happen to meet ten Conservatives or ten Labour supporters. If you judged election results by that small a sample, you might conclude that one party or the other would win unanimously, which actually never happens.

Second, the sample must be neither intentionally nor unintentionally biased. A political pollster could, for example, make a poll come out any way he wanted to by choosing to question only people in districts known to be heavily Democratic or heavily Republican. This would be intentional bias, and any political pollster who made a practice of intentionally biasing his samples would soon have to go out of business because he would be proved wrong so often.

Unintentional bias, however, is often very difficult to avoid unless the sample is very large. Within the major universes there may be minor universes – and by giving each its proper proportion in the sample, the researcher may get good results with much smaller samples. This is known as 'stratified sampling'. In a sample designed for a political poll, the major universe is made up of all the voters, but each income bracket constitutes a minor universe. So does each section of the country. So do farmers. And there are many other minor universes. These must be represented in the stratified sample in the same proportion as they are represented in the total universe. And it is very difficult sometimes to identify all the minor universes and to ensure that they're represented in the sample in the proper proportions.

For example, a skilled statistician noted that the political pollsters who went wrong in 1948 may have unintentionally biased their samples in favour of more conservative voters.

The people who were hired to poll the voters were permitted, at their own discretion, to question any of the families in given buildings. When they came to a walk-up apartment building, they naturally chose to poll those on the ground floor to avoid climbing stairs. But the people living on the ground floor were generally older people who had chosen to live on the ground floor for that reason. Since older voters tended to be more conservative than younger voters, the sample tended to be biased.

No matter how large a sample is, it will not produce reliable results if it is biased. But even when all the minor universes have been identified correctly and included in the proper proportion, the sampling can still give incorrect results if the sample is too small.

Suppose a market researcher were trying to determine which of two brands of laundry soap women preferred. If his sample were too small, he might happen to question women whose preferences differed from those of the majority. This could be true even though he had included women in various sections of the country, those in various income brackets, women in various age groups, and so on – all in proportion to the number in each group in the general population.

A common-sense way of determining when a sample is large enough, though more exact methods exist, is to keep adding to it until further additions don't change the results. If the results are graphed, this will be when the line straightens out, like this:

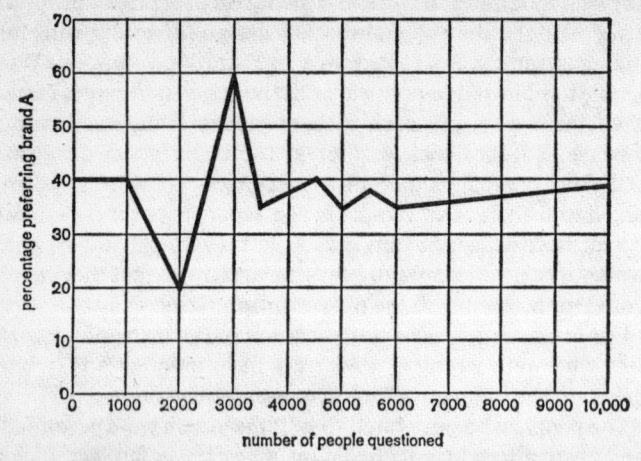

Figure 10.1 The effect of sample size on accuracy

In this case each new group of people questioned must be of the same size, and each must include all the minor universes in the proper proportions.

Finally, a sample can never be completely representative of the universe from which it is drawn, so there's always a degree of probable error. Since the statistician can never be absolutely sure, he calculates what the probable error may be and includes that in his final results. But when he does this, he automatically has a range of accuracy rather than a single accurate figure.

For this reason the statistician is constantly involved with what we call 'probability analysis'. In other words he's likely to say that it is highly probable, rather than absolutely true, that such and such is so.

THE NORMAL CURVE[1]

There are many cases, however, in which results are not a simple choice between two political parties or among two or more products.

1. For a good presentation of this material, see L. L. Thurstone: *The Fundamentals of Statistics* (New York, The Macmillan Company, 1935).

Let's say we give a problem-solving test to a large group of people. The chances are that the results would be similar to those shown in the 'frequency distribution' below, which has been tabulated according to a class interval of 10 – in this case *40–49, 50–59,* and so on. If we trace the approximate curve for these data, we have a frequency polygon or *frequency distribution curve*. And in this case its shape is what is known as a *normal curve* – that is, the typical bell-shaped curve shown in the figure.

In a normal distribution the average score of the group falls at the approximate centre of the curve, and this average or arithmetic mean also coincides with the median and the mode.

The extent to which the scores in the sample group cluster around the midpoint shows how homogeneous the group is – and we call this a *measure of central tendency*. Another fact the curve brings out is the *measure of dispersion* – that is, by studying the difference between the lowest scores and the highest scores, the statistician can determine how much the group *varies* in problem-solving ability.

There are various statistical measures for evaluating the dispersion characteristics of a group, whether it be made up of people, parts, or data relating to opinions. But perhaps the most popular ranking methods are *quartiles*, *percentiles*, and *standard deviation scores* of one kind or another.

In the case of quartiles, we divide the group into four equal parts, according to their scores. Then a person in the lowest quartile would be in the lowest 25 per cent of the group taking the test, even though his actual score might be fairly high. On the other hand those in the highest quartile would be in the highest 25 per cent.

There are times, however, when we want to know the exact relationship of a particular case to a given number of cases. In this instance we can use percentile ranking. Here we take the highest score in the group and assign it a rank of 100 per cent, and then scale down all the other scores in the group. Thus if a person occupies the 70th percentile in a group, 30 per cent of the group would have higher scores and 69 per cent would have lower scores.

To learn more about the characteristics of dispersion we use what is called the *standard deviation*, which helps us decide how the group spreads out *above* or *below* the average or mean score. The lines on the curve represent standard deviations from the mean for the particular group. And the Greek letter sigma (σ) is used to signify standard deviation.

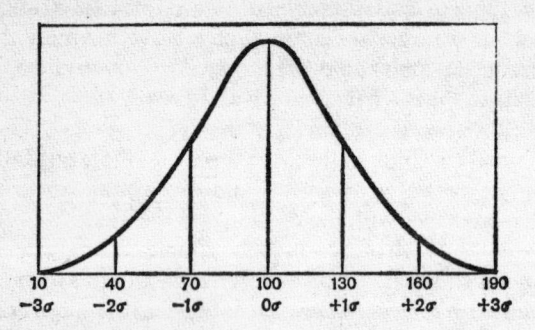

Figure 10.2 The normal distribution curve

In the illustration we can see that, in a normal curve, almost all the cases lie within a range of $\pm$ 3 sigmas. In this case each standard deviation stands for a difference of 30 points in test results, and plus and minus signs show whether the point is above or below the mean score.

STATISTICAL QUALITY CONTROL[2]

One of the important uses of statistical procedures is in quality control. Obviously, it's much easier to inspect a sample of the products in a batch than to inspect every single one of them.

Suppose a company is turning out shaft-type parts with relatively close tolerances, and 50 of these parts are taken at random from a batch of parts and their outside diameters are measured and classified according to their actual dimensions. We would probably obtain the dimensional pattern shown in the illustration – that is, a normal curve. The dimensions cluster close to the mathematical average of the group, so the sample has good 'central tendency'.

Then if we divide the frequency distribution into the six standard deviation zones, 68 per cent of the parts will be within $\pm$ 1 sigma;

2. The material in this section is adapted from L. C. Michelon: *Industrial Inspection Methods* (New York, Harper & Brothers, 1950), pp. 344–7.

INTRODUCTORY STATISTICS FOR MANAGEMENT

95·5 per cent will be within ± 2 sigmas; and 99·75 per cent will be within ± 3 sigmas.

Experience proves that it is not economical to control a process so closely that no marginal work is produced. Therefore ± 3 sigmas

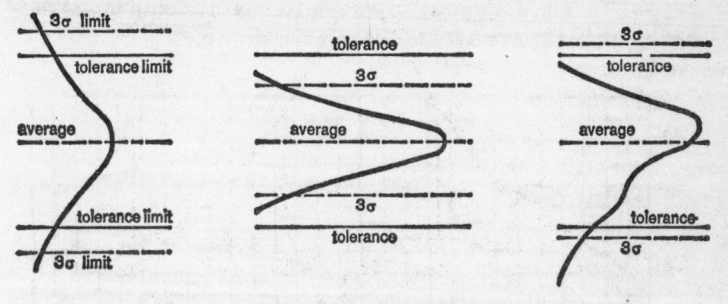

Figure 10.3 Typical distribution curves and tolerance limits

SOURCE: Courtesy of Federal Products Corporation.

can be adopted as limits for quality control. Then a control chart can be constructed, as in the illustration, and more than 99 per cent of the sample should fall within those limits if the process is in control.

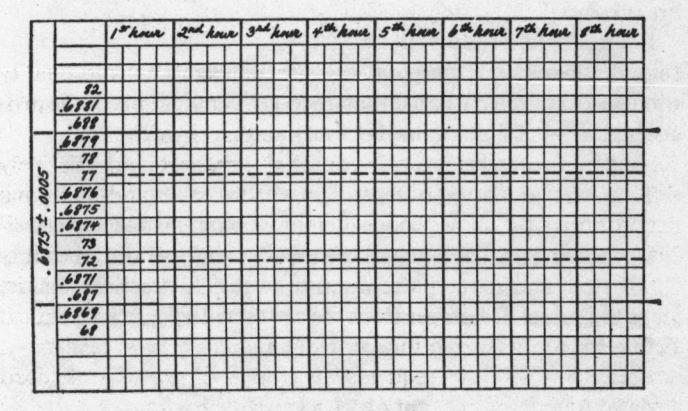

Figure 10.4 A control chart with limits set

SOURCE: Courtesy of Federal Products Corporation.

In typical shop practice, a continuous sampling process is most often used. Instead of waiting until an entire batch has been produced and taking as many as 50 samples, it is possible to take, say, 5 samples at a time as the process continues and to graph the results as you go along. Then you can plot the results in a continuous manner by using the averages of the samples drawn.

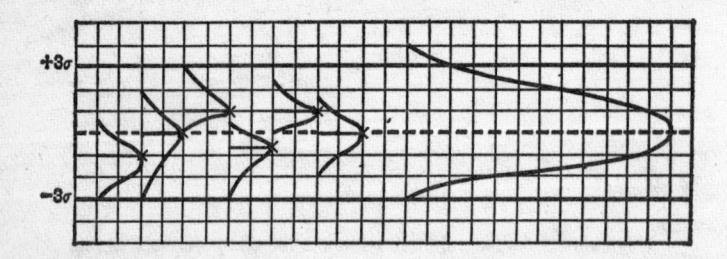

Figure 10.5 Plotting the averages of small samples

SOURCE: Courtesy of Federal Products Corporation.

When these sample averages approach the upper or lower control limits, we know what is happening and why, and can take steps to bring the process under control before too many defective parts are produced.

For example, if the part is a shaft whose outside diameter is being turned down, the cutting tool will gradually get dull and tend to produce oversized parts. Measurements will begin to creep towards the high or $+3$ sigma side of the tolerance, and we can change the tooling immediately.

Thus, statistical quality control, in which we sample only a small proportion of the items produced, is more economical than inspection of every item. It makes it unnecessary to inspect all of the items in a batch, and reduces the number of rejects drastically, since steps to correct deviations from the proper tolerance can be taken before the results exceed the control limits.

CORRELATION

Another important statistical measure of great use in business is correlation, which is simply the extent to which one factor is related to another. Managers constantly need a measure of this kind as a basis for their decisions.

Correlations may be *simple, non-linear, multiple,* or *partial.* But we will merely present a few examples of simple and non-linear correlations.

A simple correlation can be illustrated by a scattergram which tells us that the average cricket chirps more frequently when it's hot and less frequently as the temperature goes down. The chirps per

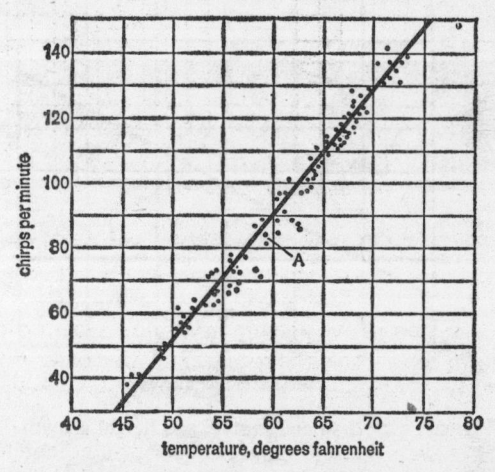

Figure 10.6 Temperature and chirps per minute of 115 crickets

SOURCE: Data furnished by Bert E. Holmes. See Bert E. Holmes: 'Vocal Thermometers', *The Scientific Monthly,* Vol. XXV, September 1927, pp. 261–4.

minute are shown by the dots, and a straight line of 'best fit' is drawn through the raw data. The slope of the line is then expressed by a mathematical equation that permits us to calculate how many chirps per minute will take place at any given temperature.

Another simple correlation is shown, which compares the heights of trees with their diameters. This has a practical application because it is fairly easy to estimate the heights of trees by checking their diameters. In this case, however, the scatter has more

MODERN MANAGEMENT METHODS

dispersion and the range up and down would give us a much greater standard deviation.

Sometimes a correlation is non-linear – that is, the line of best fit is curved rather than straight. For example, take the graph that compares man-hours per ton of corn and the yield in tons per acre. Man-hours per ton go down substantially as yield per acre goes up, which is to be expected. But they do not go down in a straight-line

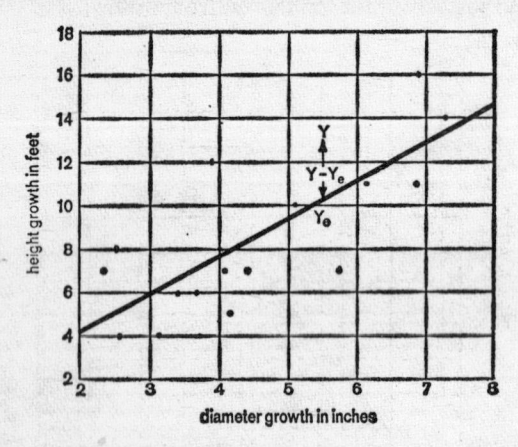

Figure 10.7 Breast-high diameter growth and height growth of 20 forest trees

SOURCE: Frederick E. Croxton and Dudley J. Cowden: *Applied General Statistics* (New York, Prentice-Hall, Inc., 1939), pp. 655–6. From: Donald Bruce and F. X. Schumacher, *Forest Mensuration* (New York, McGraw-Hill, 1935), p. 124.

relationship – in exactly the same proportion as the yield goes up. Corn is used in this example, but the same approach can be applied to steel, textiles, or other types of continuous production. In other words the volume of operation would definitely affect the man-hours per ton needed.

The correlation between two factors is shown by the coefficient of correlation, which may vary between $+1$ and -1. Thus if we were correlating the results attained on a psychological test with success on the job, there would be a correlation of $+1$ if everyone who did well on the test was a success on the job and everyone who did poorly failed to pass it. If *those who failed the test proved, without exception, to be good workers* and those who did well on it failed on the job, there would be a correlation of − 1.

For a correlation to be significant it generally must be well above ·5. Also the sample must be large enough and not biased in any way if we expect to use one factor to predict another – for example, to predict success on the job from test results.

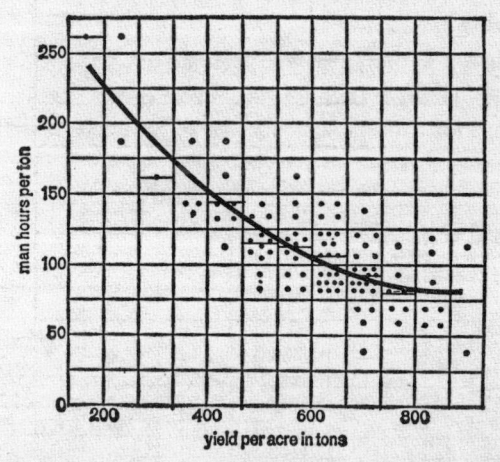

Figure 10.8 Yield per acre and man-hours per ton required to harvest broomcorn

SOURCE: 'An Economic Study of Broomcorn Production', by R. S. Washburn and J. H. Martin (Washington, D.C., U.S. Department of Agriculture, Technical Bulletin, No. 349, February 1933), p. 27.

It might also be noted that if the correlation is less than + 1 and we reject everyone who fails the test and accept all those who pass it, we will inevitably be rejecting some good candidates and accepting some poor ones. No test or group of tests yet developed shows a perfect correlation with success on any job. And that's why psychological tests can do no more than help the manager decide between candidates. They can't do his selection job for him.

PREDICTING FUTURE TRENDS

In industry, time scales are often correlated with production or market data. This is of real value to companies interested in measuring their markets or future growth potential.

As a rule an industry goes through four broad stages:[3]

1. Experimentation
2. Growth
3. Growth at a diminishing rate
4. Stability.

To show this pattern over a period of time a Gompertz plot can conveniently be used. Because such a plot shows size (here size of output) on a logarithmic scale the rise of the curve over any given

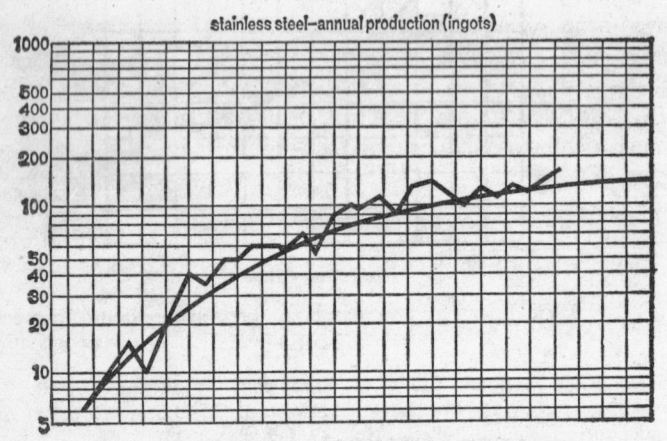

Figure 10.9 Annual production of stainless steel

period of time measures the growth over that period as a proportion of the size at the start of the period. Thus growth at a steady compound rate (e.g. 10 per cent per year) would be represented by a straight line on such a scale. The growth depicted in figure 10.9 is at a rate diminishing with time.

3. See Frederick E. Croxton and Dudley J. Cowden: *Applied General Statistics*, 2nd ed. (Englewood Cliffs, N.J., Prentice-Hall, Inc., 1955).

The curve shown is a forecast of stainless steel production, and it gives companies a pretty good idea of what their sales may be if they maintain their current share of the market. The actual figures on sales to date are shown by the jagged line. But the trend line is relatively clear despite the ups and downs due to temporary conditions, and the trend may be projected into the future.

SOURCES OF MISCONCEPTIONS

Some of the ways in which statistics can mislead have already been noted. The samples may be too small. They may be biased in some way and thus not be representative of the universe one is trying to measure. Or a person may use the term 'average' to mean typical, when the arithmetic average is very far from representative.

Other misconceptions may occur by confusing the various terms used in measuring wages. For example, take the terms *hourly wages*, *wage costs*, *employment costs*, and *labour costs*. Many people use them as though they were all the same thing, but they are not. Hourly wage generally means the basic wage rate in money, or so much an hour. And this doesn't include fringe benefits, or what we now prefer to call supplemental wage payments. When hourly wages are added to supplemental wage payments, we get wage roll employment costs in money.

The term *labour or wage cost* is generally employed to designate the percentage of total product cost that's represented by manpower cost. In some industries labour costs make up 40 per cent of every pound of total costs. In other industries labour costs may be 5 per cent or less.

Because of this difference, a wage increase of 10 per cent will have entirely different impacts on different industries. In an industry in which labour cost is only 5 per cent, it will add only $\frac{1}{2}$ of 1 per cent to total costs. But a 10 per cent increase in an industry in which labour costs are 40 per cent adds a full 4 per cent to total costs. The impact here is, therefore, eight times as great.

This would be true, also, if a 10 per cent rise in hourly rates were accompanied by as great a rise in supplemental benefits. And the rise often is as great or greater because other components of cost may be figured on a percentage basis also. Thus if the hourly wage rate were ten shillings, overtime at time and a half would be fifteen shillings an hour. If the basic hourly wage were raised by 10 per cent to eleven shillings, time and half would then be sixteen shillings and sixpence.

Let's consider profits. There are several figures that may be used to state them: profits before taxes, profits after taxes, profits as a percentage of sales, profit as a percentage of investment.

Profits before taxes don't mean much, since the money that goes for taxes is not available to the company for dividends to stockholders or for reinvestment in the company. Also, profits before or after taxes in absolute amounts may give no indication of how well the company is doing. A company may make a million pounds a year; but if it had to invest £50 million to do so, it would be earning only 2 per cent on its investment and would be better off if it put its money in the bank or into government bonds.

Profits as a percentage of sales may indicate how much leeway a company has to cut its prices, although there it would have to consider the effect of taxes at both the higher and the lower figure. But like the absolute figure, profits as a percentage of sales can be misleading.

Thus, a high profit margin on a company's total volume of sales doesn't necessarily indicate leeway in specific products. The figure is a weighted average, so for some products the margin may be small or even non-existent. To be guided by the total figure may be misleading, because it may create the impression that there are no costs problems whereas actually these may be acute in many instances.

Profits as a percentage of total investment or as a percentage of net worth is perhaps the best measure of company success because it shows how well the stockholders' assets are being utilized. Also to be considered, however, is share of the market. The absolute share of the market is immaterial; but if the company's share is shrinking, the prognosis may not be too good because it may be losing ground to competitors. Share of the market by itself, however, is not a good measure since a company may spend too much to increase or to maintain a dominant position. One also must consider whether the market itself is shrinking or growing. A larger share of a smaller market might mean a loss of both sales and profits.

From the viewpoint of a stockholder or a potential stockholder, earnings per share may be a very good measure coupled with growth in the stockholders' equity per share. A company may double the profit figure and its total assets; but if it has also doubled the number of shares, the original stockholders are no better off unless they have received more shares through a stock split or stock dividends.

Thus, it's very easy to use statistics, entirely accurate in themselves, to create almost any impression one wishes to – that wages are too high or too low, that profits are inadequate or exorbitant, and so on, merely by the choice of terms. Only if one understands the meaning of the terms is it possible to judge the accuracy of statements that cite statistics.

Even more misleading effects can be achieved by comparing incomparable things. For example, if the rise in wage rates since 1950 were compared with the rise in profits since 1934, the latter would show an enormously greater percentage rise. Or if one wanted to prove that wages had risen much faster than profits, one could take wage rates for a depression year and profits in a prosperous year as the bases of comparison.

Or the comparison may be perfectly valid but give the wrong impression to those who don't understand how the figures were arrived at. Thus one might read that life expectancy in the United States is around 70 years, whereas in some undeveloped country it is around 25. He might conclude from this that a young citizen of an undeveloped country, 21 years old, would probably not live over four years, while an American of 21 could expect to live another 50 years.

This is not true. The catch is that the figures are for life expectancy at birth – and infant mortality rates, which are likely to be extremely high in undeveloped countries, distort the picture. Actually the average person who reaches 21, either in the U.S. or in an underdeveloped country, can expect to live to an older age than he could at birth. The comparison still favours the U.S., but the difference would be much less. And if a person survives to age 70, he can expect to live to a still older age.

Perhaps nowhere is it easier to deceive people than in the use of correlations. Where a correlation between two variables exists they are generally only two of the variables in the situation and the others may be more important. For example, one statistician was able to show a negative correlation between church membership and crime – that is, an indication that church members were less likely to commit crimes than non-members, which of course sounds perfectly logical. But by excluding certain groups in turn from his sample, he found *first* a positive correlation, and *then* a negative correlation again.

'The mathematician can only help out the specialist ... not replace him,' says a mathematician. 'The best advice we can give to the man who finds a correlation and starts to say "It's obvious," is: Think again. Ten to one there's a catch in it.'[4]

'Think again and look for the catch' is good advice whenever statistics are cited to 'prove' a controversial point.

SUGGESTED QUESTIONS FOR YOUR CONSIDERATION

1. What is the difference between the *average* and the *mean*? Between the *mean* and the *median*? Between the *median* and the *mode*?

2. What do we mean by measures of central tendency? Measures of dispersion? Give specific examples and applications.

3. When is an average *typical*? *Non-typical*? How does the number of cases affect the average, all other factors being equal?

4. What is a universe? Can you give several examples?

5. What are the basic standards for a reliable sample?

6. What is meant by probable error? What has it to do with probability reporting?

7. How does a *weighted* average differ from a *regular* average? Can you give an example?

8. What's the difference between quartiles, percentiles, and standard deviation scores? Which is most likely to classify *a single case* in relation to all other cases of a given group?

9. How does a logarithmic graph differ from a standard graph? When are we apt to use a logarithmic graph?

10. Can you take a specific situation in your work, and apply the statistical procedures described in this chapter?

4. M. J. Moroney: *Facts From Figures* (Penguin Books, 1951), pp. 303–4.

CHAPTER 11

Payoff Tables and Decision Trees

THE consequences of any business decision lie in the future because nothing we do today will change the past. Therefore an essential part of any business decision is a forecast of the future results of decisions made under conditions of uncertainty.

A good way to deal with business uncertainty is to analyse our decisions on the basis of the various alternatives that might occur. For example, we can calculate how profitable a given new product will be at different sales volumes. Then we can use market research data and judgement to determine the likelihood of attaining various sales volumes.

Another practical method is to divide a complex business decision into smaller parts, decide on each part, and then come up with an overall decision through a process of reconstruction.

Two other factors enter into decision making under conditions of uncertainty:

1. We need reliable criteria to help us choose among alternatives when their consequences cannot be predicted with certainty.

2. We may at times want to buy additional information to make our decisions more reliable. In the case of a new product, for example, we can do extensive market research, but we will have to spend money for it. We must decide, therefore, how much money it is reasonable to spend.

The payoff tables and decision trees employed by Professor Paul Vatter of the Harvard Graduate School of Business may be used when considering these problems.[1] Here's how the technique works.

1. We are indebted to Professor Paul Vatter and the Harvard Graduate School of Business for permission to adapt the case examples used in this chapter. For a thorough explanation, the full case materials should be obtained from the Harvard Graduate School of Business.

A NEW PRODUCT

Let's suppose you're the head of a toy company that's considering a new toy for its product line. You talk over the idea with your production people, and they come up with the following alternatives:

1. The company can use Process A by leasing a machine for £1,000. But if it uses this process, its variable costs will be £1·00 a toy.

2. Or it can use Process B by leasing a machine for £5,000 – and in that case, its variable costs will be £0·50 a toy.

In either case the company plans to sell the toy for £1·50, which is the most it can hope to get for toys in this category.

How can the company decide whether to produce the toy – and if so, which process to use?

The amount of investment in each case is known, but the fixed cost for each unit is not known because that depends upon how many units are sold. If the company can sell 10,000 units, fixed costs will be only £0·10 a toy for the first process, and £0·50 a toy for the second. But variable costs are £1·00 per unit if Process A is chosen and only £0·50 for Process B. If you knew for certain that 10,000 units would be sold, you would choose Process B.

With Process A the profit on each toy would be £0·40 – £1·50 selling price minus £0·10 fixed costs and £1·00 variable cost. With Process B, however, it would be £0·50 – £1·50 minus £0·50 fixed costs and £0·50 variable cost.

But this is for only one possible sales volume, 10,000 units. What of other possible volumes? Further, how do you take into account the probabilities that you will sell any given number of units?

The first step is to set up what is called a payoff table that shows the possible courses of action and the possible levels of demand. In our toy example the table might look as follows:

Demand	Price	No-Go	Process A	Process B
1,000	£1·50	0		
5,000	£1·50	0		
10,000	£1·50	0		

PAYOFF TABLES AND DECISION TREES

The price has been decided, so that the figure is the same in each case.

There are, then, three possible courses of action:

1. The product may not be produced at all.
2. It may be produced by Process A.
3. It may be produced by Process B.

The No-Go column contains three zeros because there will be neither profit nor loss if the decision is not to produce the product at all.

The next step is to fill in the other two columns:

Demand	Price	No-Go	Process A	Process B
1,000	£1·50	0	− £500	− £4,000
5,000	£1·50	0	£1,500	0
10,000	£1·50	0	£4,000	£5,000

At sales of 1,000 units the result would be a loss with either process. The revenue would be £1,500 – but in the case of Process A, the company would have total costs of £2,000–£1,000 for rental of the equipment and £1,000 for variable costs. At the same volume the loss for Process B would be £4,000 since costs would be £5,000 for rental of equipment and £500 variable cost.

If sales were 5,000 units, the company would make £1,500 using Process A, and would break even using Process B.

At 10,000 units it would make more on Process B. Thus the possibility of reaching each sales level is quite pertinent to the decision.

Let's say you think the odds are 50/50 that 1,000 units will be sold, 1 chance in 3 that the volume will be 5,000 units, and 1 chance in 6 that it will be as much as 10,000 units. You can now proceed to use the *Principle of Expected Monetary Value* (EMV) to help you make your decision. And to do this you simply apply the percentage odds to each profit or loss figure:

EXPECTED MONETARY VALUE (EMV)

Odds	Process A		Odds	Process B
½ of − £ 500 =	− £250		½ of − £4,000 =	− £2,000
⅓ of £1,500 =	£500		⅓ of £ 0 =	£ 0
⅙ of £4,000 =	£667		⅙ of £5,000 =	£ 833
EMV =	£917		EMV =	− £1,167

EMV is weighted to take into account the probabilities if you follow different courses of action. In this case it is easy to see that your expected gain is greater if you choose Process A. Notice, however, that if your chances of selling 10,000 units were good, Process B might be more attractive.

By breaking down a problem into its constituent parts and assigning numerical values to qualitative factors, you can arrive at fairly logical conclusions that will help you make reasonably good management decisions to maximize returns under conditions of uncertainty.

Now let's determine what would be the value of getting additional information in this case.

Let's say the new toy could be market-tested, but that it would cost £600 to have this done. Should you go ahead and spend the £600 before you make the decision to use Process A?

To make the problem simpler, let's pretend that all you have to do to get perfect information about the market is make a telephone call. But, this telephone call would cost £600. Would it be worthwhile? Well, let's see.

If the source reports back that no more than 1,000 units can be sold, the decision will be no-go. But if the company goes ahead with Process A and sells only 1,000 units it will have lost only £500. In making the call, you would be spending £600 to save £500, which means that the company would be £100 better off if the call had not been made.

Suppose the source says that 5,000 units can be sold. Using Process A would still be the logical course, but the money spent on the call would be wasted since it didn't change the decision arrived at from the payoff table.

If the company bought perfect information for £600, that act would entail an expected loss of £183. Less accurate information would be even less desirable.

$$\frac{1}{2} \text{ of } - £100 = - £\ 50$$
$$\frac{1}{3} \text{ of } - £600 = - £200$$
$$\frac{1}{6} \text{ of } + £400 = + £\ 67$$

$$\text{EMV} = - £183$$

Of course, the less sure you are of your odds, the more alike they

PAYOFF TABLES AND DECISION TREES

will be – probably $\frac{1}{6}$, $\frac{1}{3}$, and $\frac{1}{2}$ – and the more willing you would be to pay for information to make your decisions more reliable. Also, the more difficult the problem or the more serious the effects, the more inclined you would be to gain confidence through more and better information.

DECISION TREES

A payoff table is satisfactory for a simple problem, but there's a much better way to analyse more complicated problems. This is by the use of decision trees.

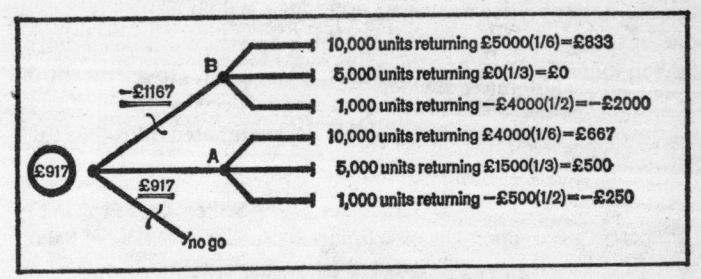

```
                              ┌─ 10,000 units returning £5000(1/6) = £833
                          B ──┼─ 5,000 units returning £0(1/3) = £0
                 -£1167 ╱     └─ 1,000 units returning -£4000(1/2) = -£2000
                       ╱      ┌─ 10,000 units returning £4000(1/6) = £667
              (£917) ──── A ──┼─ 5,000 units returning £1500(1/3) = £500
                    £917      └─ 1,000 units returning -£500(1/2) = -£250
                       ╲
                        no go
```

Figure 11.1 A typical decision tree

SOURCE: Harvard University Graduate School of Business Administration. Developed by Paul A. Vatter, Administrative Director.

Each possible act becomes a main branch of the tree, and the table of values is put in skeletal form. The illustration shows the tree that might be developed for the problem described above. This indicates very quickly that Branch A is probably the better course of action.

We always go along the branch that gives the highest value. In the example shown, the payoff table is as simple to use as the tree, but decision trees are much easier to use for more complex decisions.

For example, let's suppose that a client asks a real estate man to sell three properties – A, B, and C – and agrees to pay him a 5 per cent commission in each case. However, he specifies certain conditions:

1. The real estate man must sell *A* first. And the whole deal is off if he doesn't sell it within thirty days.

2. If *A* is sold, the real estate man will get the 5 per cent commission on that sale. Then he can stop there or try to sell either of the two remaining properties within thirty days. But if he does not sell *one* of them, he will not have the opportunity to sell the other.

3. When the first two properties are sold, he can sell the third.

There are several decisions to be made here. First, should the real estate man accept the deal at all? He will incur certain costs in each case whether or not he makes a sale. Furthermore, if he succeeds in selling *A*, he must decide whether to sell one of the two remaining properties or stop at that point. And if he decides to sell one of the remaining properties, which one should it be? Finally, having sold two properties, should he go on and try to sell the third?

The real estate man's first step in using a decision tree will be to set down the facts, together with his best estimated odds that each sale will be made.

Property	Price	Income, if Sold	Selling Costs	Probability of Sale
A	£25,000	£1,250	£800	70/30
B	50,000	2,500	450	60/40
C	100,000	5,000	900	50/50

Next he diagrams the alternatives and writes in the money results of each approach. This is done on a conditional basis to help him decide whether one course of action is better than another, bearing in mind risk and opportunity.

In other words, if he doesn't sell *A*, he's out £800. If he sells *A* – and the chances that he will be able to seem pretty good – he's made £450. Then if he tries to sell *B* next, and fails to do so, he loses what he made on *A*, but he breaks even on the whole deal. If he sells *B* and then stops, he's made £2,500. Then if he tries to sell *C* and fails, he's only £1,600 ahead, but if he succeeds in selling *C*, he will have a total gain of £6,600.

The same reasoning is then applied to the other branch of the tree, which shows what the possibilities are if the real estate man tries to sell *C* instead of *B*, after he has sold *A*. If he fails, he's out

PAYOFF TABLES AND DECISION TREES

£450 instead of breaking even. But if he succeeds, he makes more.

The next step is to apply the odds to the tree and produce the EMVs as shown in the boxes.

At this point the real estate man starts at the right-hand side of the tree, and goes back to the point where the last decision – the decision to try to sell the third property – must be made. Following the lower line, he sees that if he fails to sell *C* after selling *A* and *B*, he will wind up with £1,600. And if he succeeds in selling the property, he will have total net of £6,600.

The chances of selling *C* are 50/50. Therefore, applying these odds to the gains or losses, it becomes clear that the decision to go to *C* is worth £4,100.

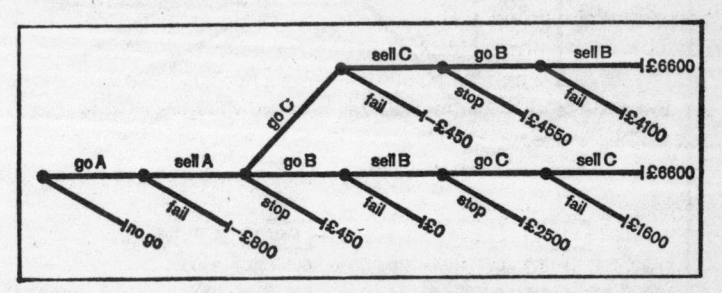

Figure 11.2 A specific decision tree

SOURCE: Harvard University Graduate School of Business Administration. Developed by Paul A. Vatter, Administrative Director.

Once the value of that decision is known, the real estate man goes back to the decision to sell *B*. There is a 40 per cent chance that he will not and will wind up with nothing. The conditional value of that decision, therefore, is £2,460.

Assuming that he decides to try to sell *A*, the value of that decision is £1,482, provided he goes on to *B*. But if he next sells *C* the value of the decision is £1,562. Thus he might do better to follow the procedure indicated by the upper main branch. He would be further ahead each step of the way.

The beauty of this method is that it's applicable to a wide variety of problems, and doesn't require the use of the computer. With a little practice, anyone can use it.

MODERN MANAGEMENT METHODS

There is another point worth noting. Those who want to be ultra-conservative can go the route A, B, then C knowing that, although they don't maximize income at every step, they do avoid loss if they cannot sell B after selling A. In a sense this might be considered 'minimax decision-making'. It is a way of trying to earn commissions without incurring the risk of loss.

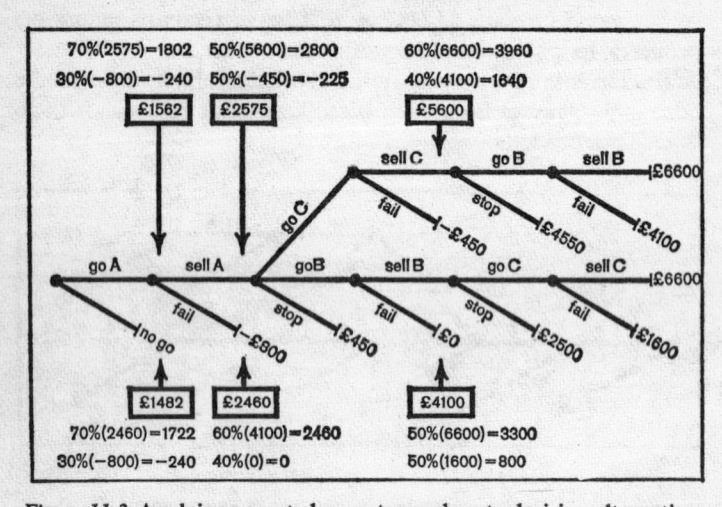

```
70%(2575)=1802   50%(5600)=2800      60%(6600)=3960
30%(-800)=-240   50%(-450)=-225      40%(4100)=1640
   £1562            £2575               £5600
```

Figure 11.3 Applying expected monetary values to decision alternatives

SOURCE: Harvard University Graduate School of Business Administration. Developed by Paul A. Vatter, Administrative Director.

AN INVENTORY PROBLEM

A problem often encountered in business involves inventory – how much inventory should be stocked when there's no certainty of selling any given amount. Too much inventory means extra expense; too little means lost sales.

Let's say a retailer has to decide how many units of a certain commodity to order. The commodity is perishable, and can't be kept in stock for more than a day. For this reason the retailer would like to order a day's supply at a time.

Suppose each unit costs the retailer £2, and he sells it for £5. Thus each demand he fails to satisfy represents a loss of £3 in income.

If the retailer knew exactly what the demand would be on a particular day, he would order exactly the units needed to meet his demand. But he never knows for sure, and yet he must decide how much to stock each day.

To simplify the arithmetic, we'll limit the retailer's shelf space to no more than 5 units. Thus his possible decisions are to stock anywhere from 0 to 5 units.

On this basis we can analyse his alternative courses of action by a payoff table based on income and cost.

Payoff Table Inventory

Demand	0	1	2	3	4	5
0	£0	−2	−4	−6	−8	−10
1	0	3	1	−1	−3	−5
2	0	3	6	4	2	0
3	0	3	6	9	7	5
4	0	3	6	9	12	10
5	0	3	6	9	12	15

A brief check will show that because the markup is high in this case, the retailer will be better off stocking up on the full side, at least at the 3 *unit* level. If he stocks four units, he may lose £8, but he has a possibility of gaining £12, and begins to make money when just 2 units are sold.

RISK AND THE MANAGER

Basically, payoff tables and decision trees improve our decision-making when we can't be sure of the outcome. We do this by quantifying in income and cost terms all possible alternatives as we see them. The purpose is to handle risk in a more certain and objective manner.

Risk is always present in today's rapidly changing world. Managers must make heavy financial commitments with no real assurance that the results they hope for will come to pass. How much risk to take and how to reduce risk in situations containing opportunity – these are vital questions that must be tackled by managers everywhere.

Finally, we must remember that many management decisions are determined by the degree of risk rather than by possible monetary value. For example, suppose you were asked to match pennies for £10,000 a throw. If they match, you would win £10,000, but if they don't you would pay your opponent £9,500. Since the chances are 50/50, the EMV would be £250:

$$\frac{1}{2} \times £10,000 \quad £5,000$$
$$\frac{1}{2} \times £\ 9,500 \quad -\ 4,750$$
$$EMV = £\ 250$$

None the less, the chances are that few of us would be willing to flip coins in this case because the risk of losing is too great, even with a sizeable EMV in our favour. The possible loss of £9,500 is more important than the statistical sureness of a gain. An economist would say that the utility of the £9,500 is far greater than the added utility of the money that might be gained by winning.

Thus decisions cannot be made simply on the basis of EMV, for the degree of risk is of the utmost importance. For that reason there should be a company policy on how much risk the organization will take in any given situation – and wherever possible, payoff tables and decision trees should be used to quantify the factors.

SUGGESTED QUESTIONS FOR YOUR CONSIDERATION

1. Can you think of situations in your own company where alternative courses of action could be analysed profitably by means of payoff tables and decision trees?

2. Take an actual situation that you're familiar with, construct a payoff table, and then diagram the decision tree.

3. Should a company decide to risk its very existence if it has a chance of making 100 times as much as it is now making and the odds are 50/50 that it will succeed in producing this result? What would you say the odds should be before it should be willing to take the risk?

PAYOFF TABLES AND DECISION TREES

4. Suppose you're the head of a small company which has no market research department and can't spare any money to pay an outside group to do research for it. How would you try to evaluate the chances of success of a proposed new product?

5. Does your company employ this general approach to decision making under conditions of risk? If not, what methods are used to minimize risk and maximize opportunity?

CHAPTER 12

Critical Path Analysis – PERT

IF you are in the composing room of a newspaper near press time, you may see the foreman take a four-page story and give one page to each of four typesetters. Thus the four pages are put into type in the same time it would take to set a single page.

In this case it is quite easy to see how different parts of the work can be done simultaneously to shorten total time. But decisions of this nature may be extremely difficult in a project that includes thousands of steps and requires many different skills.

Also, comparatively few steps are involved in getting out a newspaper, and it is clear where speeding up one part of the work will shorten the total time. But in complicated projects, it's easy to become confused because it is beyond the power of any human being to keep all the tasks and their interrelationships in mind and figure out the effect of speeding up one step on the total project time. In many cases speeding up several of the steps would merely be hurrying up to wait for something else to be done.

Critical path analysis is used to get around these difficulties and to help management determine where it is worthwhile to speed up a given activity. Almost any task can be speeded up if more people are put to work or overtime is used, but it wouldn't be smart to spend extra money to get some of the work done more quickly unless the total time required for the entire project would be shortened.

In critical path analysis the planner examines each job in the project to determine:

1. What other work must be completed before the job can be started

2. What other work can be started as soon as the job is completed

3. What other work can be going on while the job is in progress.

He produces a diagram showing the interrelationships between the jobs. With this diagram spread before him, he is in a much better position to judge where extra effort can be used to shorten total project time or to get back on schedule if there have been delays.

For example, in the production of the Polaris missile, some 3,000 contractors and agencies had to be coordinated, and the use of one form of critical path planning and control advanced the programme more than two years. The form of critical path analysis used in the Polaris programme was PERT, or *P*rogramme *E*valuation and *R*eview *T*echnique.[1]

Now when a project is very complicated and involves a large number of interrelated tasks, a computer is often necessary to make the essential computations. But on projects that are not too complicated, the same technique can be used without employing computers or higher mathematics.

THE ARROW DIAGRAM

Figure 12.1 shows a network using the PERT technique.

The arrows represent *tasks to be done*, while the circles show *what are known as* 'events'. Events, in PERT terminology, are simply stages in the progress of the project.

The tasks, or activities, require manpower, material, facilities and/or other resources, while events represent specific accomplishments that are the result of work. Therefore, an event requires no expenditure of resources and takes no time.

If you were building a house, for example, the first activity might be digging the foundation. This would be an activity or task that would require the use of resources and would be indicated on the diagram by an arrow. The completion of this task, which would mean you were ready to go on to the next step, would be an event and would be indicated by a circle.

The *critical path* is the *longest* path in terms of time through the

[1]. A substantial amount of the material in this chapter was adapted with permission from *PERT ... A Dynamic Project Planning & Control Method* (White Plains, New York, IBM, Technical Publications Department) Form E20-8067-1.

See also A. Battersby: *Network Analysis for Planning and Scheduling* (Macmillan, London, 1964).

MODERN MANAGEMENT METHODS

network. It indicates a series of jobs which must be done in sequence and which will take longer than the other sequences of jobs that can be going along simultaneously. It is critical because the time spent on the jobs that lie along the path must be shortened if the total time of the project is to be shortened. The critical path in the diagram is indicated by the heavy line.

You can see from the diagram that there are several activities that must be completed before you reach Event 43: the tasks represented by the two arrows from the starting date to Events 40 and 41; the tasks represented by the arrow between Events 40 and

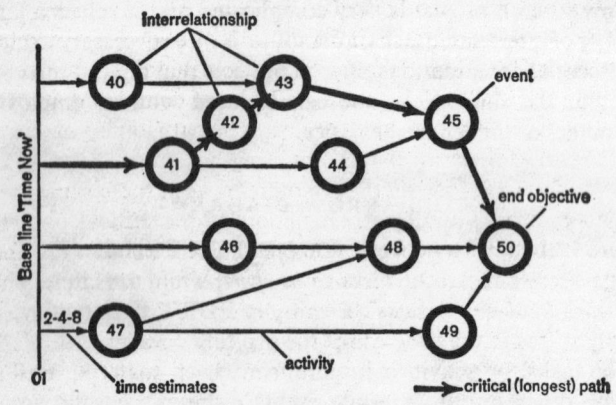

Figure 12.1 PERT network of events and activities

SOURCE: *PERT ... A Dynamic Project Planning & Control Method*, International Business Machines.

43 and by the arrow between Events 41 and 42 and the arrow between Events 42 and 43. Once having reached Event 43, you can go on to the next activity and reach Event 45, *provided* you also had people working in the meantime on the activities indicated by arrows 41–44 and 44–45. Event 50, the end objective, can be reached only when all the activities indicated by the arrows have been completed. Thus the diagram shows that:

1. You can start the four activities indicated by the four arrows at the extreme left simultaneously
2. As soon as you have reached Event 40, you can go on to Activity 40–43

CRITICAL PATH ANALYSIS – PERT

3. As soon as you have reached Event 41, you can go on to Activity 41–42 – and when that is completed, to Activity 42–43. If Activity 40–43 is also completed, you are now at Event 43 and can go on to Activity 43–45

4. When the first task in the third line is completed, you can go on to the second, 46–48

5. To arrive at Event 48 on the third line, you must have completed both Activity 46–48 and Activity 47–48

6. You can start on Activity 47–49 as soon as you have reached Event 47 – that is, completed the first task on the bottom line – regardless of progress on other parts of the job.

Now if all this were stated in words only, as above, it would be almost impossible to keep the relationships straight. But a glance at the network makes quite clear the effect of completing or not completing each task in the total project. The path joining any two events is part of the critical path if its length (in terms of time) is greater than that of any alternative path between these same two events. This means that the completion of the critical path is awaited by the workers following the alternative paths. Thus the critical path in diagram 12.1 from event 41 to event 50 is that joining 41–42–43–45–50 because the completion of each one of these steps takes longer than the completion of any parallel path there may be (e.g. 41–44–44–45 is in parallel with 41–43–43–45 but is shorter in time).

In its completed form the network would show the time needed for each task, and would indicate that there's plenty of time to complete the other activities while those lying along the critical path are in progress. This means that the total project time can be shortened only if we can speed up some or all of the jobs along the critical path. To speed up Activity 40–43, for example, would do no good because the activities that form the critical path will take longer anyway, and we cannot reach Event 43 until they are completed.

The extra time available for an activity is known as 'slack time' in the PERT network or as 'float' in other types of critical path analysis. If the tasks lying along the critical path can be speeded up sufficiently, however, the slack time along other paths may disappear, and the critical path may change. For example, suppose

MODERN MANAGEMENT METHODS

we could reach Event 41 and complete Tasks 41–42 and 42–43 *before* we could get to Event 43 on the top line. Then the critical path would lie from the starting point to Event 40 and along the arrow 40–43.

CONSTRUCTING A NETWORK

In constructing a PERT network, the first thing to do is to determine the various stages in the completion of the programme – that is, the events. At this point in the procedure the PERT chart is a

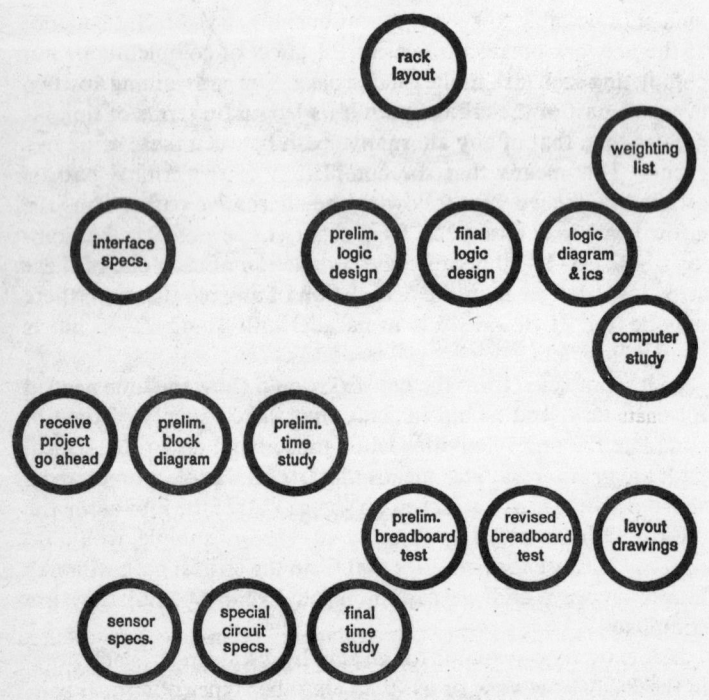

Figure 12.2 PERT event layout

SOURCE: *PERT ... A Dynamic Project Planning & Control Method*, International Business Machines.

CRITICAL PATH ANALYSIS – PERT

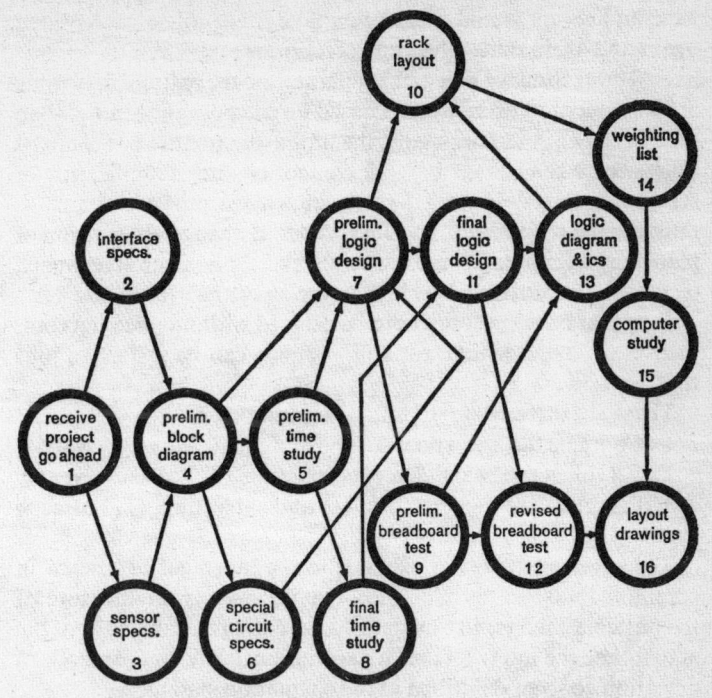

Figure 12.3 PERT activity layout (connecting events)

SOURCE: *PERT ... A Dynamic Project Planning & Control Method*, International Business Machines.

series of circles or squares containing written descriptions. And when all events have been placed on the chart, identification numbers are assigned to each.

Then the events are linked by arrows indicating the activities necessary to arrive at the various stages of completion represented by the events. At this point we examine each activity to determine:

1. The *optimistic time* – the shortest possible time in which the activity can be accomplished if there are no hitches whatsoever

2. The *most likely time*. This is the time estimate you would probably give your superior if he requested the information. It is the

time an activity would most often take if the job were repeated again and again under the same conditions

3. The *pessimistic time* – the longest time the activity may take.

The three time estimates are based on calendar time rather than on workdays. And once made, the time estimates are not changed unless there is a change in work content or rate of application of resources, or unless we get more knowledge that enables us to estimate the time better. Possible causes of change are revision of plans, application of more resources, changes in personnel, technical difficulties or breakthroughs.

Jobs that have slack time can be delayed without affecting completion dates; so manpower and/or funds can be shifted to jobs that are critical.

There are three basic steps in computing slack:

1. Compute the mean time (t_e) and variance (t_e^2) of each activity
2. Establish the calculated expected time (T_E) of each event.
3. Establish the calculated latest allowable time (T_L) of each event.

The expected value corresponds to the 'average' or 'mean' in common statistical terminology. The variance is the measure of the possible changes in this time because of uncertainty about the actual time the job will take. It depends basically on the standard deviation concept described in the chapter on statistics.

If the variance is large – that is, if the optimistic and pessimistic estimates are far apart – there is great uncertainty about the time an activity will take. If the variance is small, we can be fairly certain the job will be completed in the time allowed. Various normal-type curves are possible, according to the different degrees of variability in the duration of activities.

Now let's look at a section of a network. In Figure 12.7 the three estimates – most optimistic, most likely, and most pessimistic – are shown above the arrow.

These estimates correspond to *a*, *m* and *b* respectively in the frequency curve illustrated on page 194.

From the three elapsed time estimates, the mean time, t_e, and its associated variance, t_e^2, is computed for each activity. (See page 195.)

Next, the expected time, or T_E, is calculated for each event in the

CRITICAL PATH ANALYSIS – PERT

network. This is the time, from the start of the whole project, that it will take to reach that event, or stage, in the progress of the project. This is obtained by adding up the t_e's for the activities necessary to reach the event. Thus it will take 58 days to reach Event 44 – 56 days to reach Event 8, the stage of the project at

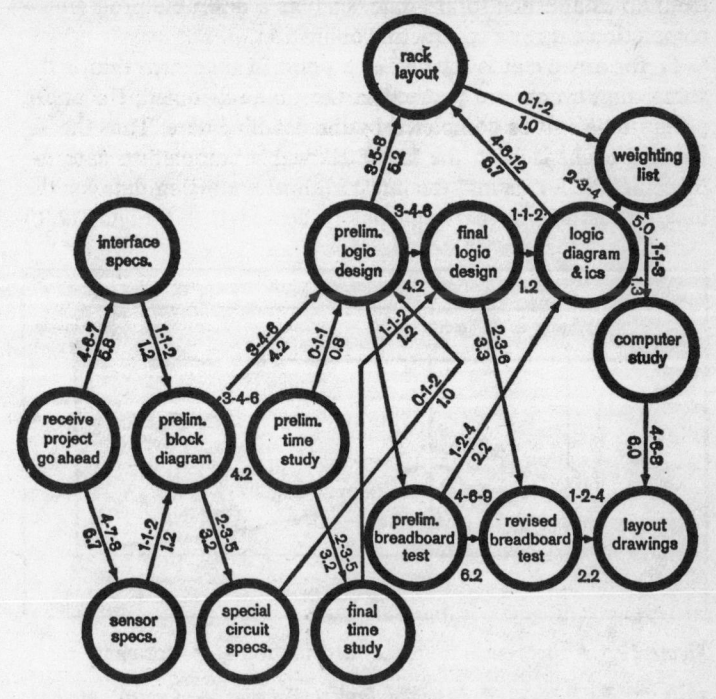

Figure 12.4 Completed PERT network

SOURCE: *PERT ... A Dynamic Project Planning & Control Method*, International Business Machines.

which work can start on Activity 8–44. And since Activity 8–44 will probably take two more days, we cannot get to Event 44 at an earlier date.

Activities 8–7 and 8–33 are independent of Activity 8–44 and can be carried on whether it is completed or not. However, the middle path to Event 6 will take a total of 65 days, and the lower path will take 61. There is, therefore, slack time for Activities 8–33, 33–6. 8–44 and 44–6. The middle path through this section of the network is critical, and the estimated time for the completion of this part of the project is 65 days.

The latest allowable time to reach each event, the T_L, is derived from an established future date, such as a desirable programme completion date or a contractual obligation.

T_L for any event is located at a point in time such that if the succeeding events are reached at the time scheduled, the entire programme will be completed by the deadline date. Thus the T_L for any event is both the latest allowable completion date for preceding activities and the latest allowable starting date for the most critical activity that immediately succeeds it. (See Figure 12.9.)

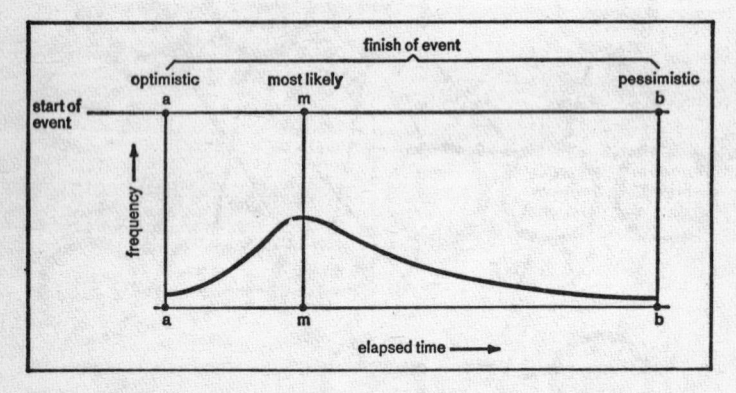

Figure 12.5 A theoretical frequency distribution of performance times

SOURCE: *PERT ... A Dynamic Project Planning & Control Method*, International Business Machines.

Now the estimated time needed to reach any event is calculated by adding all the mean times of the preceding activities. In calculating the latest allowable time we work backwards from the deadline for completion and subtract the activity mean times cumulatively.

If the deadline for reaching Event 6 in the diagram is 65 days, we subtract the t_e for activity 44–6, that is 4 days, from this figure and arrive at the conclusion that we must reach Event 44 in 61 days. But the estimated time for reaching this event is only 58 days; therefore we have three days' slack time here. But there is no slack time between Event 7 and Event 6 because we estimate we cannot get to Event 7 in less than 60 days, and the next activity on that line, which is part of the critical path, will take 5 days.

If you were a contractor who is asked to bid on a construction job that had to be completed by a definite deadline, this method would be of great help in determining how high you would have to bid to cover your costs and make an adequate profit. Naturally you would want to bid as low as possible to get the job, but there's

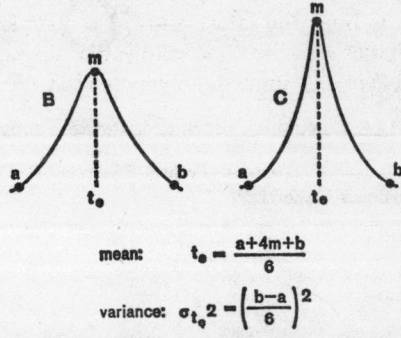

mean: $t_e = \frac{a+4m+b}{6}$

variance: $\sigma_{t_e}^2 = \left(\frac{b-a}{6}\right)^2$

Figure 12.6 Mean and variance of performance time distributions

SOURCE: *PERT ... A Dynamic Project Planning & Control Method*, International Business Machines.

no point in getting it if you have to bid so low you will lose money.

Therefore, if your network shows that you cannot meet the deadline using normal crews eight hours a day, you will have to figure out how much time you can save along the critical path by using extra men, overtime, and/or extra equipment. Then you add these costs into your bid.

Or let's say you work for an oil company and are in charge of a 'turn-around', which is a complete overhaul of a major piece of equipment. As a rule you would be told the length of time you would have to complete the entire job – let's say you're allowed three weeks. But the network diagram might show that if the job is done in the normal way it will take five weeks. Then you may examine the jobs with slack time to see whether you can use some of the

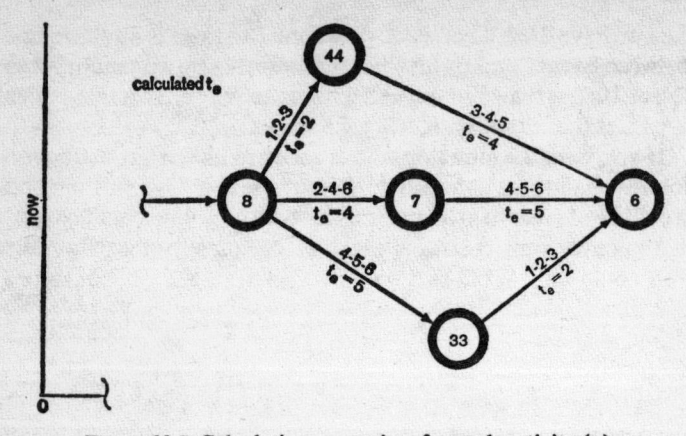

Figure 12.7 Calculating mean time for each activity (t_e)

SOURCE: *PERT ... A Dynamic Project Planning & Control Method*, International Business Machines.

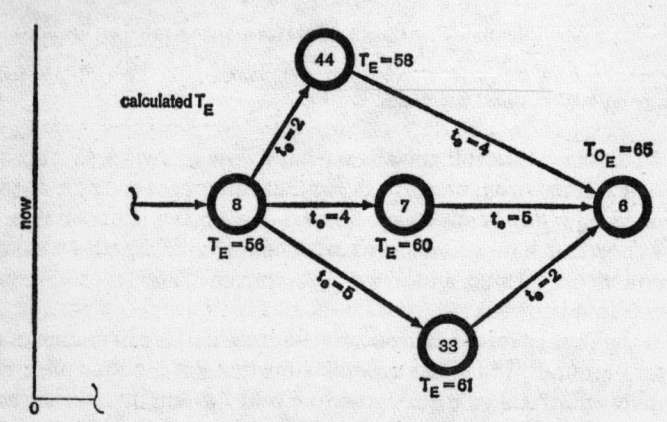

Figure 12.8 Calculating expected times of events (T_E)

SOURCE: *PERT ... A Dynamic Project Planning & Control Method*. International Business Machines.

CRITICAL PATH ANALYSIS – PERT

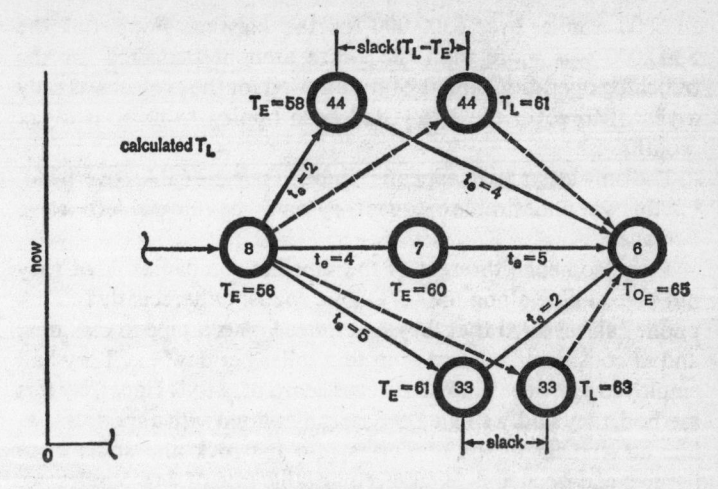

Figure 12.9 Calculating latest allowable time of an event (T_L)

men assigned to them on the more critical jobs, and in this way you may reduce the time necessary to proceed along the critical path. But if it proves impossible to get all the work done by the deadline, you can go to your superior and present clear-cut alternatives:

1. The deadline must be extended
2. More men must be hired or transferred from other work
3. Overtime must be used
4. Some of the jobs normally done on the turn-around must be postponed until the next turn-around.

Sometimes a search for better ways of doing things will produce even greater time saving. For example, the Canadian Army was constructing a large group of buildings to house communication gear, and one part of the work was to install buried cables to connect the various buildings. The blasting and digging necessary to provide trenches for the cable were given to a contractor, and the work was not given much attention in the original planning. Then critical path analysis was used, and this made it apparent that blasting was the critical job. Blasting experts predicted that the work would take more than two and a half years and would cost

$17,000 a mile, over $300,000 for the blasting alone. But the $300,000 was more than the entire amount budgeted for the trenching operation, and the time allowed for the project was only a year. Moreover the Army had been hoping to finish it in six months.

The only alternative appeared to be to put the cables overhead, but this was undesirable because they would be vulnerable to storm damage.

Then 'someone thought of the pipeline companies. Had they not placed pipe along the very same roads, only recently? ... A phone call revealed that they had indeed placed pipe in our area, and at considerable speed – up to 5 miles per day! ... They had employed a device ... we had never heard of, a rock ripper. By this method, they said, a single D9 Caterpillar fitted with a special clawlike attachment at the rear, rips into the rock and splits open fissures can-opener style, at a remarkable rate of 3 to 5 miles per day ... Even more remarkable was the cost – about $150.00 per mile.'[2]

Where a job is extremely complicated, a computer will be valuable in working out the critical path. It can print out a list of jobs showing the sequence, the number of days or weeks required to complete each one, the earliest time that each one can be completed after the start of the project, the latest time for completion if the deadline for the entire job is to be met, and the slack time. The critical path runs through the jobs with zero slack time; and it is easy to see that if each of them is not completed by the latest finish date, the time must be made up somehow or the completion of the entire project will be delayed.

Such a print-out may also include the estimated cost of each job.

In addition, computer runs may be used to determine what is possible in view of the number of people available and the skills required. The first step is to assume that enough men are available in each craft to start each activity at the earliest possible date. Then

2. Major E. S. Steben: *The Critical Path Method as Used in the Canadian Army* (Fort Washington, Pa., Mauchly Associates, Inc., 1961), p. 7. A speech presented at a critical path planning seminar in Montreal, 12 May 1961.

the computer will determine how many in each craft will be needed each day during the entire project. If this shows that manpower resources will be inadequate if every activity starts on schedule, it doesn't necessarily mean that the completion date of the project will be delayed. Many of the activities will have slack time, and the manager can schedule them to start at a later date.

CRITICAL PATH ANALYSIS WITHOUT A COMPUTER

Often a computer is not necessary, and a simple hand tabulation can be used. For example, the next illustration shows such a

Job		Dur.	Start Early	Start Late	Finish Early	Finish Late	Float Total	Float Free
0·1	Crew	1	0	0	1	1	0	*
1·2	Drawings	3	1	1	4	4	0	*
1·5	Deactivate	1	1	6	2	7	5	2
2·3	Procure pipe	3	4	4	7	7	0	*
2·6	Procure valves	4	4	5	8	9	1	1
3·6	Fabricate pipe	2	7	7	9	9	0	*
4·5	Erect scaffold	3	1	4	4	7	3	0
5·6	Remove old	2	4	7	6	9	3	3
6·7	Install new	6	9	9	15	15	0	*
6·9	Insulate	3	9	12	12	15	3	3
7·8	Pressure Test	1	15	15	16	16	0	*
8·10	Start up	1	16	16	17	17	0	*
9·10	Remove scaffold	2	15	15	17	17	0	*

* *Critical Jobs*

Figure 12.10 A list of jobs, job durations, and deadlines

SOURCE: Thomas C. Hunter, IBM.

tabulation for the installation of new piping. The critical jobs are marked with a star in the last column. They have no float or slack time.

The numbers in the first column indicate the arrows on the diagram. For example job 2–3 is the arrow that lies between Events 2 and 3. Event 2 is the stage at which the drawings are complete, and it is obvious that procurement of the pipe and valves is not possible until the drawings are ready because only then will the manager know what to order. After the pipe is purchased and delivered, the job has reached Event 3 and the fabrication can be started, but installation – Activity 6–7 – cannot be started until the fabrication is complete and the valves have been procured, Event 6.

After the listing of the job, by the arrows and by description, comes a column showing the expected duration. Then the next columns show the earliest possible starting date and the latest date on which the jobs can be started if the project is to be completed in the time allowed. The columns after that show the earliest possible completion date and the latest date by which the activity must be complete to meet the deadline. In each case the figures show the number of days as measured from the start of the project. Thus Activity 0–1 will take a day and Activity 1–2 will take three days. Therefore, Event 2 cannot be reached earlier than four days after the start of the project.

For the critical jobs, those which have no float or slack time, the earliest and latest starting dates are naturally the same and so are the earliest and latest completion dates. But there's a difference in each case when there's float. For example, deactivating the old pipe will take only a day, and it can be started as soon as the crew is assembled or one day after the beginning of the project. Therefore it could be completed two days after the start. But this is unnecessary. It could either start five days later or take five days longer to complete, or it could start two days later and take a day longer, leaving a 'free float' of two days. On the other hand, Activity 4–5 has no free float because Activity 5–6 cannot be started until it is completed – and if the float is used up in erecting the scaffold, there will be none left for Activity 5–6, removing the old pipe. The earliest date on which installation of the new pipe can start is nine days after the beginning of the project – and removing the old pipe, for which the scaffold is necessary, will take two days. Therefore if the scaffold were not erected until the seventh day, the removal of the old pipe would have to start immediately and be completed within two days. Since the removal of the old pipe is more likely to overrun the estimated time than the erection of the scaffold, the free float is assigned to the latter job.

Many companies are using some form of critical path analysis without employing a computer. For example, the maintenance department of Sandia Corporation in Albuquerque, New Mexico, has developed a form of it that it calls PPN, or Project Planning Network, and networks are distributed to all first-line foremen who will participate in a project.[3]

First of all, a planner develops a tentative diagram from work orders issued in connexion with a project and the accompanying blueprints. As each activity arrow is drawn in sequence, he places a code notation at the tail of the arrow to indicate the craft that will be needed to do the work – for example, *Pn* for painters. Then he adds the work order number and the number of the specific item on the work order that covers the activity.

When he has a rough draft network with this information completed, he visits the job site, often in company with the craft foreman who will supervise the work. This is to determine whether there are any conditions that will necessitate extra activities – such as dismantling a machine to make way for construction. The planner then revises his network accordingly.

Then he numbers the events in sequence, using even numbers only so that the odd numbers remain in case extra jobs develop. After that he estimates the man-hours required and the optimum crew size for each activity and translates these data into clock hours. For example, if the painters will spend 32 man-hours on an activity, and four painters are required, he will note the activity as requiring 8 clock hours.

At this point the planner examines the diagram to determine the critical path, and the total time needed to complete the project by adding up the clock hours and dividing the total by 8. This gives the number of days required to complete the project without using overtime.

With the network complete, the planner can then go to the scheduling board and determine where the project activities will fit in and what other jobs will have to be rescheduled to allow time for them. Calendar dates for the start of the activities are placed on the network, and since the schedule board is set up by date and by

3. 'Use of PPN at the First-Line Foreman Level', *Techniques of Plant Engineering and Maintenance*, Vol. 16 (New York, Clapp & Poliak, Inc., 1965).

craft, any excessive requirements for certain crafts become immediately apparent.

Copies of the network are distributed along with the work orders and drawings to all the foremen who will supervise the activities. In this way each supervisor knows when his part of the project will start, and which activities must be completed before his men can begin working. The network also provides a simplified language in which to discuss the progress of the work. Since all supervisors concerned have copies, each one knows what is meant if it is stated that Activity 8–10 has been delayed a day or completed a day ahead of time, and can judge how it will affect his own work.

ADVANTAGES OF CRITICAL PATH ANALYSIS

Everyone who uses the critical path method appears to agree that it makes for more careful planning of projects. Where the plan takes the form of a simple work list, it is much easier to overlook some of the necessary activities. The network also makes it easier to determine whether a project can be completed in the time allowed with the resources available – and if not, where the application of more resources will do the most good.

In addition, the technique makes it easier to determine the progress made to date at any time during the life of the project, and to report to management on what is needed. If there is slippage along the critical path, that fact is easy to see.

Perhaps the greatest saving, however, is that the critical path methods make it easy to determine what activities can proceed simultaneously and when each activity should start. This results in better utilization of both men and machines.

APPLICATIONS OF CRITICAL PATH ANALYSIS

At present the critical path method is probably used most commonly on construction projects and major maintenance projects, such as turn-arounds in oil companies. Some companies even insist that all contractors they employ use the method, both in developing their bids and in following the progress of the jobs. It is also widely used in planning computer installations.

There are many possible uses of the method; although some of them have not been widely tried as yet. For example, it is a natural for the introduction of a new product, the start-up of a new plant, or for production control systems.

It can be valuable also in long-range planning of overall company activities for five or ten years ahead. As in a construction project, it could be used to determine just what should be accomplished by given dates if the company is to reach a certain sales volume, share of the market, and profit position five, ten or twenty years from now.

The technique also could be used in many types of marketing jobs, where coordination of many different activities is necessary. For example, it has happened that products were advertised before they were available for purchase, with the result that the impact of the advertisements was lost before the customers could obtain the products. Conversely, the products may be available before the advertising is ready.

Some form of critical path analysis is likely to be useful, in fact, whenever there are a number of activities to be coordinated and it is necessary either to meet a deadline or to give a firm estimate of the time when an entire project will be completed.

An important point about the technique is that it can be used by anyone with a knowledge of arithmetic. As R. L. Martino, an authority on the subject, has observed;

Mathematics is used to develop, justify, and prove the rules, *which require only simple arithmetic to apply*, or which are programmed into a computer ...
Mathematics justifies the rules, and computers can speed the result. We don't really need to know anything further about either.[4]

SUGGESTED QUESTIONS AND PROJECTS FOR YOUR CONSIDERATION

1. Draw up a network for the pipe replacement job for which the tabulation is given in this chapter. (Note: There is no Activity 1–4. This is indicated by a dotted line between Events 1 and 4.)

4. R. L. Martino: 'Finding the Critical Path', *Project Management and Control*, Vol. I (New York, American Management Association, 1964), p. 16.

2. Make a list of the activities that would be necessary to complete some project of which you are in charge or have been in charge. What parts of this job can be done concurrently? What are the events or stages in progress towards its completion?

3. Draw a network or arrow diagram for the project.

4. Estimate the shortest possible time in which each activity can be completed, the most pessimistic time, and the mean or average. Calculate the variances.

5. Trace the critical path through the network.

6. What is the earliest possible date on which the entire project could be completed? Is there any way in which the time needed for the activities along the critical path could be shortened?

CHAPTER 13

Management and the Computer

BUSINESS and industry began using computers only about a dozen years ago, but the number of computers and the uses to which they are put have mushroomed and are still increasing. Thus it is important that managers understand how computers work and the ways in which they can be used.

Computers are of two main types – *analogue* and *digital* – although there are hybrid computers with features of both. Analogue computers are used in scientific computations and process control, while digital computers are preferred for business transactions and calculations.

An analogue computer measures physical relationships, solves equations, and presents the solutions as a continuous record. It is called 'analogue' because it presents a record that's analogous to what's happening. This can be explained by referring to an automobile speedometer for, although a speedometer is not a computer and solves no equations, it is an analogue device. It really measures the speed of a rotating shaft and not miles per hour. Then it presents the information continuously in the form of miles per hour because this is the form in which the driver can best make use of it.

William Baumol presents the following simple illustration of how a measuring device may perform calculations. *Voltage* is equal to the *amperes* of current multiplied by the *resistance*. Therefore, if a current of 36 amperes is run through a resistance of 53 ohms, one could read the product of 36 × 53 on a voltmeter.[1]

A digital computer, on the other hand, simply counts electronic impulses, and is more accurate than the analogue computer.

Essentially a digital computer is a high-speed adding machine whose output depends on what has been stored or put into it. Computer experts have a saying, 'Garbage in, garbage out', or

1. William Baumol: *Economic Theory and Operations Analysis* (New York, Prentice-Hall, Inc., 1961), p. 415.

GIGO for short, meaning that if a computer is fed incorrect or incomplete information, it will not produce the right answers.

For this reason computers must be properly programmed – that is, they must be told what to do at each step if correct answers are to be obtained. And that's why the programme – or 'software' as it is called – is as important as the 'hardware' (the machine and its accessories).

More elaborate computers and more sophisticated programmes are being developed to simulate the thinking or logical processes carried on by the central nervous systems and brains of human beings. But, as yet, the typical computer still finds its most practical applications in situations calling for massive memory, repetitive calculations, and quick feedback of information.

For example, a common application is the calculation of payrolls. Once a computer has the necessary information fed into its memory, it can calculate an individual's pay from time cards, taking overtime rates and all the different deductions into account.

Or consider this example. An airline has more than 1,100 ticket offices in the United States tied into one large computer. The ticket agent puts information about where the prospective passenger wants to go into a console at his desk, and transmits it directly to the central computer. The computer scans its memory unit to find available space on the flight requested; and if space is available, it schedules the passenger on the flight and sends back a confirming notice. It also records in its memory that one more seat has been sold and is no longer available.

Even if all 1,100 agents were to transmit information to the central computer at approximately the same time, the longest delay, that in answering the agent whose request is received last, would be just two and a half seconds.

HOW A COMPUTER WORKS

The central processing unit of a digital computer is most commonly referred to as the computer itself, and it contains three sections:

1. Storage
2. Arithmetic unit

3. Control unit.[2]

The storage system in a digital computer generally consists of a magnetic tape, drum, or core on which impulses are stored in a series of what might be called 'electronic mailboxes', although they are not in any sense boxes but merely sections of the memory unit. Each box has an identifying number so that the stored information may be used at will – that is, there's what's called 'random access' to the memory.

That's why Internal Revenue is now using computers. It will not be easy for a taxpayer to 'forget' about bank interest or stock dividends and not be called to account. The taxpayer gives his Social Security number or some other identifying number to the bank or the company in which he holds stock, and the amounts of interest, dividends, and salary paid him – as reported – can be stored under that number. Then the total can be compared with the total income he reports for the year.

Similarly the New York Police Department is now storing the licence numbers of stolen cars in the memory unit of a computer. In a demonstration the number of a car entering a bridge was radioed by a policeman in a car parked there to a teletype operator whose machine was connected to the computer. In millionths of a second, the computer searched in memory for the number, and the answer was radioed back in time for a police car at the other end of the bridge to stop the car.

The capacity of the storage unit determines the total amount of information that can be held within the system. Storage capacities may range from 1,400 characters on small machines to millions of digits or characters on the larger ones.

The arithmetic section of the processing unit performs such applications as addition, subtraction, multiplication, division, shifting, transferring, comparing, and storing.[3]

The control unit directs the steps to be performed when a series of instructions, or programmes, has been fed into the computer.

2. Much of the material in this section was adapted from material supplied by IBM, White Plains, New York, and from special training material which was furnished by The Goodyear Tire & Rubber Company, Akron, Ohio.

3. For a good description of the way arithmetic operations can be performed through the opening and closing of circuits, see Baumol, op. cit., pp. 424–5.

Once a programme has been developed, it can be used again and again.

The key point about a digital computer is that it has a multiplicity of circuits which may be opened or closed in any combination to create a large number of different channels. But each single circuit has only two possible states: *It may be open*, or *it may be closed*. It is for this reason that 'binary arithmetic' is used in programming.

Ordinary arithmetic uses ten different digits from 0 to 9, and multiples of 10 are written by shifting the figure further to the left of the decimal point. Thus if we want to indicate 10 × 10 we write 100; for 10 × 10 × 10, we shift the 1 one place further and write 1,000.

In binary arithmetic there are only two digits, to represent the two possible states of a circuit, and these digits may be 0 and 1. Yet it is still possible to write a number of any size simply by shifting a figure further to the left of the decimal point. Thus

Decimal Numbers	Binary Numbers
0	0
1	1
2	10
3	11
4	100
5	101
6	110
7	111
8	1000
9	1001
10	1010

In decimal arithmetic, shifting a figure one place to the left of the decimal point means that the figure is multiplied by 10. In binary arithmetic, the shift means that the figure is multiplied by two. Thus in binary arithmetic the number 2 is written 10, and 4 as 100; 8 which is 2 × 2 × 2 is written as 1,000. The symbol 11 in decimal arithmetic means 10 + 1, in binary arithmetic, it means 2 + 1.

There's no real reason why 10 has to be the point at which the shift occurs. Our system was probably adopted originally because fingers and thumbs were used for counting. In the past some peoples have used 12, and it has even been suggested that this would be a better system for ordinary arithmetic because 12 is divisible by more numbers than 10 is.

Many computers can translate decimal numbers into binary numbers, perform the calculations in binary arithmetic, then translate the answers back into decimal numbers. In addition some computer languages that look more like English have been developed. The best-known of these are FORTRAN (formula translation), which is used for scientific work, and COBOL (Common Business Oriented Language).

Computer manufacturers have also developed libraries of programmes suitable for use in common computer applications, such as the calculation of payrolls or the comparison of alternate capital investments.

Information given to a computer may be presented in the form of punched cards, cards marked with a magnetic pencil, or magnetic tape. More recently, computers that can read printed or typed material have come into use.

The output may be a set of cards, a tape, or typewritten material, depending on the use to which the output is to be put. Where the output is used to control a machine, for example, it will take the form of cards or tape. If it is a report to be read by a human being, a type-written document is necessary.

PROGRAMME

In programming, a human being works out the steps a computer must perform to produce the results needed from a particular application – and if any step is omitted from the programme the results will not be correct. When a computer has been programmed to produce a payroll, its instructions might include something like the following:

1. Compare the number of hours for each employee with 40
2. If the number is less than 40, find the individual's hourly rate, which is already stored in the memory unit under his clock number
3. Multiply the hours by the rate

4. Find in memory the applicable income tax deduction, and subtract it from the total.

Another set of instructions would be needed to tell the computer what to do if the number were more than 40. If the man had worked more than 40 hours during the week, the computer would multiply the hourly rate by 40, and then multiply the number of hours over 40 by the appropriate premium rate, and then add the two figures.

These instructions would be translated into computer language, and the entire programme stored to be used when a human being directed the computer to use it. If the input were a set of punched cards, they would be fed into the machine automatically, and the cheques would come out automatically at the other end, produced by a printer, which would be 'peripheral equipment' rather than part of the computer. Each card, in this case, would be punched to indicate the man's clock number and the time he had worked.

Changes would be made in the programme only when the system of payment was changed – for example, by the introduction of incentive payments for higher production. However, all input data would be constantly updated as people were added or dropped from the payroll or as wage increases were given or changes made in tax rates or other deductions.

A programme is similar to a flow chart, except that it is translated into computer language – that is, it details the steps necessary to complete the operation. In developing a programme or checking one, the programmer may draw up a chart somewhat similar to a flow chart. This is called a block diagram.

ROUTINE JOBS FOR COMPUTERS

One big advantage of computers is that they can perform mathematical operations much more quickly than human beings can. Another is that they don't make mistakes as long as they are operating properly and the programme has been planned correctly.

This makes computers a natural for jobs that require many routine calculations, like making up a payroll or calculating insurance premiums. Often they can do in minutes what would take a large number of clerks several days to perform.

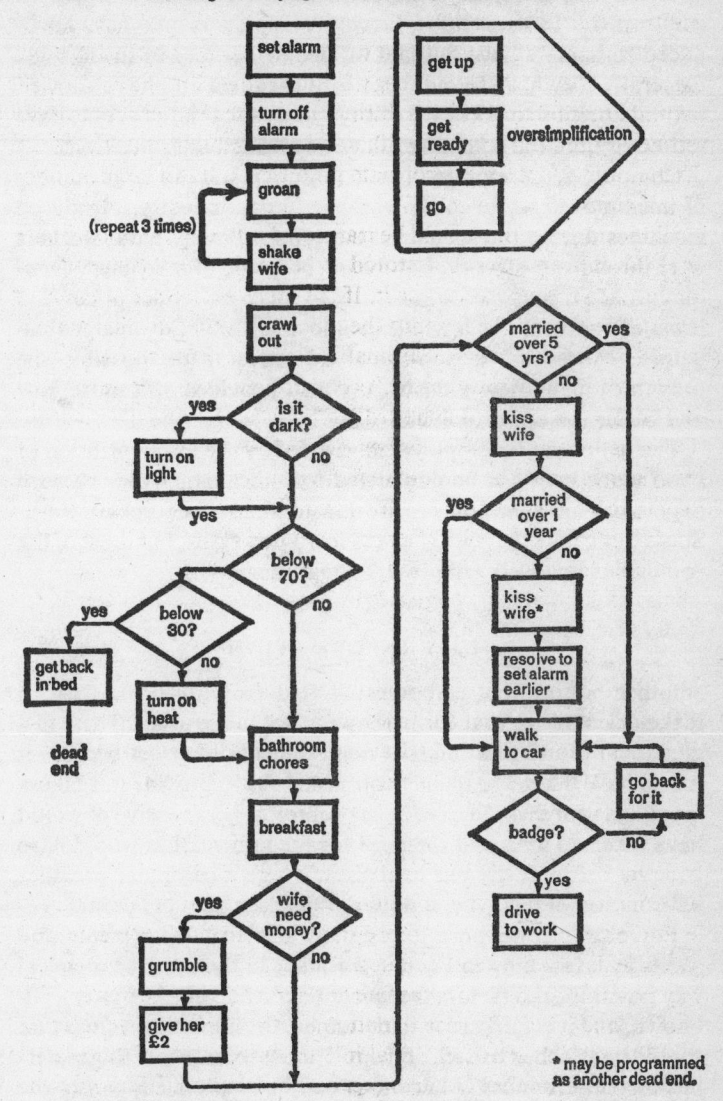

Figure 13.1 Block diagram for getting to work in the morning

That's why computers are sometimes viewed as a threat to employment. In most cases, however, employers who have introduced computers have not laid off people because of the change. Generally they have found other jobs for them and have allowed natural attrition to take care of any excess – that is, as people have retired or quit, the companies have not refilled their positions.

Computers, therefore, will probably not result in a large number of unemployed white-collar workers. When industry introduced machines during the Industrial Revolution, many hand workers were thrown out of work. But the introduction of machinery eventually made it possible for industries to cut costs, reduce prices, and broaden markets. As a result, employment was far greater than before. Moreover, technological advances made possible the growth of many new industries, which provided still more jobs and better job opportunities.

The temporary unemployment created by the mechanization of hand work may not be duplicated for office employees because paperwork has a tendency to grow faster than other types of work. Some clerical workers will have to learn new skills, but most of the companies involved will provide the training.

MORE INFORMATION

Another point about computers is that they are being used to make calculations that formerly were not made at all. There is a great deal of information that management didn't get because it would have taken too many people too long to provide it. Making the calculations would have been prohibitively expensive or would have taken so long that the need for the information would have gone by before it became available. Where a computer provides information of this type, it does not displace human labour.

For example, suppose a company has ten departments and wants to know how to lay out the plant in the most economical way possible. The factors that must be considered are pretty well-known, and it is fairly easy to determine the numerical values that should be attached to each of them. The cost of transporting materials certain distances is known or can be determined, as can the cost of a trip from one department to another and the average number of trips from Department A to Department B, and so on, each day. To determine the cost of a technician's trip from his department to another department, it is simply necessary to know the location of the departments, the distance between them, and the man's hourly rate.

But with ten departments, there are 3·5 million possible ways in which they might be arranged – and to figure out the cost of each arrangement would take so many man-hours or man-years that it would be impractical to make the calculations. But a computer can make the calculations very quickly and print out ten or more of the most economical layouts, thus narrowing down the choice to a manageable number. In so doing it will automatically discard layouts that transgress certain necessary restrictions if these have been provided in the programme, such as:

Department A and Department E cannot be placed together.
Department B must be next to an outside wall.
Department G must remain where it is.[4]

Again, most maintenance departments try to maintain a record of how much money is spent on repair and adjustment of each machine, and this can be done by keeping a card for each machine and adding the costs shown on the work orders as the jobs are completed. By looking over the record, it is possible to determine whether it is a single part that's at fault – in which case it should probably be redesigned – or whether the entire machine is simply getting to the end of its useful life.

The computer can easily provide the same information by machine and by parts. It can break down the information in several other ways: by department, by cost centre, by the length of time the machine has run, by equipment manufacturer, and so on. All this information could be collected by clerks if there were enough of them, but generally, there are not. As a result, only the data considered essential will appear in the reports based on manual record-keeping. With a computer the manager can get almost any type of breakdown he wants, and get it very quickly.

4. Drawn from William J. Smith (Computer Equipment Dept., General Electric Co.): 'Use of a Computer in Determining Optimum Plant Layout', *Techniques of Plant Engineering and Maintenance*, Vol. XVI (New York, Clapp & Poliak, Inc., 1965), pp. 17–20.

Or take a chain-store operation in which a central buying office purchases the staple merchandise for all outlets. The clerical workers in the individual store offices may not be numerous enough to provide reports on sales often enough to ensure that some stores don't run out of some items or sizes.

A computer system introduced by one chain-store company works as follows. As merchandise is sold, small punched tickets coded to describe the merchandise are detached and sent each day to a central location where they are converted into punched cards to be fed into a central computer. The computer adds up the sales of each item and subtracts the sales of each one from the inventory of the previous day to determine what's left. Then every two weeks it compares the inventory with the planned level for each item and sends out an order to buy and the shipping instructions. Some chains have even worked out systems that provide daily reports on stock.

'In theory,' says *Business Week*, 'it has always been true that a store's buyers could give management a daily report on stock conditions and what was sold the preceding day . . . But as a matter of hard, cruel fact – as opposed to theory – this just hasn't been so.'[5]

Also pertinent to the inventory problem is a programme recently developed by IBM–IMPACT. For a long time there has been a formula to determine the most economic order quantities, taking into account the fact that as the cost of placing orders falls, the cost of carrying inventory rises, and vice versa. If large orders are placed, there can be fewer of them, but the inventory will be larger, while smaller orders mean less inventory, but more orders. There are also rules by which one can determine the optimum inventory *levels* and rules to minimize the cost of shipments between stores and warehouses.

But in each case, the result is only a suboptimum, because all these factors interact. The advantage of the IMPACT programme is that it enables the user to take account of all the variables and their interaction with each other. This would be very difficult to do without a computer to make the calculations.

5. 'Computers Begin to Solve the Marketing Problem', *Business Week* (17 April 1965), p. 115.

A computer also makes possible much more refinement of marketing research and predictions of future markets. For example, cosmetics manufacturers once used only two variables in gauging future markets: the number of females over fourteen years of age, and disposable income. With a computer it is possible to consider more variables and make forecasts of possible sales more accurate. Instead of taking merely 'females over fourteen' as one of the variables, the researchers are able to take account of different age groups within the over-fourteen category, and of the change in disposable income from the previous year as well as of the absolute amount of disposable income. When the calculations had to be performed with paper and pencil and an ordinary desk calculator, the mathematical models employed had to be kept fairly simple. With a computer it became fairly easy to solve much more complicated equations.

The advantages of using more variables in forecasting are obvious. For example, it is valuable for automobile companies to know what the total demand for automobiles is likely to be, but it is more valuable for them to know what the demand will be for various types of cars and in various sections of the country.

Another very useful technique possible with computers is simulation. In the payoff-table technique described in the last chapter, the manager first works out what would happen if various volumes of sales materialized, then takes account of the probability of each sales volume. In this case only three possible sales volumes were considered, and the arithmetic was easy to do. But there might be many more possible sales volumes to consider, to say nothing of the probable effects of price changes on both sales volume and profits. To simulate all the possibilities with paper and pencil, even with the help of an automatic desk calculator, would take an immense amount of time.

Engineers can use computers to simulate the effect of various combinations of design changes on the total performance of a piece of equipment or of various types of operation on output and equipment.

The value of the simulation process is that it makes possible penalty-free trial and error. One can simulate various possible courses of action, and see what the results will be merely by changing the terms in a mathematical model. As a Du Pont executive once explained:

> If the output of your simulator indicates the pressure vs. time curve going off the top of the chart, you have not broken up any equipment. If you wish to determine the effect of doubling the size of a piece of equipment, you do not have to spend £100,000 to build it, you merely change the term in an equation or change the setting on an analogue.[6]

REAL TIME

True management control of operations is possible only if managers get information on how their plans are working out soon enough to make corrections before any great harm has been done. In many applications it is not necessary that the manager get the information the minute the events occur, but in others, the smaller the time lag between occurrences and presentation of pertinent information, the better the control. That's why computer manufacturers and users are interested in what are called 'real time' systems – that is, systems in which the report of an event is practically simultaneous with the event itself.

There are many instances of real time information systems that don't involve computers. For all practical purposes, a speedometer is a real time system in that changes in the speed of the car are shown almost at the instant they occur. Similarly a live television broadcast of a news event might be said to be presented in real time, whereas a film of the event is not.

One of the important applications of real-time computer systems is to production control. At one aircraft company, for example, a continuous stream of information is fed into the central computer through typewriter-like devices on the production floor at every stage in the production cycle. Then practically up-to-the-minute information on any job order, the location of materials, or other factors pertinent to the production cycle can be obtained at any time.[7]

6. R. C. Ficke: 'Simulation as a Systems Performance Prediction Tool', *Proceedings of the 1964 Systems Engineering Conference* (New York, Clapp & Poliak, Inc., 1964), p. 444.

7. 'Keeping Ahead on Real Time', *Business Week* (27 March 1965), p. 167.

Even closer approximations to making the information simultaneous with the event may be valuable in cases where computers control and adjust machines.

TOTAL SYSTEMS

There has been a great deal of talk about 'total systems' of computerization, but so far no real total systems seem to have materialized in larger businesses. In a total system, all the pertinent data would be caught up at its source, screened, classified and stored, and forwarded to those who can use it. Any manager in any department could obtain any information he needed at any time.

Parts of total systems do exist. For example, when a customer's order is translated into machine language and fed into a computer, it may be merged in the master production schedule, the parts and sub-assemblies determined and compared with an inventory, and shop schedules created. There may also be feedback in the form of information from the production floor on the status of the orders, and so on, as in the aircraft company described above. But this is really a 'sub-total' system covering one part of the total company operation – the filling of orders.

COMPUTERS AND DECISION-MAKING

Some more pessimistic observers have predicted that computers will make some middle management skills, as well as many types of clerical skills, obsolete. They visualize real-time systems so total that all the information needed to run the business can be transmitted to and examined at the top, and all the decisions made there. Some have even predicted that top management decisions themselves will be made by computers.

Both possibilities seem unlikely for a long time to come. In 1964 one of the authors conducted a survey[8] of thirty-two representative companies that had been using computers for some time, including companies from many different fields ranging from aerospace to

8. Ernest Dale: *The Decision-Making Process in the Commercial Use of High-Speed Computers* (Ithaca, New York, Graduate School of Business and Public Administration, Cornell University, 1964).

banking and retailing. In no case had the computers taken over top-management decision-making, and the middle management decisions that they were handling were mainly of a routine nature.

There are other good reasons why 'all' decisions can't be made at the top. If one or a very few people are to make decisions on the data provided, data must of necessity be put in very succinct form because there's a limit to the amount of material a few people can read and consider. So there's a question whether a wise decision can be made on the basis of figures when many of them must necessarily be estimates, for there are always factors that cannot be quantified exactly.

Moreover, at each point where data are fed into the system, someone must decide which data to use and how to evaluate the intangibles quantitatively, and no one can do this unless he has a knowledge of the business itself. Many companies, in fact, prefer training their operating people in computerization to training computer experts in the fine points of the business. It's easier, they say, for the man who knows the business to learn about computers than for the man who knows all about computers to learn about the business.

Finally, since computers increase the number of alternatives that can be considered, they may increase the need for human decision-making. For example, an engineer may investigate 100 different designs for 1 per cent of the cost of calculating a single one by hand. Since he's relieved of the routine calculations, he will be able to weigh many more alternatives than he could otherwise possibly consider.

DO COMPUTERS THINK?

Are computers brains? Do they really think? The answer is a flat no! And this answer is true quite aside from the fact that no computer so far built is anywhere near as complex as the physical human brain.

A desk calculator also performs addition, subtraction, multiplication, and division but no one contends that it thinks. A thermostat 'feels' that the house is too warm and turns down the heat, but it doesn't feel it in the same way that a human being does.

Nor can it decide that the person who set it considered only his own comfort, then adjust itself to take account of the feelings of the rest of the family.

Many of the more exotic reports of what machines can do are based on pure speculation. As one expert has written: '... the statement that a flow chart could be written for a non-existent programme for a non-existent machine establishes the existence of the machine... many non-existent devices have been named in the literature and are referred to as though they existed.'[9]

The fact that a computer has been programmed to play checkers and has even beaten the man who programmed it at the game does not eliminate the inexorable truth of GIGO. And this is even true of the so-called 'learning machines' that learn from their own mistakes and do better in the future.

Norbert Wiener was a mathematician who pioneered in developing many of the concepts of cybernetics – which is the science of communication and control of which many of the proposed machines are practical applications – yet he once likened what could happen with so-called 'thinking machines' to what happened in the story by W. W. Jacobs, *The Monkey's Paw*. The monkey's paw enabled its possessor to wish for something and get it. When the man in the story wished for a sum of money, he got it – but only because his son had been killed on the job and the company offered the money as compensation.

'The point is,' said Wiener, 'that magic is terribly literal-minded. It will give you what you ask for, not what you should have asked for, nor necessarily what you want.... If you do not put into the programming the important restriction that you do not want £200 at the cost of having your son ground up in the machinery, you cannot expect the machine itself to think of this restriction.'[10]

9. Mortimer Taube: *Computers and Common Sense* (New York, Columbia University Press, 1961) quoted in Robert A. Solo, 'Automation: Technique, Mystique, Critique', *The Journal of Business*, Graduate School of Business, University of Chicago (April 1963), p. 172.

10. *Management and the Computer of the Future*, Martin Greenberger, ed. (Cambridge, Mass., The M.I.T. Press, 1962), reprinted in Ernest Dale: *Readings in Management: Landmarks and New Frontiers* (New York, McGraw-Hill, Inc., 1965), pp. 465–6.

SUGGESTED QUESTIONS FOR YOUR CONSIDERATION

1. 'The computer will revolutionize the practice of management by taking over the key decision-making functions.' Comment on this statement.

2. Do you believe the computer will reduce the present number of white collar jobs? Why or why not?

3. Why are binary numbers used in computer work?

4. Why is the programme, or 'software', so important in computer applications?

5. What, fundamentally, is the difference between an analogue and a digital computer? Why are digital computers preferred for precise mathematical computations?

6. What do we mean by a total information system? A real time system?

7. Can you list five impending, practical uses for the computer? Why do you think they will be important in the years ahead?

8. What is a flow chart? A block diagram?

9. Can you make a suggested block diagram for getting a cup of coffee, with cream and sugar, from a dispensing machine?

10. What is meant by input and output devices? By the central processing unit?

CHAPTER 14

Management and the Future

Any forecast of the future must rest on certain assumptions because there are always many developments that could completely reverse present trends.

In this forecast we're assuming:

1. There will be no conflict between major powers involving widespread nuclear destruction.
2. There will be no major depression on the scale of the 1930s.

The consequences of either of these developments are incalculable. A nuclear war could mean the practical annihilation of the human race or its reduction to a few colonies living by primitive means.

A major depression could produce revolution, or it could bring about a series of palliative measures and a lower standard of living for most people for a period of several years.

But assuming no nuclear war or major depression, what qualities should the potential or rising manager acquire to meet the demands of the years ahead?

THE NEED FOR EDUCATION

First, future managers will need more education than those of the past. An academic degree will be distinctly advantageous. But in the future, the manager may have to supplement this with knowledge of what the novelist C. P. Snow has called 'the two cultures' – the humanities (literature, history, and so on) and the sciences. A knowledge of the humanities will be needed for a balanced viewpoint and for the sensitivity necessary to estimate the social and human consequences of business decisions. Scientific knowledge will be required to distinguish between good and bad expert advice, for the area of management is replete with disagreements between experts.

Of course the easiest way to get on the management ladder is to acquire a knowledge of the sciences and humanities through college and graduate courses. But a manager who doesn't have a degree is not necessarily barred from acquiring it. More company-sponsored courses are likely to be offered, and there is 'programmed learning' which enables people to learn new skills on their own.

The person who's already a manager has a big advantage over the recent college graduate because he knows more about what's to be managed. Probably none of the techniques of management described in this book can be applied successfully without some knowledge of the business itself.

In a recent magazine article,[1] a manager described his own frustration when he tried to apply techniques learned in business school to the construction industry. He was anxious to reduce costs by the introduction of such things as accurate costing, methods study, and the rest – all of which did help, of course. But he missed a key point about the industry of which the older managers were conscious – *the need for close relations with the clients*. 'The costs to be saved in economic design by using the contractor's experience at the design stage far exceeded the costs to be saved by trying to build efficiently something which should never have been built at all.' The older hands did not know *why* the close relationship paid off. They only knew from experience that it did.

The eventual answer to the company's problems turned out to be a combination of the old and the new. The close relations with the clients – formerly maintained merely by expense account luncheons – were ensured through a new type of contract which was awarded at the design stage, thus enabling the contractor to suggest changes – along the lines of value analysis – that would reduce construction costs.

Neither experience alone nor academic knowledge of the latest management techniques is sufficient for the manager. He needs to know *what* experience has shown will work in a particular industry, and *why* it works so that he can obtain the greatest possible benefit for his company. This is true today, and it will be increasingly true in the future as changes accelerate.

Most of all the new manager needs a flexible outlook – the will-

[1]. H. F. R. Catherwood: 'Management Techniques and Real Life', *The Journal of Management Studies* (May 1965), pp. 129–37.

ingness to accept new ways of doing things and an equal willingness to learn new skills. Some observers insist that future managers will have to change their fields as many as three times in their business careers if they're to remain promotable or even employable.

THE NEED FOR AN INTERNATIONAL OUTLOOK

Second, most managers will have to begin to think in terms of international competition and their relations with foreign customers and associates. International trade will continue to expand as world population increases and barriers to trade and investment decline. The potential growth of capacity in many industries because of technical advances will mean that increasing ingenuity will be required to dispose of the output through export and exchange.

In multinational companies, which will become more numerous, increased sensitivity to foreign conditions will be vital. In countries that are striving to become industrialized, there will be joint ventures in which British companies team up with foreign companies to start new businesses. There will be many cases where British companies contract to build a plant, train the workers, manage the start-up, then retire from the organization, taking their pay in the form of an agreed-upon fee rather than maintaining an interest in the business and its profits.

INCREASED DOMESTIC RESPONSIBILITY

Third, as the international responsibilities of management increase, so too domestic responsibility to the community will receive greater stress. The widespread feeling that all that is necessary is to avoid the attention of government officials is likely to give way to more active participation.

This is true because many investments being made today – in space, atomic energy, and international ventures – are so large that no one company can undertake them. Another reason why industry will have to develop closer government relations is that the government is likely to show increasing concern with private industry's decisions – as in the case of wage-price relations in key industries and the shifting of labour and work from declining to expanding areas.

ACCURATE FORECASTING AND IMPROVED PLANNING

Managers can look forward to greater accuracy in their forecasts of the future. Projections of the gross national product are likely to increase in accuracy because of recent improvements in forecasting techniques. In recent years, for example, forecasts by the Council of Economic Advisers have been accurate within 1 per cent.

Industry forecasts are also likely to gain in accuracy because of improved work by trade associations. Even more important is the impact of computer information in individual companies, since it makes possible much more detailed breakdowns of market potential.

One observer[2] has visualized the possibility of a 'national economic computer' in which an enormous quantity of information on general conditions can be stored and which individual companies can use to simulate the results of their own decisions. Because of its complexity, however, this is not likely to be developed within the next ten years.

Despite the improvement in techniques, speed, and machines, it is not likely that foresight will become perfect.

In the first place, not all the facts will be available. This is particularly true in regard to the behaviour of key individuals and changes in political influences. Many of these facts simply cannot be anticipated.

For example, the increase in the money supply in relation to the increase in business activity is an important factor in forecasting the state of business. But this relationship may be upset by political decisions prompted by the need to maintain the foreign exchange stability of the pound. This need may necessitate a smaller increase in the money supply than would otherwise have been made.

Second, basic assumptions may often be incorrect because they are fundamentally assumptions that the future will be an extension

2. Sir Leon Bagrit: *The Age of Automation* (New York, The New American Library, 1965), pp. 59–60.

of the past. But perhaps the one certain feature of the future is that new factors or a different combination of old factors is likely to arise.

Third, managers may ask the wrong questions about the future or neglect to ask some of the important ones. A common mistake is to make studies of the market without considering what the reaction of competitors is likely to be. Thus, in many situations, the share of the market plans of competitors adds up to more than 100 per cent, and the result is over-capacity.

Finally, many companies and individual managers may underestimate the size of the gap between forecasts and actual accomplishments. Thus 'gap filling' strategy will become of increasing importance, and the man who can think of new and original ways of narrowing the gap by reducing costs or developing extra revenue is likely to be in demand.

As management by objectives becomes more popular, every manager may be asked to draw up a plan for his own segment of the organization and develop 'wedges' to fill the gap between forecast and actual performance. If he is wise, he will make a range of forecasts – optimistic, pessimistic, and an average between the two. Then he will begin thinking of possible courses of action if the circumstances change so as to make his most pessimistic forecast likely to materialize. He will have to keep his plans more flexible than in the past and be ready to change them quickly.

ORGANIZATION AND COORDINATION

There's likely to be some trend away from decentralization through semi-autonomous divisions in the next few years. Back in the 1950s there was great enthusiasm for this form of decentralization because of the increasing size of many companies and the need to decentralize decision-making. But in many companies divisionalization was undertaken too hastily and without provision for sufficient review and control of what the divisions were doing. In recent years there has been a reaction against too great decentralization and this is likely to continue for several more years.

Computer information is likely to be more centralized to permit greater utilization of expensive equipment. Some companies are already visualizing electronic data processing as a centralized department that plans and manages the flow of information for the entire company.

If this develops, however, it will not mean that the computer section will make the decisions based upon the information. Quite a number of companies have established regional information centres that are handling accounting work for the divisions and plants. But the actual decisions are still made on a more decentralized basis. The only difference is that the plant and division managers have more information on which to base their decisions.

It doesn't seem probable, either, that there will be any basic change in the line and staff type of organization – although there's room for imaginative innovation in this respect. The hard fact is that no line manager can possibly have complete knowledge of all the specialized fields that impinge on his job, and staff assistance seems the best way to get around that difficulty.

STAFFING

Any decrease in the number of managerial jobs as a result of computerization or centralization is likely to be offset by the increasing number of staff managers that will be needed as complexities increase. For example, there will probably be more coordinators of various types, to say nothing of specialists in various sciences.

In the way of hiring practices, there has been some turning away from the view that it is better to get a man who has no major faults, even if that means that he has no major virtues as well and is pretty close to an 'average' man. There's a growing emphasis on the all-importance of 'creativity' as companies realize that merely keeping things running is not enough in an age of accelerating change.

Emphasis on good human relations – with subordinates, men on the same level, and superiors – will undoubtedly continue to be strong, however, if only to the extent that it will continue to be true that more executives and employees are fired for personality difficulties than for lack of capacity in their jobs. This is partly because almost everyone hates to fire anyone who is generally pleasant and obviously trying hard, whereas discharging a man who is always getting into fights is comparatively easy and can be done without any feeling of guilt.

Since human nature is not likely to change radically in this respect, the ability to get along with people – or at least to avoid constant difficulties with associates – will not only make a better manager but provide an insurance against loss of job.

Psychological testing will probably be improved and will be used even more widely than at present. Where tests are used in the selection of managers, however, there is likely to be an attempt to develop tests that pick out innovators and less emphasis on identifying men who will not rock the boat.

DIRECTION

Some observers have forecast the development of psychology to the point where it will be possible to solve all human relations problems by the application of scientific laws, possibly with the aid of computers to sort out all the variables and produce conclusions. If this prediction ever comes true, however, it will probably not be within the lifespan of today's managers and certainly not within the next ten years.

Managers will undoubtedly get more psychological help in directing subordinates, but it will still be necessary for them to use personal judgement in applying the theories and in conducting face-to-face contacts with their employees and with customers and members of the general public. The generalizations about what people want and what will motivate them are valuable, but they apply only in a broad sense and take little cognizance of the vast difference between individuals. The manager will still have to study his subordinates and apply the generalizations with discernment.

There is unlikely to be a return to the autocratic management of the past, but there will be less emphasis placed on being 'nice' to employees as the principal factor in successful supervision, and more on organization of the work to make possible a sense of achievement.

The manager's job may be facilitated in this respect because many of the deadening routine jobs may disappear with the advent of automation and computerization.

CONTROL

Control, in the sense of frequent checking on plans to determine how they are working out, will become much easier for managers at all levels through the use of the computer. In a sense this will make some of the manager's decisions less risky because he will be able to reverse them before the results are too serious.

But it may also put a greater premium on creative innovation because, in many cases where plans are not working out as expected, it is necessary to do a great deal more than simply rescind a decision. It is essential to discover an entirely new course of action, to think of many new alternatives, and to select the best one very quickly.

And in some cases, the computer may make it necessary that managers be right the first time. Some highly automated and computerized suppliers can produce and ship products so quickly that a manager who cancels an order a short time after he has dispatched it may find that the shipment has already been made. This has already happened in a few cases, and will happen more frequently in the future.

Incidentally, even small companies that cannot afford to purchase computers can now get computer services from outside organizations. A recent development that makes this easier is what is known as 'time sharing'. In this system the data for many companies may be stored in one large computer; then through an elaborate system of programming, the computer can be instructed to shift from one company's problem to another's.

SMALL BUSINESS

The big companies will continue to get bigger through growth in their sales volume, building new plants, and acquisition and merger. Moreover, many of the industries in which a number of small businesses now exist will, through merger, eventually become the domain of big business.

MANAGEMENT AND THE FUTURE

But opportunities for small business will not disappear, or even suffer much curtailment. A recent survey conducted for the Federal Government's Small Business Administration[3] concludes that opportunities for the small businessman who is both owner and manager will continue to be available, and that they may multiply faster than the number of potential entrepreneurs. Because of population trends, the number in the age group 35–45, which is the group from which most new entrepreneurs come, will remain constant, while the opportunities tend to rise.

In manufacturing, the report predicts, the real opportunity for new entrepreneurs will lie in producing goods for other businesses rather than for the general consumer. Also, the scale of business in the service industries – self-service laundries, beauty parlours and barber shops, office services, and so on – will remain quite small.

In retailing, many types of independent stores – the corner grocery, for example – will find the going harder as chains proliferate and spread themselves further. But speciality retail outlets of various kinds are likely to multiply.

It might also be said that the bigger big business grows, the more opportunities there are likely to be for small business. A huge business with heavy investment in automated equipment must aim at a very large market if it is to cover its fixed costs, and it cannot afford to adapt itself to consumers with specialized needs and wants. Thus there remain many interstices that the small businessman can claim as his own.

It is true that many small businesses fail during their first year and few survive as long as five years, but the opportunities remain for those who know how to recognize them and who are good managers in their own right.[4]

---

3. Conducted by economists of Robert R. Nathan Associates. Reported on in *Business Week* (31 July 1965).

4. For anyone interested in starting his own business, see Kurt B. Mayer and Sidney Goldstein: *The First Two Years: Problems of Small Firm Growth and Survival* (Washington, D.C., Small Business Administration, 1961). This not only discusses the causes of survival and failure, but offers a number of enlightening case histories of success and failure.

SUGGESTED QUESTIONS FOR YOUR CONSIDERATION

1. Do you believe that further knowledge of one of the physical sciences – physics, chemistry, and so on – would help you in the understanding of your business? If so, have you made plans for acquiring it?

2. What is the key factor in the success of a company such as your own? Keeping costs down? Close relations with customers? Development of new products? High quality? Or something else? Why is it the key factor?

3. If you had to change industries, is there any other in which your experience and knowledge would be valuable?

4. Have you tried to look ahead – and plan ahead – to capitalize on changes and opportunities affecting your company? Your industry?

5. Looking back over the past *five* years, what have you personally done to achieve greater flexibility and better personal characteristics on the job?

Index

Ackoff, E., 135
Administrative law, 115–16
Analogue computers, 105
Antitrust, laws, 115–16
Area maintenance, 56
Argyris, Chris, 28, 59
Attitudinal bias, 82–4
Authority, 48
Average, statistical, 157–60

Backward integration, 97–8
Barnard, Chester I., 127
Bata Shoe Company, 76
Battersby, A., 187
Baumol, William, 205
Behaviouristic sciences, 43–4
Binary numbers, 208
Breech, Ernest R., 22
Budgeting, 18, 102–3
Burns, Tom, 59–60
Business, future opportunities, 228–9; trends, planning finance, and control, 92–112; predicting the future, 170–71

Chain of command, 51
Charismatic leadership, 37–8
COBOL (Common Business Oriented Language), 209
Communication, 81–91; by action, 85–6; a management function, 21; mental set, 82–4; by objectives, 66–80; organizational, 81–91; process, 84–5; purpose of, 82; spoken, 89–90; tips on, 90; written, 86–9
Company image, 123–5
Competition, foreign, 93
Computers, 205–20; analogue, 205; applications, 210–16; basic functional units, 205–20; in decision making, 217–18; do computers think?, 218–19; how computer works, 206–9; more information, 212–16; programming, 209–10; real time, 216–17; routine jobs for, 210–12; total systems, 217
Consumer price index, 157
Control, 92–113; budgeting, 102–3; deciding what's needed, 94–5; defining objectives, 93–4; as management function, 18; in long-range planning, 111–12; quality control, 164–6
Coordination, future management need, 225–6; in organization, 46–7
Corporate development plan, 104
Correlation in statistics, 166–9
Costs, 142–55; areas of examination, 147–8; preventing costs by value analysis, 144–6; related techniques, 148–51; value analysis, 151–4; wage, 171–2
Critical path analysis – PERT, 186–204; advantages of, 202; application of, 202–3; arrow diagrams, 187–90; constructing a PERT network, 190–202; critical path analysis without a computer, 199–202
Crowder, Norman A., 27
Customers, creating and retaining them, 73; production capacity and, 95

Decision making, 127–41; broad process of, 130–32; computers and, 217–18; degree of risk, 128–30; improving decisions, 138–41;

Decision making – *contd.*
  management science or OR, 134–8; methematical decision making, 132–4
Decision trees and payoff tables, 175–85; decision trees, 179–82; in inventory analysis, 182–3; in new product analysis, 176–9; risk and the manager, 183–4
Delegation, how to delegate, 49–50; in organization, 49
Dickens, Charles, on paperwork, 66–7, 87
Dickson, W. J., 32
Digital computers, 205–9
Direction, as future management need, 227; in human relations and leadership, 28–9; as management function, 17
Disposable income, 97, 99
Divisionalization, in organization, 56–8
Drucker, Peter, 33–4, 62, 149
Duckworth, W. E., 135
Duncan, A. R. C., 132, 138

Education of managers, 221–3
Elections, their effect on business climate, 120–21
Emerson, Harrington, 67, 144
Employment, costs, 171–2; interview, 24–6
Enthoven, Alain, 138
Executives, line and staff, 51–4
Expected monetary value (EMV), 177–8
Expenditures, expense vs capital, 102–3

Fayol, Henri, 48
Financing, 92–113; budgeting, 102–3; control, 111–12; deciding what will be needed, 94–5; defining objectives, 93–4; forecasting the business cycle, 100; how one company plans, 104–9; making the plan, 98–9; making things happen, 110–11; sources of statistics, 100–102; trends, long-term, 96–8
Flow charts, 150
Follett, Mary Parker, 81
Ford, Henry, 21; Ford, Henry II, 22
Forecasting, future management needs, 224–5; in planning, finnance and control, 100; in short and long-range planning, 94–100
Fortran (formula translation), 209
Forward integration, 97–8
Free enterprise, theory of, 117
Frequency distribution curve, 163
Future management needs, 221–30; accurate forecasting and improved planning, 224–5; control, 228; increased domestic responsibility, 223–4; need for education, 221–3; need for international outlook, 223; organization and coordination, 225–6; staffing, 226–7

'Gangplanks,' in coordination, 47
Gantt, Henry Laurence, 30
Gompertz curve, 170–71
Government, agencies, 119–20; regulation of business, 117–20
Government - business relations, 114–26; company image, 123–5; dealing with officials, 121–2; effect of elections, 120–21; importance of administrative law, 115–16
Graicunas, L. A., 50
Gross national product, 96–100
Growth, and growth companies, 14–16; stages of, 170–71
Gulick, Luther, 54–8

Hawthorne experiments, 31–4, 63–4, 83
Herzberg, Frederick, 33, 63
Hourly wages, 171–2

INDEX

Human relations and leadership, 24–42; achievement motive, 32–7; direction, 28–9; leadership, 37–42; money motive, 29–31; selection, 24–6; sense of belonging, 31–2, training, 26–8

Human wants, economic and non-economic, 85

Incentives, achievement objective, 32–7; money motive, 29–31, 35–6; organizing for motivation, 61–3; sense of belonging, 31–2

Informal organization, 63–5

Innovation, as a management function, 18–20

International outlook, need for in future management, 223

International minerals and chemicals, 137

Inventory, impact programme, 214

Jacobs, W. W., 219
Job definition, 59–61
Job Instructor Training Programme, 26
Job Relations Training, 40, 132

Labour costs, 171–2
Lag and lead indicators, 100
Law of the situation, in communication, 81–2
Laws, anti-trust, 115–16
Lead and lag indicators, 100
Leadership, 37–42; charismatic, 37; qualities, 37–42
Likert, Rensis, 33, 40
Line and staff, 51–4

McGregor, Douglas, 33, 41
Maintenance area, 56
Management, 11–23; accurate forecasting and improved planning, 224–5; communicating by objectives, 21, 66–80; controlling, 18, 228; decision making, 127–41; directing, 17; functions of, 12–21; increased domestic responsibility, 223–4; innovating, 18–20; introductory statistics for, 157–74; management and the computer, 205–20; management and the future, 221–30; management by objectives, 66–80; need for an international outlook, 223; need for management education, 221–3; organizing, 16–17, 225–6; planning, 12–16; representing, 20–21; staffing, 17, 226–7

Managing by objectives, 66–80; analysis of opportunities, 74–80; new approach, 68–9; objectives vs tasks, 69–74

Martino, R. L., 203
Massarik, Fred, 28
Mathematics, in decision making, 132–5
Mayo, Elton, 31–2, 34
Measures of central tendency, 163; of dispersion, 163
Medians in statistics, 158–9
Mental set, in communication, 82–4
Miles, Lawrence D., 143, 146
Modes, in statistics, 158–9
Monopolies and Mergers Acts, 115–16
Mooney, James D., 43
Motivating factors, 28–37; achievement, 32–7; feeling of belonging, 31–2; hygiene, 33; money, 29–31, 35–6

National Income, 97
Normal curve, 162–4

Objectives, 45, 66–80; communicating by, 66–80; defining objectives, 93–4; managing by, 66–80; organizational, 45; planning, 12–16
O'Brien, Robert P., 94

233

INDEX

Odiorne, George S., 28
Operations plan, 104
Operations, research in decision making, 135-8
Opportunities, in managing and communicating by objectives, 74-80
Optimum, in operations research, 135
Organization, 43-65; authority, 48; behavioural sciences and, 58-61; chain of command, 51; challenge of, 43-65; classical theories, 45; communication in, 81-91; co-ordination, 46-7; definition, 43-5; delegation, 49-50; divisionalization, 55-8; informal, 63-5; line and staff, 51-4; objectives, 45; organizing as a future management need, 225-6; organizing as a management function, 16-17; organizing for motivation, 61-3; principles of, 54-5; reorganization, 58; responsibility, 48-9; span of control, 50-51; specialization, 45-6
Organizational networks, 139-40

Payoff tables, 175-85; and decision trees, 179-82; an inventory problem, 182-3; and new products, 176-9; risk evaluation, 183-4
Personnel, direction of, 28-9; incentives of achievement, money, sense of belonging, 29-37; training of, 26-8
PERT terminology, 190-92
Planning, 92-113; corporate development plan, 104; deciding what will be needed, 94-5; defining objectives, 93-4; forecasting the business cycle, 100; how one company plans, 105-9; improved planning as a future management need, 224-5; long-term trends, 96-8; making the plan, 98-9; making things happen, 110-11; as a management function, 12-16; operations plan, 104; planning through budgeting, 102-3; purpose of, 92-3; sources of planning statistics, 100-102; strategic plan, 104
Pollution, 123
Population trends, 96
Production capacity, 95
Profit variables, 111
Profits, defined, 172
Programmed learning, 27-8
Programming, computers, 209-10
Psychological tests, in selection of employees, 24-5

Qualities, leadership, 37-42
Quality control, statistical, 164-6

Random access, 207
Rathenau, Walter, 89-90
Real time computers, 216-17
Regulatory agencies, 119-20
Reorganizations, 58
Representation, as a management function, 20-21
Responsibility, commensurate with authority, 223; in organization, 48-9
Return on investment, 133-4
Rivett, B. H. P., 135
Risk and decision making, 128-30
Roethlisberger, Fritz, 32-4

Sales forecasting, 98-9
Samples, characteristics of, 160-62
Sampling methods, 160-62
Sandia Corporation, 201-2
Schleh, Edward C., 79-80
Selection, of personnel, 24-6
Sensitivity training, 28
Snow, C. P., 221
Span of Control, 50-51
Specialization, 45-6, 61-3
Staffing, future management needs,

INDEX

226–7; as a management function, 17
Stalker, G. M., 59–60
Standard deviation, 163–4
Statistical methods, 157–74; averages, medians, and modes, 157–60; correlations, 166–9; normal curve, 162–4; predicting future trends, 170–71; sampling methods, 160–62; sources of misconceptions, 171–4; statistical quality control, 164–6
Statistical sources, 100–102
Statutory orders, 115–16
Stock, *see* Inventory
Strategic plan, 104
Systems, managerial applications, 217

Tannenbaum, Robert, 28
Taylor, Frederick W., 29–35, 63, 92–3
Technological change, effect on product life cycles, 92

Theory X and Theory Y, 33
Time value of money, 133–4
Total systems, 217
Training, in human relations and leadership, 26–8

Value analysis, 142–56; areas of examination, 147–8; importance of, 151–4; related techniques, 148–51; value analysis technique, 144–6
Vatter, Paul, 175–9

Wage costs, 171–2
Weighted average, 158–9
Weir, Ernest T., 72
Weschler, Irving W., 28
Whitehead, T. N., 64
Whyte, William F., Jr, 19
Wiener, Norbert, 219
Work, division of, 55; simplification, 149–50
Written communications, 86–9

MORE ABOUT PENGUINS, PELICANS AND PUFFINS

For further information about books available from Penguins please write to Dept EP, Penguin Books Ltd, Harmondsworth, Middlesex UB7 0DA.

In the U.S.A.: For a complete list of books available from Penguins in the United States write to Dept DG, Penguin Books, 299 Murray Hill Parkway, East Rutherford, New Jersey 07073.

In Canada: For a complete list of books available from Penguins in Canada write to Penguin Books Canada Limited, 2801 John Street, Markham, Ontario L3R 1B4.

In Australia: For a complete list of books available from Penguins in Australia write to the Marketing Department, Penguin Books Australia Ltd, P.O. Box 257, Ringwood, Victoria 3134.

In New Zealand: For a complete list of books available from Penguins in New Zealand write to the Marketing Department, Penguin Books (N.Z.) Ltd, Private Bag, Takapuna, Auckland 9.

In India: For a complete list of books available from Penguins in India write to Penguin Overseas Ltd, 706 Eros Apartments, 56 Nehru Place, New Delhi 110019.

Management Classics in the Penguin Business Library

SELF-HELP
Samuel Smiles

Self-Help, published the same year as *The Origin of Species* and *On Liberty*, brought into common usage the maxim 'God helps those who help themselves'.

An advocate of capitalism, Smiles celebrates the effort of the individual, the value of achievement over that of birth (although he was opposed to entirely self-seeking opportunism) and the role of the entrepreneur in economic development, and argues that those who want to be good citizens and successful in business must learn to be self-reliant, self-disciplined and industrious.

Management Classics in the Penguin Business Library

MY YEARS WITH GENERAL MOTORS
Alfred P. Sloan, Jr

A classic account of one of the great business success stories of all time.

When Alfred P. Sloan retired from General Motors in 1957, it was the largest private industrial enterprise in the world, producer of about half the passenger cars and trucks in the United States and Canada. Since Sloan had taken over an ailing company in 1918, his was an almost unparalleled personal achievement. No one else could describe with such authority how a major business is built up, run and kept at the top; how a flexible and decentralized management structure at the head of 600,000 employees worldwide can remain ruthlessly efficient; and how, more particularly, the great battle with Ford was waged in the early 1920s, when Sloan's firm belief in progress and rising living standards led him to the revolutionary policy of 'a car for every purse and purpose'.

This edition contains a new introduction by John Egan (Chairman of Jaguar) and it makes available again a book which is as fascinating and enjoyable as it is informative – and may well be the most famous management book ever written.

'There's no one better qualified to tell the story of a triumph that has fascinated students of business for decades' – *Wall Street Journal*